THE WORKS OF
HERMAN MELVILLE

STANDARD EDITION

VOLUME

X

THE PIAZZA TALES

BY

HERMAN MELVILLE

NEW YORK
RUSSELL & RUSSELL · INC
1963

THE STANDARD EDITION OF

THE WORKS OF HERMAN MELVILLE

IN SIXTEEN VOLUMES

REISSUED, 1963, BY RUSSELL & RUSSELL, INC.

L. C. CATALOG CARD NO: 63–18862

PRINTED IN THE UNITED STATES OF AMERICA

CONTENTS

	PAGE
THE PIAZZA	1
BARTLEBY	19
BENITO CERENO	66
THE LIGHTNING-ROD MAN	171
THE ENCANTADAS ; OR, ENCHANTED ISLANDS . .	181
THE BELL-TOWER	253

THE PIAZZA TALES

THE PIAZZA

'With fairest flowers,
Whilst summer lasts, and I live here, Fidele——'

WHEN I removed into the country, it was to occupy an
old-fashioned farm-house, which had no piazza—a de-
ficiency the more regretted, because not only did I like
piazzas, as somehow combining the cosiness of indoors
with the freedom of outdoors, and it is so pleasant to
inspect your thermometer there, but the country round
about was such a picture, that in berry time no boy
climbs hill or crosses vale without coming upon easels
planted in every nook, and sunburnt painters painting
there. A very paradise of painters. The circle of the
stars cut by the circle of the mountains. At least, so
looks it from the house ; though, once upon the mountains, no circle of them can you see. Had the site been
chosen five rods off, this charmed ring would not have
been.

The house is old. Seventy years since, from the heart
of the Hearth Stone Hills, they quarried the Kaaba, or
Holy Stone, to which, each Thanksgiving, the social
pilgrims used to come. So long ago, that, in digging
for the foundation, the workmen used both spade and
axe, fighting the Troglodytes of those subterranean parts
—sturdy roots of a sturdy wood, encamped upon what
is now a long landslide of sleeping meadow, sloping

A

away off from my poppy-bed. Of that knit wood, but one survivor stands—an elm, lonely through stead-fastness.

Whoever built the house, he builded better than he knew; or else Orion in the zenith flashed down his Damocles' sword to him some starry night, and said, ' Build there.' For how, otherwise, could it have entered the builder's mind, that, upon the clearing being made, such a purple prospect would be his ?—nothing less than Greylock, with all his hills about him, like Charlemagne among his peers.

Now, for a house, so situated in such a country, to have no piazza for the convenience of those who might desire to feast upon the view, and take their time and ease about it, seemed as much of an omission as if a picture-gallery should have no bench; for what but picture-galleries are the marble halls of these same lime-stone hills ?—galleries hung, month after month anew, with pictures ever fading into pictures ever fresh. And beauty is like piety—you cannot run and read it; tranquillity and constancy, with, nowadays, an easy-chair, are needed. For though, of old, when reverence was in vogue, and indolence was not, the devotees of Nature, doubtless, used to stand and adore—just as, in the cathedrals of those ages, the worshippers of a higher Power did—yet, in these times of failing faith and feeble knees, we have the piazza and the pew.

During the first year of my residence, the more leisurely to witness the coronation of Charlemagne (weather per-mitting, they crown him every sunrise and sunset), I chose me, on the hill-side bank near by, a royal lounge of turf—a green velvet lounge, with long, moss-padded back; while at the head, strangely enough, there grew (but, I suppose, for heraldry) three tufts of blue violets in a field-argent of wild strawberries; and a trellis, with honeysuckle, I set for canopy. Very majestical lounge, indeed. So much so, that here, as with the reclining majesty of Denmark in his orchard, a sly earache invaded me. But, if damps abound at times in Westminster Abbey, because it is so old, why not within this monastery of mountains, which is older?

A piazza must be had.

The house was wide—my fortune narrow; so that, to build a panoramic piazza, one round and round, it could not be—although, indeed, considering the matter by rule and square, the carpenters, in the kindest way, were anxious to gratify my furthest wishes, at I 've forgotten how much a foot.

Upon but one of the four sides would prudence grant me what I wanted. Now, which side?

To the east, that long camp of the Hearth Stone Hills, fading far away toward Quito; and every fall, a small white flake of something peering suddenly, of a coolish morning, from the topmost cliff—the season's new-dropped lamb, its earliest fleece; and then the Christmas dawn, draping those dun highlands with red-barred plaids and tartans—goodly sight from your piazza, that. Goodly sight; but, to the north is Charlemagne—can't have the Hearth Stone Hills with Charlemagne.

Well, the south side. Apple-trees are there. Pleasant, of a balmy morning, in the month of May, to sit and see that orchard, white-budded, as for a bridal; and, in October, one green arsenal yard; such piles of ruddy shot. Very fine, I grant; but, to the north is Charlemagne.

The west side, look. An upland pasture, alleying away into a maple wood at top. Sweet, in opening spring, to trace upon the hill-side, otherwise gray and bare—to trace, I say, the oldest paths by their streaks of earliest green. Sweet, indeed, I can't deny; but, to the north is Charlemagne.

So Charlemagne, he carried it. It was not long after 1848 ; and, somehow, about that time, all round the world, these kings, they had the casting vote, and voted for themselves.

No sooner was ground broken, than all the neighbourhood, neighbour Dives, in particular, broke, too—into a laugh. Piazza to the north! Winter piazza! Wants, of winter midnights, to watch the Aurora Borealis, I suppose; hope he 's laid in good store of Polar muffs and mittens.

That was in the lion month of March. Not forgotten are the blue noses of the carpenters, and how they scouted at the greenness of the cit, who would build his sole piazza to the north. But March don't last forever ; patience, and August comes. And then, in the cool elysium of my northern bower, I, Lazarus in Abraham's bosom, cast down the hill a pitying glance on poor old Dives, tormented in the purgatory of his piazza to the south.

But, even in December, this northern piazza does not repel—nipping cold and gusty though it be, and the north wind, like any miller, bolting by the snow, in finest flour—for then, once more, with frosted beard, I pace the sleety deck, weathering Cape Horn.

In summer, too, Canute-like, sitting here, one is often reminded of the sea. For not only do long ground-swells roll the slanting grain, and little wavelets of the grass ripple over upon the low piazza, as their beach, and the blown down of dandelions is wafted like the spray, and the purple of the mountains is just the purple of the billows, and a still August noon broods upon the deep meadows, as a calm upon the Line ; but the vastness and the lonesomeness are so oceanic, and the silence and the sameness, too, that the first peep of a strange house, rising beyond the trees, is for all the world like spying, on the Barbary coast, an unknown sail.

And this recalls my inland voyage to fairyland. A true voyage ; but, take it all in all, interesting as if invented.

From the piazza, some uncertain object I had caught, mysteriously snugged away, to all appearance, in a sort of purpled breast-pocket, high up in a hopper-like hollow, or sunken angle, among the north-western mountains— yet, whether, really, it was on a mountain-side, or a mountain-top, could not be determined ; because, though, viewed from favourable points, a blue summit, peering up away behind the rest, will, as it were, talk to you over their heads, and plainly tell you, that, though he (the blue summit) seems among them, he is not of them (God forbid !), and, indeed, would have you know that he considers himself—as, to say truth, he has good right— by several cubits their superior, nevertheless, certain ranges, here and there double-filed, as in platoons, so shoulder and follow up upon one another, with their irregular shapes and heights, that, from the piazza, a nigher and lower mountain will, in most states of the atmosphere, effacingly shade itself away into a higher and further one ; that an object, bleak on the former's crest, will, for all that, appear nested in the latter's flank. These mountains, somehow, they play at hide-and-seek, and all before one's eyes.

But, be that as it may, the spot in question was, at all events, so situated as to be only visible, and then but vaguely, under certain witching conditions of light and shadow.

Indeed, for a year or more, I knew not there was such a spot, and might, perhaps, have never known, had it not been for a wizard afternoon in autumn—late in autumn—a mad poet's afternoon ; when the turned maple woods in the broad basin below me, having lost their first vermilion tint, dully smoked, like smouldering towns, when flames expire upon their prey ; and rumour

had it, that this smokiness in the general air was not all
Indian summer—which was not used to be so sick a thing,
however mild—but, in great part, was blown from far-off
forests, for weeks on fire, in Vermont ; so that no wonder
the sky was ominous as Hecate's cauldron—and two
sportsmen, crossing a red stubble buckwheat field,
seemed guilty Macbeth and foreboding Banquo ; and
the hermit-sun, hutted in an Adullam cave, well toward
the south, according to his season, did little else but, by
indirect reflection of narrow rays shot down a Simplon
Pass among the clouds, just steadily paint one small,
round, strawberry mole upon the wan cheek of north-
western hills.   Signal as a candle.   One spot of radiance,
where all else was shade.

Fairies there, thought I ; some haunted ring where
fairies dance.

Time passed ; and the following May, after a gentle
shower upon the mountains—a little shower islanded in
misty seas of sunshine ; such a distant shower—and
sometimes two, and three, and four of them, all visible
together in different parts—as I love to watch from the
piazza, instead of thunder-storms, as I used to, which
wrap old Greylock, like a Sinai, till one thinks swart
Moses must be climbing among scathed hemlocks there ;
after, I say, that gentle shower, I saw a rainbow, resting
its further end just where, in autumn, I had marked the
mole.   Fairies there, thought I ;   remembering that
rainbows bring out the blooms, and that, if one can but
get to the rainbow's end, his fortune is made in a bag
of gold.   Yon rainbow's end, would I were there, thought
I.   And none the less I wished it, for now first noticing
what seemed some sort of glen, or grotto, in the mountain-
side ;   at least, whatever it was, viewed through the
rainbow's medium, it glowed like the Potosi mine.   But
a workaday neighbour said, no doubt it was but some

old barn—an abandoned one, its broadside beaten in,
the acclivity its background. But I, though I had never
been there, I knew better.

A few days after, a cheery sunrise kindled a golden
sparkle in the same spot as before. The sparkle was
of that vividness, it seemed as if it could only come
from glass. The building, then—if building, after all, it
was—could, at least, not be a barn, much less an abandoned one ; stale hay ten years musting in it. No ; if
aught built by mortal, it must be a cottage ; perhaps
long vacant and dismantled, but this very spring magically
fitted up and glazed.

Again, one noon, in the same direction, I marked,
over dimmed tops of terraced foliage, a broader gleam,
as of a silver buckler, held sunward over some croucher's
head ; which gleam, experience in like cases taught,
must come from a roof newly shingled. This, to me,
made pretty sure the recent occupancy of that far cot
in fairyland.

Day after day, now, full of interest in my discovery,
what time I could spare from reading the *Midsummer
Night's Dream*, and all about Titania, wishfully I gazed
off toward the hills ; but in vain. Either troops of
shadows, an imperial guard, with slow pace and solemn,
defiled along the steeps ; or, routed by pursuing light,
fled broadcast from east to west—old wars of Lucifer
and Michael ; or the mountains, though unvexed by
these mirrored sham fights in the sky, had an atmosphere
otherwise unfavourable for fairy-views. I was sorry ;
the more so, because I had to keep my chamber for some
time after—which chamber did not face those hills.

At length, when pretty well again, and sitting out, in
the September morning, upon the piazza, and thinking
to myself, when, just after a little flock of sheep, the
farmer's banded children passed, a-nutting, and said,

'How sweet a day'—it was, after all, but what their
fathers call a weather-breeder—and, indeed, was become
so sensitive through my illness, as that I could not bear
to look upon a Chinese creeper of my adoption, and
which, to my delight, climbing a post of the piazza, had
burst out in starry bloom, but now, if you removed the
leaves a little, showed millions of strange, cankerous
worms, which, feeding upon those blossoms, so shared
their blessed hue, as to make it unblessed evermore—
worms, whose germs had doubtless lurked in the very
bulb which, so hopefully, I had planted : in this ingrate
peevishness of my weary convalescence, was I sitting
there ; when, suddenly looking off, I saw the golden
mountain-window, dazzling like a deep-sea dolphin.
Fairies there, thought I, once more ; the queen of fairies
at her fairy-window ; at any rate, some glad mountain-
girl ; it will do me good, it will cure this weariness, to
look on her. No more ; I'll launch my yawl—ho,
cheerly, heart ! and push away for fairyland—for rainbow's end, in fairyland.

How to get to fairyland, by what road, I did not
know ; nor could anyone inform me ; not even one
Edmund Spenser, who had been there—so he wrote me—
further than that to reach fairyland, it must be voyaged
to, and with faith.   I took the fairy-mountain's bearings,
and the first fine day, when strength permitted, got into
my yawl—high-pommelled, leather one—cast off the fast,
and away I sailed, free voyager as an autumn leaf.   Early
dawn ; and, sallying westward, I sowed the morning
before me.

Some miles brought me nigh the hills ; but out of
present sight of them. I was not lost ; for roadside
golden-rods, as guide-posts, pointed, I doubted not, the
way to the golden window. Following them, I came to
a lone and languid region, where the grass-grown ways

were travelled but by drowsy cattle, that, less waked
than stirred by day, seemed to walk in sleep. Browse,
they did not—the enchanted never eat. At least, so
says Don Quixote, that sagest sage that ever lived.

On I went, and gained at last the fairy-mountain's
base, but saw yet no fairy-ring. A pasture rose before
me. Letting down five mouldering bars—so moistly
green, they seemed fished up from some sunken wreck—
a wigged old Aries, long-visaged, and with crumpled
horn, came snuffing up ; and then, retreating, decorously
led on along a milky-way of white-weed, past dim-
clustering Pleiades and Hyades, of small forget-me-nots ;
and would have led me further still his astral path, but
for golden flights of yellow-birds—pilots, surely, to the
golden window, to one side flying before me, from bush
to bush, toward deep woods—which woods themselves
were luring—and, somehow, lured, too, by their fence,
banning a dark road, which, however dark, led up. I
pushed through ; when Aries, renouncing me now for
some lost soul, wheeled, and went his wiser way. Forbidding and forbidden ground—to him.

A winter wood road, matted all along with winter-
green. By the side of pebbly waters—waters the cheerier
for their solitude ; beneath swaying fir-boughs, petted
by no season, but still green in all, on I journeyed—my
horse and I ; on, by an old saw-mill, bound down and
hushed with vines, that his grating voice no more was
heard ; on, by a deep flume clove through snowy marble,
vernal-tinted, where freshet eddies had, on each side,
spun out empty chapels in the living rock ; on, where
Jacks-in-the-pulpit, like their Baptist namesake, preached
but to the wilderness ; on, where a huge, cross-grain
block, fern-bedded, showed where, in forgotten times,
man after man had tried to split it, but lost his wedges
for his pains—which wedges yet rusted in their holes ;

on, where, ages past, in step-like ledges of a cascade, skull-hollow pots had been churned out by ceaseless whirling of a flint-stone—ever wearing, but itself unworn ; on, by wild rapids pouring into a secret pool, but soothed by circling there a while, issued forth serenely ; on, to less broken ground, and by a little ring, where, truly, fairies must have danced, or else some wheel-tyre been heated—for all was bare ; still on, and up, and out into a hanging orchard, where maidenly looked down upon me a crescent moon, from morning.

My horse hitched low his head. Red apples rolled before him ; Eve's apples ; seek-no-furthers. He tasted one, I another ; it tasted of the ground. Fairyland not yet, thought I, flinging my bridle to a humped old tree, that crooked out an arm to catch it. For the way now lay where path was none, and none might go but by himself, and only go by daring. Through blackberry brakes that tried to pluck me back, though I but strained toward fruitless growths of mountain-laurel ; up slippery steeps to barren heights, where stood none to welcome. Fairyland not yet, thought I, though the morning is here before me.

Footsore enough and weary, I gained not then my journey's end, but came ere long to a craggy pass, dipping toward growing regions still beyond. A zigzag road, half overgrown with blueberry bushes, here turned among the cliffs. A rent was in their ragged sides ; through it a little track branched off, which, upward threading that short defile, came breezily out above, to where the mountain-top, part sheltered northward, by a taller brother, sloped gently off a space, ere darkly plunging ; and here, among fantastic rocks, reposing in a herd, the foot-track wound, half beaten, up to a little, low-storied, grayish cottage, capped, nun-like, with a peaked roof.

On one slope, the roof was deeply weather-stained,

and, nigh the turfy eaves-trough, all velvet-napped ; no
doubt the snail-monks founded mossy priories there.
The other slope was newly shingled. On the north side,
doorless and windowless, the clap-boards, innocent of
paint were yet green as the north side of lichened pines,
or copperless hulls of Japanese junks, becalmed. The
whole base, like those of the neighbouring rocks, was
rimmed about with shaded streaks of richest sod ; for,
with hearth-stones in fairyland, the natural rock, though
housed, preserves to the last, just as in open fields, its
fertilising charm ; only, by necessity, working now at a
remove, to the sward without. So, at least, says Oberon,
grave authority in fairy-lore. Though setting Oberon
aside, certain it is, that, even in the common world, the
soil, close up to farm-houses, as close up to pasture rocks,
is, even though untended, ever richer than it is a few
rods off—such gentle, nurturing heat is radiated there.

But with this cottage, the shaded streaks were richest
in its front and about its entrance, where the ground-
sill, and especially the door-sill, had, through long eld,
quietly settled down.

No fence was seen, no enclosure. Near by—ferns,
ferns, ferns ; further—woods, woods, woods ; beyond—
mountains, mountains, mountains ; then—sky, sky, sky.
Turned out in aerial commons, pasture for the mountain
moon. Nature, and but nature, house and all ; even a
low cross-pile of silver birch, piled openly, to season ;
up among whose silvery sticks, as through the fencing of
some sequestered grave, sprang vagrant raspberry bushes
—wilful assertors of their right-of-way.

The foot-track, so dainty narrow, just like a sheep-
track, led through long ferns that lodged. Fairyland
at last, thought I ; Una and her lamb dwell here. Truly,
a small abode—mere palanquin, set down on the summit,
in a pass between two worlds, participant of neither.

A sultry hour, and I wore a light hat, of yellow sinnet, with white duck trowsers—both relics of my tropic sea-going. Clogged in the muffling ferns, I softly stumbled, staining the knees a sea-green.

Pausing at the threshold, or rather where threshold once had been, I saw, through the open doorway, a lonely girl, sewing at a lonely window. A pale-cheeked girl, and fly-specked window, with wasps about the mended upper panes. I spoke. She shyly started, like some Tahiti girl, secreted for a sacrifice, first catching sight, through palms, of Captain Cook. Recovering, she bade me enter ; with her apron brushed off a stool ; then silently resumed her own. With thanks I took the stool ; but now, for a space, I, too, was mute. This, then, is the fairy-mountain house, and here, the fairy-queen sitting at her fairy-window.

I went up to it. Downward, directed by the tunnelled pass, as through a levelled telescope, I caught sight of a far-off, soft, azure world. I hardly knew it, though I came from it.

' You must find this view very pleasant,' said I, at last.

' Oh, sir,' tears starting in her eyes, ' the first time I looked out of this window, I said, " Never, never shall I weary of this." '

' And what wearies you of it now ? '

' I don't know,' while a tear fell ; ' but it is not the view, it is Marianna.'

Some months back, her brother, only seventeen, had come hither, a long way from the other side, to cut wood and burn coal, and she, elder sister, had accompanied him. Long had they been orphans, and now, sole inhabitants of the sole house upon the mountain. No guest came, no traveller passed. The zigzag, perilous road was only used at seasons by the coal wagons. The

brother was absent the entire day, sometimes the entire
night. When at evening, fagged out, he did come home,
he soon left his bench, poor fellow, for his bed ; just as
one, at last, wearily quits that, too, for still deeper
rest. The bench, the bed, the grave.

Silent I stood by the fairy-window, while these things
were being told.

' Do you know,' said she at last, as stealing from her
story, ' do you know who lives yonder ?—I have never
been down into that country—away off there, I mean ;
that house, that marble one,' pointing far across the
lower landscape ; ' have you not caught it ? there, on
the long hill-side ! the field before, the woods behind ;
the white shines out against their blue ; don't you mark
it ? the only house in sight.'

I looked ; and after a time, to my surprise, recognised,
more by its position than its aspect, or Marianna's
description, my own abode, glimmering much like this
mountain one from the piazza. The mirage haze made
it appear less a farm-house than King Charming's palace.

' I have often wondered who lives there ; but it must be
some happy one ; again this morning was I thinking so.'

' Some happy one,' returned I, starting ; ' and why
do you think that ? You judge some rich one lives
there ? '

' Rich or not, I never thought ; but it looks so happy,
I can't tell how ; and it is so far away. Sometimes I
think I do but dream it is there. You should see it in
a sunset.'

' No doubt the sunset gilds it finely ; but not more
than the sunrise does this house, perhaps.'

' This house ? The sun is a good sun, but it never
gilds this house. Why should it ? This old house is
rotting. That makes it so mossy. In the morning, the
sun comes in at this old window, to be sure—boarded up,

when first we came; a window I can't keep clean, do
what I may—and half burns, and nearly blinds me at
my sewing, besides setting the flies and wasps astir—
such flies and wasps as only lone mountain houses know.
See, here is the curtain—this apron—I try to shut it
out with then. It fades it, you see. Sun gild this
house? not that ever Marianna saw.'

'Because when this roof is gilded most, then you stay
here within.'

'The hottest, weariest hour of day, you mean? Sir,
the sun gilds not this roof. It leaked so, brother newly
shingled all one side. Did you not see it? The north
side, where the sun strikes most on what the rain has
wetted. The sun is a good sun; but this roof, it first
scorches, and then rots. An old house. They went
West, and are long dead, they say, who built it. A
mountain house. In winter no fox could den in it.
That chimney-place has been blocked up with snow,
just like a hollow stump.'

'Yours are strange fancies, Marianna.'

'They but reflect the things.'

'Then I should have said, "These are strange things,"
rather than, "Yours are strange fancies." '

'As you will'; and took up her sewing.

Something in those quiet words, or in that quiet act,
it made me mute again; while, noting, through the
fairy-window, a broad shadow stealing on, as cast by
some gigantic condor, floating at brooding poise on outstretched wings, I marked how, by its deeper and
inclusive dusk, it wiped away into itself all lesser shades
of rock or fern.

'You watch the cloud,' said Marianna.

'No, a shadow; a cloud's, no doubt—though that I
cannot see. How did you know it? Your eyes are on
your work.'

' It dusked my work. There, now the cloud is gone, Tray comes back.'

' How ? '

' The dog, the shaggy dog. At noon, he steals off, of himself, to change his shape—returns, and lies down a while, nigh the door. Don't you see him ? His head is turned round at you ; though, when you came, he looked before him.'

' Your eyes rest but on your work ; what do you speak of ? '

' By the window, crossing.'

' You mean this shaggy shadow—the nigh one ? And, yes, now that I mark it, it is not unlike a large, black Newfoundland dog. The invading shadow gone, the invaded one returns. But I do not see what casts it.'

' For that, you must go without.'

' One of those grassy rocks, no doubt.'

' You see his head, his face ? '

' The shadow's ? You speak as if *you* saw it, and all the time your eyes are on your work.'

' Tray looks at you,' still without glancing up ; ' this is his hour ; I see him.'

' Have you, then, so long sat at this mountain window, where but clouds and vapours pass, that, to you, shadows are as things, though you speak of them as of phantoms ; that, by familiar knowledge, working like a second sight, you can, without looking for them, tell just where they are, though, as having mice-like feet, they creep about, and come and go ; that, to you, these lifeless shadows are as living friends, who, though out of sight, are not out of mind, even in their faces—is it so ? '

' That way I never thought of it. But the friendliest one, that used to soothe my weariness so much, coolly quivering on the ferns, it was taken from me, never to

return, as Tray did just now. The shadow of a
birch. The tree was struck by lightning, and brother
cut it up. You saw the cross-pile outdoors—the buried
root lies under it ; but not the shadow. That is
flown, and never will come back, nor ever anywhere
stir again.'

Another cloud here stole along, once more blotting out
the dog, and blackening all the mountain ; while the
stillness was so still, deafness might have forgot itself,
or else believed that noiseless shadow spoke.

' Birds, Marianna, singing-birds, I hear none ; I hear
nothing. Boys and bob-o-links, do they never come
a-berrying up here ? '

' Birds, I seldom hear ; boys, never. The berries
mostly ripe and fall—few, but me, the wiser.'

' But yellow-birds showed me the way—part way, at
least.'

' And then flew back. I guess they play about the
mountain-side, but don't make the top their home. And
no doubt you think that, living so lonesome here, knowing
nothing, hearing nothing—little, at least, but sound of
thunder and the fall of trees—never reading, seldom
speaking, yet ever wakeful, this is what gives me my
strange thoughts—for so you call them—this weariness
and wakefulness together. Brother, who stands and works
in open air, would I could rest like him ; but mine is
mostly but dull woman's work—sitting, sitting, restless
sitting.'

' But, do you not go walk at times ? These woods
are wide.'

' And lonesome ; lonesome, because so wide. Sometimes, 'tis true, of afternoons, I go a little way ; but
soon come back again. Better feel lone by hearth, than
rock. The shadows hereabouts I know—those in the
woods are strangers,'

' But the night ? '

' Just like the day. Thinking, thinking—a wheel I cannot stop ; pure want of sleep it is that turns it.'

' I have heard that, for this wakeful weariness, to say one's prayers, and then lay one's head upon a fresh hop pillow——'

' Look ! '

Through the fairy-window, she pointed down the steep to a small garden patch near by—mere pot of rifled loam, half rounded in by sheltering rocks—where, side by side, some feet apart, nipped and puny, two hop-vines climbed two poles, and, gaining their tip-ends, would have then joined over in an upward clasp, but the baffled shoots, groping a while in empty air, trailed back whence they sprung.

' You have tried the pillow, then ? '

' Yes.'

' And prayer ? '

' Prayer and pillow.'

' Is there no other cure, or charm ? '

' Oh, if I could but once get to yonder house, and but look upon whoever the happy being is that lives there ! A foolish thought : why do I think it ? Is it that I live so lonesome, and know nothing ? '

' I, too, know nothing ; and, therefore, cannot answer ; but, for your sake, Marianna, well could wish that I were that happy one of the happy house you dream you see ; for then you would behold him now, and, as you say, this weariness might leave you.'

Enough. Launching my yawl no more for fairyland, I stick to the piazza. It is my box-royal ; and this amphitheatre, my theatre of San Carlo. Yes, the scenery is magical—the illusion so complete. And Madam Meadow Lark, my prima donna, plays her grand engagement here ; and, drinking in her sunrise note, which,

B

Memnon-like, seems struck from the golden window, how far from me the weary face behind it.

But, every night, when the curtain falls, truth comes in with darkness. No light shows from the mountain. To and fro I walk the piazza deck, haunted by Marianna's face, and many as real a story.

BARTLEBY

I am a rather elderly man. The nature of my avocations, for the last thirty years, has brought me into more than ordinary contact with what would seem an interesting and somewhat singular set of men, of whom, as yet, nothing, that I know of, has ever been written— I mean, the law-copyists, or scriveners. I have known very many of them, professionally and privately, and, if I pleased, could relate divers histories, at which good-natured gentlemen might smile, and sentimental souls might weep. But I waive the biographies of all other scriveners, for a few passages in the life of Bartleby, who was a scrivener, the strangest I ever saw, or heard of. While, of other law-copyists, I might write the complete life, of Bartleby nothing of that sort can be done. I believe that no materials exist, for a full and satisfactory biography of this man. It is an irreparable loss to literature. Bartleby was one of those beings of whom nothing is ascertainable, except from the original sources, and, in his case, those are very small. What my own astonished eyes saw of Bartleby, *that* is all I know of him, except, indeed, one vague report, which will appear in the sequel.

Ere introducing the scrivener, as he first appeared to me, it is fit I make some mention of myself, my employés, my business, my chambers, and general surroundings ; because some such description is indispensable to an adequate understanding of the chief character about to be presented. Imprimis : I am a man who, from his

19

youth upward, has been filled with a profound conviction that the easiest way of life is the best. Hence, though I belong to a profession proverbially energetic and nervous, even to turbulence, at times, yet nothing of that sort have I ever suffered to invade my peace. I am one of those unambitious lawyers who never addresses a jury, or in any way draws down public applause; but, in the cool tranquillity of a snug retreat, do a snug business among rich men's bonds, and mortgages, and title-deeds. All who know me, consider me an eminently *safe* man. The late John Jacob Astor, a personage little given to poetic enthusiasm, had no hesitation in pronouncing my first grand point to be prudence; my next, method. I do not speak it in vanity, but simply record the fact, that I was not unemployed in my profession by the late John Jacob Astor; a name which, I admit, I love to repeat; for it hath a rounded and orbicular sound to it, and rings like unto bullion. I will freely add, that I was not insensible to the late John Jacob Astor's good opinion.

Some time prior to the period at which this little history begins, my avocations had been largely increased. The good old office, now extinct in the State of New York, of a Master in Chancery, had been conferred upon me. It was not a very arduous office, but very pleasantly remunerative. I seldom lose my temper; much more seldom indulge in dangerous indignation at wrongs and outrages; but, I must be permitted to be rash here, and declare, that I consider the sudden and violent abrogation of the office of Master in Chancery, by the new Constitution, as a—premature act; inasmuch as I had counted upon a life-lease of the profits, whereas I only received those of a few short years. But this is by the way.

My chambers were upstairs, at No. — Wall Street.

At one end, they looked upon the white wall of the interior of a spacious skylight shaft, penetrating the building from top to bottom.

This view might have been considered rather tame than otherwise, deficient in what landscape painters call ' life.' But, if so, the view from the other end of my chambers offered, at least, a contrast, if nothing more. In that direction, my windows commanded an un-obstructed view of a lofty brick wall, black by age and everlasting shade ; which wall required no spy-glass to bring out its lurking beauties, but, for the benefit of all near-sighted spectators, was pushed up to within ten feet of my window panes. Owing to the great height of the surrounding buildings, and my chambers being on the second floor, the interval between this wall and mine not a little resembled a huge square cistern.

At the period just preceding the advent of Bartleby, I had two persons as copyists in my employment, and a promising lad as an office-boy. First, Turkey ; second, Nippers ; third, Ginger Nut. These may seem names, the like of which are not usually found in the Directory. In truth, they were nicknames, mutually conferred upon each other by my three clerks, and were deemed expres-sive of their respective persons or characters. Turkey was a short, pursy Englishman, of about my own age— that is, somewhere not far from sixty. In the morning, one might say, his face was of a fine florid hue, but after twelve o'clock, meridian—his dinner hour—it blazed like a grate full of Christmas coals ; and continued blazing— but, as it were, with a gradual wane—till six o'clock, P.M., or thereabouts ; after which, I saw no more of the pro-prietor of the face, which, gaining its meridian with the sun, seemed to set with it, to rise, culminate, and decline the following day, with the like regularity and un-diminished glory. There are many singular coincidences

I have known in the course of my life, not the least among
which was the fact, that, exactly when Turkey displayed
his fullest beams from his red and radiant countenance,
just then, too, at that critical moment, began the daily
period when I considered his business capacities as
seriously disturbed for the remainder of the twenty-four
hours. Not that he was absolutely idle, or averse to
business, then; far from it. The difficulty was, he was
apt to be altogether too energetic. There was a strange,
inflamed, flurried, flighty recklessness of activity about
him. He would be incautious in dipping his pen into his
inkstand. All his blots upon my documents were
dropped there after twelve o'clock, meridian. Indeed,
not only would he be reckless, and sadly given to making
blots in the afternoon, but, some days, he went further,
and was rather noisy. At such times, too, his face flamed
with augmented blazonry, as if cannel coal had been
heaped on anthracite. He made an unpleasant racket
with his chair; spilled his sand-box; in mending his
pens, impatiently split them all to pieces, and threw
them on the floor in a sudden passion; stood up, and
leaned over his table, boxing his papers about in a most
indecorous manner, very sad to behold in an elderly
man like him. Nevertheless, as he was in many ways a
most valuable person to me, and all the time before
twelve o'clock, meridian, was the quickest, steadiest
creature, too, accomplishing a great deal of work in a
style not easily to be matched—for these reasons, I was
willing to overlook his eccentricities, though, indeed,
occasionally, I remonstrated with him. I did this very
gently, however, because, though the civilest, nay, the
blandest and most reverential of men in the morning,
yet, in the afternoon, he was disposed, upon provocation,
to be slightly rash with his tongue—in fact, insolent.
Now, valuing his morning services as I did, and resolved

not to lose them—yet, at the same time, made uncomfortable by his inflamed ways after twelve o'clock—and being a man of peace, unwilling by my admonitions to call forth unseemly retorts from him, I took upon me, one Saturday noon (he was always worse on Saturdays) to hint to him, very kindly, that, perhaps, now that he was growing old, it might be well to abridge his labours ; in short, he need not come to my chambers after twelve o'clock, but, dinner over, had best go home to his lodgings, and rest himself till tea-time. But no ; he insisted upon his afternoon devotions. His countenance became intolerably fervid, as he oratorically assured me—gesticulating with a long ruler at the other end of the room—that if his services in the morning were useful, how indispensable, then, in the afternoon ?

' With submission, sir,' said Turkey, on this occasion, ' I consider myself your right-hand man. In the morning I but marshal and deploy my columns ; but in the afternoon I put myself at their head, and gallantly charge the foe, thus '—and he made a violent thrust with the ruler.

' But the blots, Turkey,' intimated I.

' True ; but, with submission, sir, behold these hairs ! I am getting old. Surely, sir, a blot or two of a warm afternoon is not to be severely urged against gray hairs. Old age—even if it blot the page—is honourable. With submission, sir, we *both* are getting old.'

This appeal to my fellow-feeling was hardly to be resisted. At all events, I saw that go he would not. So, I made up my mind to let him stay, resolving, nevertheless, to see to it that, during the afternoon, he had to do with my less important papers.

Nippers, the second on my list, was a whiskered, sallow, and, upon the whole, rather piratical-looking young man, of about five-and-twenty. I always deemed him the victim of two evil powers—ambition and indigestion. The ambition was evinced by a certain impatience of the duties of a mere copyist, an unwarrantable usurpation of strictly professional affairs, such as the original drawing up of legal documents. The indigestion seemed betokened in an occasional nervous testiness and grinning irritability, causing the teeth to audibly grind together over mistakes committed in copying ; unnecessary maledictions, hissed, rather than spoken, in the heat of business ; and especially by a continual discontent with the height of the table where he worked. Though of a very ingenious mechanical turn, Nippers could never get this table to suit him. He put chips under it, blocks of various sorts, bits of pasteboard, and at last went so far as to attempt an exquisite adjustment, by final pieces of folded blotting-paper. But no invention would answer. If, for the sake of easing his back, he brought the table lid at a sharp angle well up toward his chin, and wrote there like a man using the steep roof of a Dutch house for his desk, then he declared that it stopped the circulation in his arms. If now he lowered the table to his waistbands, and stooped over it in writing, then there was a sore aching in his back. In short, the truth of the matter was, Nippers knew not what he wanted. Or, if he wanted anything, it was to be rid of a scrivener's table altogether. Among the manifestations of his diseased ambition was a fondness he had for receiving visits from certain ambiguous-looking fellows in seedy coats, whom he called his clients. Indeed, I was aware that not only was he, at times, considerable of a ward-politician, but he occasionally did a little business at the Justices' courts, and was not unknown on the steps of the Tombs. I have good reason to believe, however, that one individual who called upon him at my chambers, and who, with a grand air, he insisted was his client, was no other than a dun, and the alleged title-deed, a bill. But, with all his failings, and the annoyances he caused me, Nippers, like his compatriot Turkey, was a very useful man to me ; wrote a neat, swift hand ; and, when he chose, was not deficient in a gentlemanly sort of deportment. Added to this, he always dressed in a gentlemanly sort of way ; and so, incidentally, reflected credit upon my chambers. Whereas, with respect to Turkey, I had much ado to keep him from being a reproach to me. His clothes were apt to look oily, and smell of eating-houses. He wore his pantaloons very loose and baggy in summer. His coats were execrable ; his hat not to be handled. But while the hat was a thing of indifference to me, inasmuch as his natural civility and deference, as a dependent Englishman, always led him to doff it the moment he entered the room, yet his coat was another matter. Concerning his coats, I reasoned with him ; but with no effect. The truth was, I suppose, that a man with so small an income could not afford to sport such a lustrous face and a lustrous coat at one and the same time. As Nippers once observed, Turkey's money went chiefly for red ink. One winter day, I presented Turkey with a highly respectable-looking coat of my own—a padded gray coat, of a most comfortable warmth, and which buttoned straight up from the knee to the neck. I thought Turkey would appreciate the favour, and abate his rashness and obstreperousness of afternoons. But no ; I verily believe that buttoning himself up in so downy and blanket-like a coat had a pernicious effect upon him—upon the same principle that too much oats are bad for horses. In fact, precisely as a rash, restive horse is said to feel his oats, so Turkey felt his coat. It made him insolent. He was a man whom prosperity harmed.

Though, concerning the self-indulgent habits of Turkey,

I had my own private surmises, yet, touching Nippers, I was well persuaded that, whatever might be his faults in other respects, he was, at least, a temperate young man. But, indeed, nature herself seemed to have been his vintner, and, at his birth, charged him so thoroughly with an irritable, brandy-like disposition, that all subsequent potations were needless. When I consider how, amid the stillness of my chambers, Nippers would sometimes impatiently rise from his seat, and stooping over his table, spread his arms wide apart, seize the whole desk, and move it, and jerk it, with a grim, grinding motion on the floor, as if the table were a perverse voluntary agent, intent on thwarting and vexing him, I plainly perceive that, for Nippers, brandy-and-water were altogether superfluous.

It was fortunate for me that, owing to its peculiar cause — indigestion — the irritability and consequent nervousness of Nippers were mainly observable in the morning, while in the afternoon he was comparatively mild. So that, Turkey's paroxysms only coming on about twelve o'clock, I never had to do with their eccentricities at one time. Their fits relieved each other, like guards. When Nippers's was on, Turkey's was off; and *vice versa*. This was a good natural arrangement, under the circumstances.

Ginger Nut, the third on my list, was a lad, some twelve years old. His father was a carman, ambitious of seeing his son on the bench instead of a cart, before he died. So he sent him to my office, as student at law, errand-boy, cleaner and sweeper, at the rate of one dollar a week. He had a little desk to himself, but he did not use it much. Upon inspection, the drawer exhibited a great array of the shells of various sorts of nuts. Indeed, to this quick-witted youth, the whole noble science of the law was contained in a nut-shell.

Not the least among the employments of Ginger Nut, as well as one which he discharged with the most alacrity, was his duty as cake and apple purveyor for Turkey and Nippers. Copying law-papers being proverbially a dry, husky sort of business, my two scriveners were fain to moisten their mouths very often with Spitzenbergs, to be had at the numerous stalls nigh the Custom House and Post Office. Also, they sent Ginger Nut very frequently for that peculiar cake—small, flat, round, and very spicy—after which he had been named by them. Of a cold morning, when business was but dull, Turkey would gobble up scores of these cakes, as if they were mere wafers—indeed, they sell them at the rate of six or eight for a penny—the scrape of his pen blending with the crunching of the crisp particles in his mouth. Of all the fiery afternoon blunders and flurried rashnesses of Turkey, was his once moistening a ginger-cake between his lips, and clapping it on to a mortgage, for a seal. I came within an ace of dismissing him then. But he mollified me by making an oriental bow, and saying—'With submission, sir, it was generous of me to find you in stationery on my own account.'

Now my original business—that of a conveyancer and title-hunter, and drawer-up of recondite documents of all sorts—was considerably increased by receiving the master's office. There was now great work for scriveners. Not only must I push the clerks already with me, but I must have additional help.

In answer to my advertisement, a motionless young man one morning stood upon my office threshold, the door being open, for it was summer. I can see that figure now—pallidly neat, pitiably respectable, incurably forlorn ! It was Bartleby.

After a few words touching his qualifications, I engaged him, glad to have among my corps of copyists a man of

so singularly sedate an aspect, which I thought might
operate beneficially upon the flighty temper of Turkey,
and the fiery one of Nippers.

I should have stated before that ground-glass folding-
doors divided my premises into two parts, one of which
was occupied by my scriveners, the other by myself.
According to my humour, I threw open these doors, or
closed them. I resolved to assign Bartleby a corner by
the folding-doors, but on my side of them, so as to
have this quiet man within easy call, in case any trifling
thing was to be done. I placed his desk close up to a
small side-window in that part of the room, a window
which originally had afforded a lateral view of certain
grimy back-yards and bricks, but which, owing to subsequent erections, commanded at present no view at all,
though it gave some light. Within three feet of the
panes was a wall, and the light came down from far above,
between two lofty buildings, as from a very small opening
in a dome. Still further to a satisfactory arrangement,
I procured a high green folding-screen, which might
entirely isolate Bartleby from my sight, though not
remove him from my voice. And thus, in a manner,
privacy and society were conjoined.

At first, Bartleby did an extraordinary quantity of
writing. As if long famishing for something to copy,
he seemed to gorge himself on my documents. There
was no pause for digestion. He ran a day and night
line, copying by sun-light and by candle-light. I should
have been quite delighted with his application, had he
been cheerfully industrious. But he wrote on silently,
palely, mechanically.

It is, of course, an indispensable part of a scrivener's
business to verify the accuracy of his copy, word by
word. Where there are two or more scriveners in an
office, they assist each other in this examination, one

reading from the copy, the other holding the original. It is a very dull, wearisome, and lethargic affair. I can readily imagine that, to some sanguine temperaments, it would be altogether intolerable. For example, I cannot credit that the mettlesome poet, Byron, would have contentedly sat down with Bartleby to examine a law document of, say, five hundred pages, closely written in a crimpy hand.

Now and then, in the haste of business, it had been my habit to assist in comparing some brief document myself, calling Turkey or Nippers for this purpose. One object I had, in placing Bartleby so handy to me behind the screen, was, to avail myself of his services on such trivial occasions. It was on the third day, I think, of his being with me, and before any necessity had arisen for having his own writing examined, that, being much hurried to complete a small affair I had in hand, I abruptly called to Bartleby. In my haste and natural expectancy of instant compliance, I sat with my head bent over the original on my desk, and my right hand sideways, and somewhat nervously extended with the copy, so that, immediately upon emerging from his retreat, Bartleby might snatch it and proceed to business without the least delay.

In this very attitude did I sit when I called to him, rapidly stating what it was I wanted him to do—namely, to examine a small paper with me. Imagine my surprise, nay, my consternation, when, without moving from his privacy, Bartleby, in a singularly mild, firm voice, replied, ' I would prefer not to.'

I sat a while in perfect silence, rallying my stunned faculties. Immediately it occurred to me that my ears had deceived me, or Bartleby had entirely misunderstood my meaning. I repeated my request in the clearest tone I could assume ; but in quite as clear a one came the previous reply, ' I would prefer not to.'

'Prefer not to,' echoed I, rising in high excitement, and crossing the room with a stride. 'What do you mean? Are you moon-struck? I want you to help me compare this sheet here—take it,' and I thrust it toward him.

'I would prefer not to,' said he.

I looked at him steadfastly. His face was leanly composed; his gray eye dimly calm. Not a wrinkle of agitation rippled him. Had there been the least un-easiness, anger, impatience, or impertinence in his manner; in other words, had there been anything ordinarily human about him, doubtless I should have violently dismissed him from the premises. But as it was, I should have as soon thought of turning my pale plaster-of-paris bust of Cicero out of doors. I stood gazing at him a while, as he went on with his own writing, and then reseated myself at my desk. This is very strange, thought I. What had one best do? But my business hurried me. I concluded to forget the matter for the present, reserving it for my future leisure. So calling Nippers from the other room, the paper was speedily examined.

A few days after this, Bartleby concluded four lengthy documents, being quadruplicates of a week's testimony taken before me in my High Court of Chancery. It became necessary to examine them. It was an im-portant suit, and great accuracy was imperative. Having all things arranged, I called Turkey, Nippers, and Ginger Nut, from the next room, meaning to place the four copies in the hands of my four clerks, while I should read from the original. Accordingly, Turkey, Nippers, and Ginger Nut had taken their seats in a row, each with his document in his hand, when I called to Bartleby to join this interesting group.

'Bartleby! quick, I am waiting.'

I heard a slow scrape of his chair legs on the uncarpeted floor, and soon he appeared standing at the
entrance of his hermitage.

'What is wanted ? ' said he mildly.

'The copies, the copies,' said I hurriedly. 'We are
going to examine them. There '—and I held toward him
the fourth quadruplicate.

'I would prefer not to,' he said, and gently disappeared
behind the screen.

For a few moments I was turned into a pillar of salt,
standing at the head of my seated column of clerks.
Recovering myself, I advanced toward the screen, and
demanded the reason for such extraordinary conduct.

'*Why* do you refuse ? '

'I would prefer not to.'

With any other man I should have flown outright into
a dreadful passion, scorned all further words, and thrust
him ignominiously from my presence. But there was
something about Bartleby that not only strangely disarmed me, but, in a wonderful manner, touched and
disconcerted me. I began to reason with him.

'These are your own copies we are about to examine.
It is labour saving to you, because one examination will
answer for your four papers. It is common usage.
Every copyist is bound to help examine his copy. Is it
not so ? Will you not speak ? Answer ! '

'I prefer not to,' he replied in a flute-like tone. It
seemed to me that, while I had been addressing him, he
carefully revolved every statement that I made ; fully
comprehended the meaning ; could not gainsay the irre-
sistible conclusion ; but, at the same time, some paramount
consideration prevailed with him to reply as he did.

'You are decided, then, not to comply with my request—a request made according to common usage and
common sense ? '

He briefly gave me to understand, that on that point my judgment was sound. Yes : his decision was irreversible.

It is not seldom the case that, when a man is browbeaten in some unprecedented and violently unreasonable way, he begins to stagger in his own plainest faith. He begins, as it were, vaguely to surmise that, wonderful as it may be, all the justice and all the reason is on the other side. Accordingly, if any disinterested persons are present, he turns to them for some reinforcement for his own faltering mind.

' Turkey,' said I, ' what do you think of this ?   Am I not right ? '

' With submission, sir,' said Turkey, in his blandest tone, ' I think that you are.'

' Nippers,' said I, ' what do *you* think of it ? '

' I think I should kick him out of the office.'

(The reader, of nice perceptions, will here perceive that, it being morning, Turkey's answer is couched in polite and tranquil terms, but Nippers's replies in ill-tempered ones. Or, to repeat a previous sentence, Nippers's ugly mood was on duty, and Turkey's off.)

' Ginger Nut,' said I, willing to enlist the smallest suffrage in my behalf, ' what do *you* think of it ? '

' I think, sir, he 's a little *luny*,' replied Ginger Nut, with a grin.

' You hear what they say,' said I, turning toward the screen, ' come forth and do your duty.'

But he vouchsafed no reply. I pondered a moment in sore perplexity. But once more business hurried me. I determined again to postpone the consideration of this dilemma to my future leisure. With a little trouble we made out to examine the papers without Bartleby, though at every page or two Turkey deferentially dropped his opinion, that this proceeding was quite out of the common ; while Nippers, twitching in his chair with a dyspeptic nervousness, ground out, between his set teeth, occasional hissing maledictions against the stubborn oaf behind the screen. And for his (Nippers's) part, this was the first and the last time he would do another man's business without pay.

Meanwhile Bartleby sat in his hermitage, oblivious to everything but his own peculiar business there.

Some days passed, the scrivener being employed upon another lengthy work. His late remarkable conduct led me to regard his ways narrowly. I observed that he never went to dinner ; indeed, that he never went anywhere. As yet I had never, of my personal knowledge, known him to be outside of my office. He was a perpetual sentry in the corner. At about eleven o'clock though, in the morning, I noticed that Ginger Nut would advance toward the opening in Bartleby's screen, as if silently beckoned thither by a gesture invisible to me where I sat. The boy would then leave the office, jingling a few pence, and reappear with a handful of ginger-nuts, which he delivered in the hermitage, receiving two of the cakes for his trouble.

He lives, then, on ginger-nuts, thought I ; never eats a dinner, properly speaking ; he must be a vegetarian, then ; but no ; he never eats even vegetables, he eats nothing but ginger-nuts. My mind then ran on in reveries concerning the probable effects upon the human constitution of living entirely on ginger-nuts. Ginger-nuts are so called, because they contain ginger as one of their peculiar constituents, and the final flavouring one. Now, what was ginger ? A hot, spicy thing. Was Bartleby hot and spicy ? Not at all. Ginger, then, had no effect upon Bartleby. Probably he preferred it should have none.

Nothing so aggravates an earnest person as a passive

C

resistance. If the individual so resisted be of a not in-
humane temper, and the resisting one perfectly harmless
in his passivity, then, in the better moods of the former,
he will endeavour charitably to construe to his imagination what proves impossible to be solved by his judgment.
Even so, for the most part, I regarded Bartleby and his
ways. Poor fellow! thought I, he means no mischief;
it is plain he intends no insolence; his aspect sufficiently
evinces that his eccentricities are involuntary. He is
useful to me. I can get along with him. If I turn him
away, the chances are he will fall in with some less-
indulgent employer, and then he will be rudely treated,
and perhaps driven forth miserably to starve. Yes.
Here I can cheaply purchase a delicious self-approval.
To befriend Bartleby; to humour him in his strange
wilfulness, will cost me little or nothing, while I lay up
in my soul what will eventually prove a sweet morsel
for my conscience. But this mood was not invariable
with me. The passiveness of Bartleby sometimes irri-
tated me. I felt strangely goaded on to encounter him
in new opposition—to elicit some angry spark from him
answerable to my own. But, indeed, I might as well have
essayed to strike fire with my knuckles against a bit of
Windsor soap. But one afternoon the evil impulse in me
mastered me, and the following little scene ensued :—

' Bartleby,' said I, ' when those papers are all copied,
I will compare them with you.'

' I would prefer not to.'

' How? Surely you do not mean to persist in that
mulish vagary?'

No answer.

I threw open the folding-doors near by, and, turning
upon Turkey and Nippers, exclaimed :

' Bartleby a second time says, he won't examine his
papers. What do you think of it, Turkey?'

It was afternoon, be it remembered. Turkey sat
glowing like a brass boiler ; his bald head steaming ;
his hands reeling among his blotted papers.

'Think of it ? ' roared Turkey ; 'I think I 'll just
step behind his screen, and black his eyes for him ! '

So saying, Turkey rose to his feet and threw his arms
into a pugilistic position. He was hurrying away to
make good his promise, when I detained him, alarmed at
the effect of incautiously rousing Turkey's combativeness
after dinner.

'Sit down, Turkey,' said I, 'and hear what Nippers
has to say. What do you think of it, Nippers ? Would
I not be justified in immediately dismissing Bartleby ? '

'Excuse me, that is for you to decide, sir. I think his
conduct quite unusual, and, indeed, unjust, as regards
Turkey and myself. But it may only be a passing
whim.'

'Ah,' exclaimed I, 'you have strangely changed your
mind, then—you speak very gently of him now.'

'All beer,' cried Turkey ; 'gentleness is effects of
beer—Nippers and I dined together to-day. You see
how gentle *I* am, sir. Shall I go and black his eyes ? '

'You refer to Bartleby, I suppose. No, not to-day,
Turkey,' I replied ; 'pray, put up your fists.'

I closed the doors, and again advanced toward Bartleby.
I felt additional incentives tempting me to my fate. I
burned to be rebelled against again. I remembered that
Bartleby never left the office.

'Bartleby,' said I, 'Ginger Nut is away ; just step
around to the Post Office, won't you ? (it was but a
three minutes' walk), and see if there is anything for me.'

'I would prefer not to.'

'You *will* not ? '

'I *prefer* not.'

I staggered to my desk, and sat there in a deep study.

My blind inveteracy returned. Was there any other thing in which I could procure myself to be ignominiously repulsed by this lean, penniless wight ?—my hired clerk ? What added thing is there, perfectly reasonable, that he will be sure to refuse to do ?

' Bartleby ! '

No answer.

' Bartleby,' in a louder tone.

No answer.

' Bartleby,' I roared.

Like a very ghost, agreeably to the laws of magical invocation, at the third summons, he appeared at the entrance of his hermitage.

' Go to the next room, and tell Nippers to come to me.'

' I prefer not to,' he respectfully and slowly said, and mildly disappeared.

' Very good, Bartleby,' said I, in a quiet sort of serenely-severe self-possessed tone, intimating the un-alterable purpose of some terrible retribution very close at hand. At the moment I half intended something of the kind. But upon the whole, as it was drawing toward my dinner-hour, I thought it best to put on my hat and walk home for the day, suffering much from perplexity and distress of mind.

Shall I acknowledge it ? The conclusion of this whole business was, that it soon became a fixed fact of my chambers, that a pale young scrivener, by the name of Bartleby, had a desk there ; that he copied for me at the usual rate of four cents a folio (one hundred words) ; but he was permanently exempt from examining the work done by him, that duty being transferred to Turkey and Nippers, out of compliment, doubtless, to their superior acuteness ; moreover, said Bartleby was never, on any account, to be dispatched on the most

trivial errand of any sort ; and that even if entreated
to take upon him such a matter, it was generally understood that he would ' prefer not to '—in other words,
that he would refuse point-blank.

As days passed on, I became considerably reconciled
to Bartleby. His steadiness, his freedom from all dissi-
pation, his incessant industry (except when he chose to
throw himself into a standing revery behind his screen),
his great stillness, his unalterableness of demeanour
under all circumstances, made him a valuable acquisi-
tion. One prime thing was this—*he was always there*—
first in the morning, continually through the day, and
the last at night. I had a singular confidence in his
honesty. I felt my most precious papers perfectly safe
in his hands. Sometimes, to be sure, I could not, for
the very soul of me, avoid falling into sudden spasmodic
passions with him. For it was exceeding difficult to
bear in mind all the time those strange peculiarities,
privileges, and unheard-of exemptions, forming the tacit
stipulations on Bartleby's part under which he remained
in my office. Now and then, in the eagerness of dis-
patching pressing business, I would inadvertently summon
Bartleby, in a short, rapid tone, to put his finger, say,
on the incipient tie of a bit of red tape with which I
was about compressing some papers. Of course, from
behind the screen the usual answer, ' I prefer not to,'
was sure to come ; and then, how could a human creature,
with the common infirmities of our nature, refrain from
bitterly exclaiming upon such perverseness—such un-
reasonableness. However, every added repulse of this
sort which I received only tended to lessen the probability
of my repeating the inadvertence.

Here it must be said, that according to the custom
of most legal gentlemen occupying chambers in densely
populated law-buildings, there were several keys to my

door. One was kept by a woman residing in the attic,
which person weekly scrubbed and daily swept and
dusted my apartments. Another was kept by Turkey
for convenience sake. The third I sometimes carried in
my own pocket. The fourth I knew not who had.

Now, one Sunday morning I happened to go to Trinity
Church, to hear a celebrated preacher, and finding myself
rather early on the ground I thought I would walk
round to my chambers for a while. Luckily I had my
key with me ; but upon applying it to the lock, I found
it resisted by something inserted from the inside. Quite
surprised, I called out ; when to my consternation a
key was turned from within ; and thrusting his lean
visage at me, and holding the door ajar, the apparition
of Bartleby appeared, in his shirt-sleeves, and otherwise
in a strangely tattered dishabille, saying quietly that
he was sorry, but he was deeply engaged just then,
and—preferred not admitting me at present. In a brief
word or two, he moreover added, that perhaps I had
better walk round the block two or three times, and
by that time he would probably have concluded his
affairs.

Now, the utterly unsurmised appearance of Bartleby,
tenanting my law-chambers of a Sunday morning, with
his cadaverously gentlemanly nonchalance, yet withal
firm and self-possessed, had such a strange effect upon
me, that incontinently I slunk away from my own door,
and did as desired. But not without sundry twinges
of impotent rebellion against the mild effrontery of this
unaccountable scrivener. Indeed, it was his wonderful
mildness chiefly, which not only disarmed me, but
unmanned me as it were. For I consider that one, for
the time, is a sort of unmanned when he tranquilly
permits his hired clerk to dictate to him, and order him
away from his own premises. Furthermore, I was full

of uneasiness as to what Bartleby could possibly be doing in my office in his shirt-sleeves, and in an otherwise dismantled condition of a Sunday morning. Was anything amiss going on ? Nay, that was out of the question. It was not to be thought of for a moment that Bartleby was an immoral person. But what could he be doing there ?—copying ? Nay again, whatever might be his eccentricities, Bartleby was an eminently decorous person. He would be the last man to sit down to his desk in any state approaching to nudity. Besides, it was Sunday ; and there was something about Bartleby that forbade the supposition that he would by any secular occupation violate the proprieties of the day.

Nevertheless, my mind was not pacified ; and full of a restless curiosity, at last I returned to the door. Without hindrance I inserted my key, opened it, and entered. Bartleby was not to be seen. I looked round anxiously, peeped behind his screen ; but it was very plain that he was gone. Upon more closely examining the place, I surmised that for an indefinite period Bartleby must have ate, dressed, and slept in my office, and that, too, without plate, mirror, or bed. The cushioned seat of a rickety old sofa in one corner bore the faint impress of a lean, reclining form. Rolled away under his desk, I found a blanket ; under the empty grate a blacking box and brush ; on a chair, a tin basin, with soap and a ragged towel ; in a newspaper a few crumbs of ginger-nuts and a morsel of cheese. Yes, thought I, it is evident enough that Bartleby has been making his home here, keeping bachelor's hall all by himself. Immediately then the thought came sweeping across me, what miserable friendlessness and loneliness are here revealed ! His poverty is great ; but his solitude, how horrible ! Think of it. Of a Sunday, Wall Street is deserted as

Petra ; and every night of every day it is an emptiness.
This building, too, which of week-days hums with
industry and life, at nightfall echoes with sheer vacancy,
and all through Sunday is forlorn. And here Bartleby
makes his home ; sole spectator of a solitude which he
has seen all-populous—a sort of innocent and transformed Marius brooding among the ruins of Carthage !

For the first time in my life a feeling of overpowering
stinging melancholy seized me. Before, I had never
experienced aught but a not unpleasing sadness. The
bond of a common humanity now drew me irresistibly
to gloom. A fraternal melancholy ! For both I and
Bartleby were sons of Adam. I remembered the bright
silks and sparkling faces I had seen that day, in gala
trim, swan-like sailing down the Mississippi of Broadway ; and I contrasted them with the pallid copyist,
and thought to myself, Ah, happiness courts the light,
so we deem the world is gay ; but misery hides aloof,
so we deem that misery there is none. These sad fancy-
ings—chimeras, doubtless, of a sick and silly brain—
led on to other and more special thoughts, concerning
the eccentricities of Bartleby. Presentiments of strange
discoveries hovered round me. The scrivener's pale
form appeared to me laid out, among uncaring strangers,
in its shivering winding-sheet.

Suddenly I was attracted by Bartleby's closed desk,
the key in open sight left in the lock.

I mean no mischief, seek the gratification of no heart-
less curiosity, thought I ; besides, the desk is mine, and
its contents, too, so I will make bold to look within.
Everything was methodically arranged, the papers
smoothly placed. The pigeon-holes were deep, and
removing the files of documents, I groped into their
recesses. Presently I felt something there, and dragged
it out. It was an old bandanna handkerchief, heavy

and knotted. I opened it, and saw it was a savings-bank.

I now recalled all the quiet mysteries which I had noted in the man. I remembered that he never spoke but to answer ; that, though at intervals he had considerable time to himself, yet I had never seen him reading—no, not even a newspaper ; that for long periods he would stand looking out, at his pale window behind the screen, upon the dead brick wall ; I was quite sure he never visited any refectory or eating-house ; while his pale face clearly indicated that he never drank beer like Turkey, or tea and coffee even, like other men ; that he never went anywhere in particular that I could learn ; never went out for a walk, unless, indeed, that was the case at present ; that he had declined telling who he was, or whence he came, or whether he had any relatives in the world ; that though so thin and pale, he never complained of ill health. And more than all, I remembered a certain unconscious air of pallid—how shall I call it ?—of pallid haughtiness, say, or rather an austere reserve about him, which had positively awed me into my tame compliance with his eccentricities, when I had feared to ask him to do the slightest incidental thing for me, even though I might know, from his long-continued motionlessness, that behind his screen he must be standing in one of those dead-wall reveries of his.

Revolving all these things, and coupling them with the recently discovered fact, that he made my office his constant abiding-place and home, and not forgetful of his morbid moodiness ; revolving all these things, a prudential feeling began to steal over me. My first emotions had been those of pure melancholy and sincerest pity ; but just in proportion as the forlornness of Bartleby grew and grew to my imagination, did that same melan-

choly merge into fear, that pity into repulsion. So
true it is, and so terrible, too, that up to a certain point
the thought or sight of misery enlists our best affections ;
but, in certain special cases, beyond that point it does
not. They err who would assert that invariably this
is owing to the inherent selfishness of the human heart.
It rather proceeds from a certain hopelessness of remedy-
ing excessive and organic ill. To a sensitive being, pity
is not seldom pain. And when at last it is perceived
that such pity cannot lead to effectual succour, common-
sense bids the soul be rid of it. What I saw that morning
persuaded me that the scrivener was the victim of
innate and incurable disorder. I might give alms to
his body ; but his body did not pain him ; it was his
soul that suffered, and his soul I could not reach.

I did not accomplish the purpose of going to Trinity
Church that morning. Somehow, the things I had seen
disqualified me for the time from church-going. I walked
homeward, thinking what I would do with Bartleby.
Finally, I resolved upon this—I would put certain calm
questions to him the next morning, touching his history,
etc., and if he declined to answer them openly and
unreservedly (and I supposed he would prefer not), then
to give him a twenty-dollar bill over and above whatever
I might owe him, and tell him his services were no
longer required ; but that if in any other way I could
assist him, I would be happy to do so, especially if he
desired to return to his native place, wherever that
might be, I would willingly help to defray the expenses.
Moreover, if, after reaching home, he found himself at
any time in want of aid, a letter from him would be
sure of a reply.

The next morning came.

' Bartleby,' said I, gently calling to him behind his
screen.

No reply.

' Bartleby,' said I, in a still gentler tone, ' come here ;
I am not going to ask you to do anything you would
prefer not to do—I simply wish to speak to you.'

Upon this he noiselessly slid into view.

' Will you tell me, Bartleby, where you were born ? '

' I would prefer not to.'

' Will you tell me *anything* about yourself ? '

' I would prefer not to.'

' But what reasonable objection can you have to
speak to me ?   I feel friendly toward you.'

He did not look at me while I spoke, but kept his
glance fixed upon my bust of Cicero, which, as I then
sat, was directly behind me, some six inches above my
head.

' What is your answer, Bartleby ? ' said I, after waiting
a considerable time for a reply, during which his countenance remained immovable, only there was the faintest
conceivable tremor of the white attenuated mouth.

' At present I prefer to give no answer,' he said, and
retired into his hermitage.

It was rather weak in me, I confess, but his manner,
on this occasion, nettled me.   Not only did there seem
to lurk in it a certain calm disdain, but his perverseness
seemed ungrateful, considering the undeniable good usage
and indulgence he had received from me.

Again I sat ruminating what I should do.   Mortified
as I was at his behaviour, and resolved as I had been to
dismiss him when I entered my office, nevertheless I
strangely felt something superstitious knocking at my
heart, and forbidding me to carry out my purpose, and
denouncing me for a villain if I dared to breathe one
bitter word against this forlornest of mankind.   At last,
familiarly drawing my chair behind his screen, I sat down
and said : ' Bartleby, never mind, then, about revealing

your history ; but let me entreat you, as a friend, to comply as far as may be with the usages of this office. Say now, you will help to examine papers to-morrow or next day : in short, say now, that in a day or two you will begin to be a little reasonable :—say so, Bartleby.'

'At present I would prefer not to be a little reasonable,' was his mildly cadaverous reply.

Just then the folding-doors opened, and Nippers approached. He seemed suffering from an unusually bad night's rest, induced by severer indigestion than common. He overheard those final words of Bartleby.

'*Prefer not*, eh ? ' gritted Nippers—'I'd *prefer* him, if I were you, sir,' addressing me—'I'd *prefer* him ; I'd give him preferences, the stubborn mule ! What is it, sir, pray, that he *prefers* not to do now ? '

Bartleby moved not a limb.

'Mr. Nippers,' said I, 'I'd prefer that you would withdraw for the present.'

Somehow, of late, I had got into the way of involuntarily using this word ' prefer ' upon all sorts of not exactly suitable occasions. And I trembled to think that my contact with the scrivener had already and seriously affected me in a mental way. And what further and deeper aberration might it not yet produce ? This apprehension had not been without efficacy in determining me to summary measures.

As Nippers, looking very sour and sulky, was departing, Turkey blandly and deferentially approached.

' With submission, sir,' said he, ' yesterday I was thinking about Bartleby here, and I think that if he would but prefer to take a quart of good ale every day, it would do much toward mending him, and enabling him to assist in examining his papers.'

' So you have got the word too,' said I, slightly excited.

'With submission, what word, sir,' asked Turkey, respectfully crowding himself into the contracted space behind the screen, and by so doing, making me jostle the scrivener. 'What word, sir?'

'I would prefer to be left alone here,' said Bartleby, as if offended at being mobbed in his privacy.

'*That's* the word, Turkey,' said I—'*that's* it.'

'Oh, *prefer*? oh yes—queer word. I never use it myself. But, sir, as I was saying, if he would but prefer——'

'Turkey,' interrupted I, 'you will please withdraw.'

'Oh certainly, sir, if you prefer that I should.'

As he opened the folding-door to retire, Nippers at his desk caught a glimpse of me, and asked whether I would prefer to have a certain paper copied on blue paper or white. He did not in the least roguishly accent the word prefer. It was plain that it involuntarily rolled from his tongue. I thought to myself, surely I must get rid of a demented man, who already has in some degree turned the tongues, if not the heads of myself and clerks. But I thought it prudent not to break the dismission at once.

The next day I noticed that Bartleby did nothing but stand at his window in his dead-wall revery. Upon asking him why he did not write, he said that he had decided upon doing no more writing.

'Why, how now? what next?' exclaimed I, 'do no more writing?'

'No more.'

'And what is the reason?'

'Do you not see the reason for yourself?' he indifferently replied.

I looked steadfastly at him, and perceived that his eyes looked dull and glazed. Instantly it occurred to me, that his unexampled diligence in copying by his dim window for the first few weeks of his stay with me might have temporarily impaired his vision.

I was touched. I said something in condolence with him. I hinted that of course he did wisely in abstaining from writing for a while ; and urged him to embrace that opportunity of taking wholesome exercise in the open air. This, however, he did not do. A few days after this, my other clerks being absent, and being in a great hurry to dispatch certain letters by the mail, I thought that having nothing else earthly to do, Bartleby would surely be less inflexible than usual, and carry these letters to the Post Office. But he blankly declined. So, much to my inconvenience, I went myself.

Still added days went by. Whether Bartleby's eyes improved or not, I could not say. To all appearance, I thought they did. But when I asked him if they did, he vouchsafed no answer. At all events, he would do no copying. At last, in reply to my urgings, he informed me that he had permanently given up copying.

' What ! ' exclaimed I ; ' suppose your eyes should get entirely well—better than ever before—would you not copy then ? '

'I have given up copying,' he answered, and slid aside.

He remained as ever, a fixture in my chamber. Nay— if that were possible—he became still more of a fixture than before. What was to be done ? He would do nothing in the office ; why should he stay there ? In plain fact, he had now become a millstone to me, not only useless as a necklace, but afflictive to bear. Yet I was sorry for him. I speak less than truth when I say that, on his own account, he occasioned me uneasiness. If he would but have named a single relative or friend, I would instantly have written, and urged their taking the poor fellow away to some convenient retreat.

But he seemed alone, absolutely alone in the universe. A bit of wreck in the mid-Atlantic. At length, necessities connected with my business tyrannised over all other considerations. Decently as I could, I told Bartleby that in six days' time he must unconditionally leave the office. I warned him to take measures, in the interval, for procuring some other abode. I offered to assist him in this endeavour, if he himself would but take the first step toward a removal. ' And when you finally quit me, Bartleby,' added I, ' I shall see that you go not away entirely unprovided. Six days from this hour, remember.'

At the expiration of that period, I peeped behind the screen, and lo ! Bartleby was there.

I buttoned up my coat, balanced myself ; advanced slowly toward him, touched his shoulder, and said, ' The time has come ; you must quit this place ; I am sorry for you ; here is money ; but you must go.'

' I would prefer not,' he replied, with his back still toward me.

' You *must*.'

He remained silent.

Now I had an unbounded confidence in this man's common honesty. He had frequently restored to me sixpences and shillings carelessly dropped upon the floor, for I am apt to be very reckless in such shirt-button affairs. The proceeding, then, which followed will not be deemed extraordinary.

' Bartleby,' said I, ' I owe you twelve dollars on account ; here are thirty-two ; the odd twenty are yours—Will you take it ? ' and I handed the bills toward him.

But he made no motion.

' I will leave them here, then,' putting them under a weight on the table. Then taking my hat and cane and going to the door, I tranquilly turned and added—' After you have removed your things from these offices, Bartleby, you will of course lock the door—since everyone is now gone for the day but you—and if you please, slip your key underneath the mat, so that I may have it in the morning. I shall not see you again ; so good-bye to you. If, hereafter, in your new place of abode, I can be of any service to you, do not fail to advise me by letter. Good-bye, Bartleby, and fare you well.'

But he answered not a word ; like the last column of some ruined temple, he remained standing mute and solitary in the middle of the otherwise deserted room.

As I walked home in a pensive mood, my vanity got the better of my pity. I could not but highly plume myself on my masterly management in getting rid of Bartleby. Masterly I call it, and such it must appear to any dispassionate thinker. The beauty of my procedure seemed to consist in its perfect quietness. There was no vulgar bullying, no bravado of any sort, no choleric hectoring, and striding to and fro across the apartment, jerking out vehement commands for Bartleby to bundle himself off with his beggarly traps. Nothing of the kind. Without loudly bidding Bartleby depart—as an inferior genius might have done—I *assumed* the ground that depart he must ; and upon that assumption built all I had to say. The more I thought over my procedure, the more I was charmed with it. Nevertheless, next morning, upon awakening, I had my doubts—I had somehow slept off the fumes of vanity. One of the coolest and wisest hours a man has, is just after he awakes in the morning. My procedure seemed as sagacious as ever—but only in theory. How it would prove in practice—there was the rub. It was truly a beautiful thought to have assumed Bartleby's departure ; but, after all, that assumption was simply my own, and none of Bartleby's. The great point was, not whether I had assumed that he would quit me, but whether he would prefer so to do. He was more a man of preferences than assumptions.

After breakfast, I walked down town, arguing the probabilities *pro* and *con*. One moment I thought it would prove a miserable failure, and Bartleby would be found all alive at my office as usual; the next moment it seemed certain that I should find his chair empty. And so I kept veering about. At the corner of Broadway and Canal Street, I saw quite an excited group of people standing in earnest conversation.

' I 'll take odds he doesn't,' said a voice as I passed.

' Doesn't go ?—done ! ' said I ; ' put up your money.'

I was instinctively putting my hand in my pocket to produce my own, when I remembered that this was an election day. The words I had overheard bore no reference to Bartleby, but to the success or non-success of some candidate for the mayoralty. In my intent frame of mind, I had, as it were, imagined that all Broadway shared in my excitement, and were debating the same question with me. I passed on, very thankful that the uproar of the street screened my momentary absent-mindedness.

As I had intended, I was earlier than usual at my office door. I stood listening for a moment. All was still. He must be gone. I tried the knob. The door was locked. Yes, my procedure had worked to a charm ; he indeed must be vanished. Yet a certain melancholy mixed with this : I was almost sorry for my brilliant success. I was fumbling under the door-mat for the key, which Bartleby was to have left there for me, when accidentally my knee knocked against a panel, producing a summoning sound, and in response a voice came to me from within—' Not yet ; I am occupied.'

D

It was Bartleby.

I was thunderstruck. For an instant I stood like the man who, pipe in mouth, was killed one cloudless afternoon long ago in Virginia, by summer lightning ; at his own warm open window he was killed, and remained leaning out there upon the dreamy afternoon, till someone touched him, when he fell.

' Not gone ! ' I murmured at last. But again obeying that wondrous ascendency which the inscrutable scrivener had over me, and from which ascendency, for all my chafing, I could not completely escape, I slowly went downstairs and out into the street, and while walking round the block, considered what I should next do in this unheard-of perplexity. Turn the man out by an actual thrusting I could not ; to drive him away by calling him hard names would not do ; calling in the police was an unpleasant idea ; and yet, permit him to enjoy his cadaverous triumph over me—this, too, I could not think of. What was to be done ? or, if nothing could be done, was there anything further that I could *assume* in the matter ? Yes, as before I had prospectively assumed that Bartleby would depart, so now I might retrospectively assume that departed he was. In the legitimate carrying out of this assumption, I might enter my office in a great hurry, and pretending not to see Bartleby at all, walk straight against him as if he were air. Such a proceeding would in a singular degree have the appearance of a home-thrust. It was hardly possible that Bartleby could withstand such an application of the doctrine of assumptions. But upon second thoughts the success of the plan seemed rather dubious. I resolved to argue the matter over with him again.

' Bartleby,' said I, entering the office, with a quietly severe expression, ' I am seriously displeased. I am pained, Bartleby. I had thought better of you. I had imagined you of such a gentlemanly organisation, that in any delicate dilemma a slight hint would suffice—in short, an assumption. But it appears I am deceived. Why,' I added, unaffectedly starting, ' you have not even touched that money yet,' pointing to it, just where I had left it the evening previous.

He answered nothing.

' Will you, or will you not, quit me ? ' I now demanded in a sudden passion, advancing close to him.

' I would prefer *not* to quit you,' he replied, gently emphasising the *not*.

' What earthly right have you to stay here ? Do you pay any rent ? Do you pay my taxes ? Or is this property yours ? '

He answered nothing.

' Are you ready to go on and write now ? Are your eyes recovered ? Could you copy a small paper for me this morning ? or help examine a few lines ? or step round to the Post Office ? In a word, will you do anything at all, to give a colouring to your refusal to depart the premises ? '

He silently retired into his hermitage.

I was now in such a state of nervous resentment that I thought it but prudent to check myself at present from further demonstrations. Bartleby and I were alone. I remembered the tragedy of the unfortunate Adams and the still more unfortunate Colt in the solitary office of the latter ; and how poor Colt, being dreadfully incensed by Adams, and imprudently permitting himself to get wildly excited, was at unawares hurried into his fatal act—an act which certainly no man could possibly deplore more than the actor himself. Often it had occurred to me in my ponderings upon the subject, that had that altercation taken place in the public street, or at a private residence, it would not have terminated as it did. It was the circumstance of being alone in a solitary office, upstairs, of a building entirely unhallowed by humanising domestic associations—an uncarpeted office, doubtless, of a dusty, haggard sort of appearance—this it must have been, which greatly helped to enhance the irritable desperation of the hapless Colt.

But when this old Adam of resentment rose in me and tempted me concerning Bartleby, I grappled him and threw him. How ? Why, simply by recalling the divine injunction : ' A new commandment give I unto you, that ye love one another.' Yes, this it was that saved me. Aside from higher considerations, charity often operates as a vastly wise and prudent principle—a great safeguard to its possessor. Men have committed murder for jealousy's sake, and anger's sake, and hatred's sake, and selfishness' sake, and spiritual pride's sake ; but no man, that ever I heard of, ever committed a diabolical murder for sweet charity's sake. Mere self-interest, then, if no better motive can be enlisted, should, especially with high-tempered men, prompt all beings to charity and philanthropy. At any rate, upon the occasion in question, I strove to drown my exasperated feelings toward the scrivener by benevolently construing his conduct. Poor fellow, poor fellow ! thought I, he don't mean anything ; and besides, he has seen hard times, and ought to be indulged.

I endeavoured, also, immediately to occupy myself, and at the same time to comfort my despondency. I tried to fancy, that in the course of the morning, at such time as might prove agreeable to him, Bartleby, of his own free accord, would emerge from his heritage and take up some decided line of march in the direction of the door. But no. Half-past twelve o'clock came ; Turkey began to glow in the face, overturn his ink-

stand, and become generally obstreperous; Nippers
abated down into quietude and courtesy; Ginger Nut
munched his noon apple; and Bartleby remained
standing at his window in one of his profoundest dead-
wall reveries. Will it be credited ? Ought I to acknowledge it ? That afternoon I left the office without
saying one further word to him.

Some days now passed, during which, at leisure intervals, I looked a little into 'Edwards on the Will,' and
'Priestley on Necessity.' Under the circumstances, those
books induced a salutary feeling. Gradually I slid into
the persuasion that these troubles of mine, touching
the scrivener, had been all predestinated from eternity,
and Bartleby was billeted upon me for some mysterious
purpose of an all-wise Providence, which it was not for
a mere mortal like me to fathom. Yes, Bartleby, stay
there behind your screen, thought I; I shall persecute
you no more; you are harmless and noiseless as any of
these old chairs; in short, I never feel so private as when
I know you are here. At last I see it, I feel it; I penetrate to the predestinated purpose of my life. I am
content. Others may have loftier parts to enact; but my
mission in this world, Bartleby, is to furnish you with
office-room for such period as you may see fit to remain.

I believe that this wise and blessed frame of mind
would have continued with me, had it not been for the
unsolicited and uncharitable remarks obtruded upon me
by my professional friends who visited the rooms. But
thus it often is, that the constant friction of illiberal
minds wears out at last the best resolves of the more
generous. Though to be sure, when I reflected upon it,
it was not strange that people entering my office should
be struck by the peculiar aspect of the unaccountable
Bartleby, and so be tempted to throw out some sinister
observations concerning him. Sometimes an attorney,

having business with me, and calling at my office, and
finding no one but the scrivener there, would undertake
to obtain some sort of precise information from him
touching my whereabouts ; but without heeding his
idle talk, Bartleby would remain standing immovable
in the middle of the room. So after contemplating him
in that position for a time, the attorney would depart,
no wiser than he came.

Also, when a reference was going on, and the room
full of lawyers and witnesses, and business driving fast,
some deeply occupied legal gentleman present, seeing
Bartleby wholly unemployed, would request him to run
round to his (the legal gentleman's) office and fetch
some papers for him. Thereupon, Bartleby would
tranquilly decline, and yet remain idle as before. Then
the lawyer would give a great stare, and turn to me.
And what could I say ? At last I was made aware
that all through the circle of my professional acquaintance, a whisper of wonder was running round, having
reference to the strange creature I kept at my office.
This worried me very much. And as the idea came upon
me of his possibly turning out a long-lived man, and
keep occupying my chambers, and denying my authority ;
and perplexing my visitors ; and scandalising my professional reputation ; and casting a general gloom over
the premises ; keeping soul and body together to the
last upon his savings (for doubtless he spent but half
a dime a day), and in the end perhaps outlive me, and
claim possession of my office by right of his perpetual
occupancy : as all these dark anticipations crowded upon
me more and more, and my friends continually intruded
their relentless remarks upon the apparition in my
room ; a great change was wrought in me. I resolved
to gather all my faculties together, and forever rid me
of this intolerable incubus.

Ere revolving any complicated project, however, adapted to this end, I first simply suggested to Bartleby the propriety of his permanent departure. In a calm and serious tone, I commended the idea to his careful and mature consideration. But, having taken three days to meditate upon it, he apprised me, that his original determination remained the same ; in short, that he still preferred to abide with me.

What shall I do ? I now said to myself, buttoning up my coat to the last button. What shall I do ? what ought I to do ? what does conscience say I *should* do with this man, or, rather, ghost. Rid myself of him, I must ; go, he shall. But how ? You will not thrust him, the poor, pale, passive mortal—you will not thrust such a helpless creature out of your door ? you will not dishonour yourself by such cruelty ? No, I will not, I cannot do that. Rather would I let him live and die here, and then mason up his remains in the wall. What, then, will you do ? For all your coaxing, he will not budge. Bribes he leaves under your own paper-weight on your table ; in short, it is quite plain that he prefers to cling to you.

Then something severe, something unusual must be done. What ! surely you will not have him collared by a constable, and commit his innocent pallor to the common jail ? And upon what ground could you procure such a thing to be done ?—a vagrant, is he ? What ! he a vagrant, a wanderer, who refuses to budge ? It is because he will *not* be a vagrant, then, that you seek to count him *as* a vagrant. That is too absurd. No visible means of support ; there I have him. Wrong again : for indubitably he *does* support himself, and that is the only unanswerable proof that any man can show of his possessing the means so to do. No more, then. Since he will not quit me, I must quit him. I will change my offices ; I will move elsewhere, and give him fair notice, that if I find him on my new premises I will then proceed against him as a common trespasser.

Acting accordingly, next day I thus addressed him : ' I find these chambers too far from the City Hall ; the air is unwholesome. In a word, I propose to remove my offices next week, and shall no longer require your services. I tell you this now, in order that you may seek another place.'

He made no reply, and nothing more was said.

On the appointed day I engaged carts and men, proceeded to my chambers, and, having but little furniture, everything was removed in a few hours. Throughout, the scrivener remained standing behind the screen, which I directed to be removed the last thing. It was withdrawn ; and, being folded up like a huge folio, left him the motionless occupant of a naked room. I stood in the entry watching him a moment, while something from within me upbraided me.

I re-entered, with my hand in my pocket—and—and my heart in my mouth.

' Good-bye, Bartleby ; I am going—good-bye, and God some way bless you ; and take that,' slipping something in his hand. But it dropped upon the floor, and then—strange to say—I tore myself from him whom I had so longed to be rid of.

Established in my new quarters, for a day or two I kept the door locked, and started at every footfall in the passages. When I returned to my rooms, after any little absence, I would pause at the threshold for an instant, and attentively listen ere applying my key. But these fears were needless. Bartleby never came nigh me.

I thought all was going well, when a perturbed-looking stranger visited me, inquiring whether I was the person who had recently occupied rooms at No. — Wall Street.

Full of forebodings, I replied that I was.

'Then, sir,' said the stranger, who proved a lawyer, 'you are responsible for the man you left there. He refuses to do any copying ; he refuses to do anything ; he says he prefers not to ; and he refuses to quit the premises.'

'I am very sorry, sir,' said I, with assumed tranquillity, but an inward tremor, 'but, really, the man you allude to is nothing to me—he is no relation or apprentice of mine, that you should hold me responsible for him.'

'In mercy's name, who is he ?'

'I certainly cannot inform you. I know nothing about him. Formerly I employed him as a copyist ; but he has done nothing for me now for some time past.'

'I shall settle him, then—good morning, sir.'

Several days passed, and I heard nothing more ; and, though I often felt a charitable prompting to call at the place and see poor Bartleby, yet a certain squeamishness, of I know not what, withheld me.

All is over with him, by this time, thought I, at last, when, through another week, no further intelligence reached me. But, coming to my room the day after, I found several persons waiting at my door in a high state of nervous excitement.

'That 's the man—here he comes,' cried the foremost one, whom I recognised as the lawyer who had previously called upon me alone.

'You must take him away, sir, at once,' cried a portly person among them, advancing upon me, and whom I knew to be the landlord of No. — Wall Street. 'These gentlemen, my tenants, cannot stand it any longer ; Mr. B——,' pointing to the lawyer, 'has turned him out of his room, and he now persists in haunting the building generally, sitting upon the banisters of the stairs by day, and sleeping in the entry by night. Everybody is concerned ; clients are leaving the offices ; some fears are entertained of a mob ; something you must do, and that without delay.'

Aghast at this torrent, I fell back before it, and would fain have locked myself in my new quarters. In vain I persisted that Bartleby was nothing to me—no more than to anyone else. In vain—I was the last person known to have anything to do with him, and they held me to the terrible account. Fearful, then, of being exposed in the papers (as one person present obscurely threatened), I considered the matter, and, at length, said, that if the lawyer would give me a confidential interview with the scrivener, in his (the lawyer's) own room, I would, that afternoon, strive my best to rid them of the nuisance they complained of.

Going upstairs to my old haunt, there was Bartleby silently sitting upon the banister at the landing.

' What are you doing here, Bartleby ? ' said I.

' Sitting upon the banister,' he mildly replied.

I motioned him into the lawyer's room, who then left us.

' Bartleby,' said I, ' are you aware that you are the cause of great tribulation to me, by persisting in occupying the entry after being dismissed from the office ? '

No answer.

' Now one of two things must take place. Either you must do something, or something must be done to you. Now what sort of business would you like to engage in ? Would you like to re-engage in copying for someone ? '

' No ; I would prefer not to make any change.'

' Would you like a clerkship in a dry-goods store ? '

' There is too much confinement about that. No, I would not like a clerkship ; but I am not particular.'

' Too much confinement,' I cried, ' why, you keep yourself confined all the time ! '

'I would prefer not to take a clerkship,' he rejoined, as if to settle that little item at once.

'How would a bar-tender's business suit you? There is no trying of the eyesight in that.'

'I would not like it at all; though, as I said before, I am not particular.'

His unwonted wordiness inspirited me. I returned to the charge.

'Well, then, would you like to travel through the country collecting bills for the merchants? That would improve your health.'

'No, I would prefer to be doing something else.'

'How, then, would going as a companion to Europe, to entertain some young gentleman with your conversation—how would that suit you?'

'Not at all. It does not strike me that there is anything definite about that. I like to be stationary. But I am not particular.'

'Stationary you shall be, then,' I cried, now losing all patience, and, for the first time in all my exasperating connection with him, fairly flying into a passion. 'If you do not go away from these premises before night, I shall feel bound—indeed, I *am* bound—to—to quit the premises myself!' I rather absurdly concluded, knowing not with what possible threat to try to frighten his immobility into compliance. Despairing of all further efforts, I was precipitately leaving him, when a final thought occurred to me—one which had not been wholly unindulged before.

'Bartleby,' said I, in the kindest tone I could assume under such exciting circumstances, 'will you go home with me now—not to my office, but my dwelling—and remain there till we can conclude upon some convenient arrangement for you at our leisure? Come, let us start now, right away.'

' No ; at present I would prefer not to make any change at all.'

I answered nothing ; but, effectually dodging everyone by the suddenness and rapidity of my flight, rushed from the building, ran up Wall Street toward Broadway, and, jumping into the first omnibus, was soon removed from pursuit. As soon as tranquillity returned, I distinctly perceived that I had now done all that I possibly could, both in respect to the demands of the landlord and his tenants, and with regard to my own desire and sense of duty, to benefit Bartleby, and shield him from rude persecution. I now strove to be entirely carefree and quiescent ; and my conscience justified me in the attempt ; though, indeed, it was not so successful as I could have wished. So fearful was I of being again hunted out by the incensed landlord and his exasperated tenants, that, surrendering my business to Nippers, for a few days, I drove about the upper part of the town and through the suburbs, in my rockaway ; crossed over to Jersey City and Hoboken, and paid fugitive visits to Manhattanville and Astoria. In fact, I almost lived in my rockaway for the time.

When again I entered my office, lo, a note from the landlord lay upon the desk. I opened it with trembling hands. It informed me that the writer had sent to the police, and had Bartleby removed to the Tombs as a vagrant. Moreover, since I knew more about him than anyone else, he wished me to appear at that place, and make a suitable statement of the facts. These tidings had a conflicting effect upon me. At first I was indignant ; but, at last, almost approved. The landlord's energetic, summary disposition had led him to adopt a procedure which I do not think I would have decided upon myself ; and yet, as a last resort, under such peculiar circumstances, it seemed the only plan.

As I afterward learned, the poor scrivener, when told
that he must be conducted to the Tombs, offered not
the slightest obstacle, but, in his pale, unmoving way,
silently acquiesced.

Some of the compassionate and curious bystanders
joined the party ; and headed by one of the constables
arm in arm with Bartleby, the silent procession filed its
way through all the noise, and heat, and joy of the
roaring thoroughfares at noon.

The same day I received the note, I went to the
Tombs, or, to speak more properly, the Halls of Justice.
Seeking the right officer, I stated the purpose of my
call, and was informed that the individual I described
was, indeed, within. I then assured the functionary
that Bartleby was a perfectly honest man, and greatly
to be compassionated, however unaccountably eccentric.
I narrated all I knew, and closed by suggesting the idea
of letting him remain in as indulgent confinement as
possible, till something less harsh might be done—
though, indeed, I hardly knew what. At all events, if
nothing else could be decided upon, the almshouse must
receive him. I then begged to have an interview.

Being under no disgraceful charge, and quite serene
and harmless in all his ways, they had permitted him
freely to wander about the prison, and, especially, in
the enclosed grass-platted yards thereof. And so I found
him there, standing all alone in the quietest of the yards,
his face toward a high wall, while all around, from the
narrow slits of the jail windows, I thought I saw peering
out upon him the eyes of murderers and thieves.

' Bartleby ! '

' I know you,' he said, without looking round—' and
I want nothing to say to you.'

' It was not I that brought you here, Bartleby,' said I,
keenly pained at his implied suspicion. ' And to you,.

this should not be so vile a place. Nothing reproachful attaches to you by being here. And see, it is not so sad a place as one might think. Look, there is the sky, and here is the grass.'

' I know where I am,' he replied, but would say nothing more, and so I left him.

As I entered the corridor again, a broad meat-like man, in an apron, accosted me, and, jerking his thumb over his shoulder, said, ' Is that your friend ? '

' Yes.'

' Does he want to starve ? If he does, let him live on the prison fare, that 's all.'

' Who are you ? ' asked I, not knowing what to make of such an unofficially speaking person in such a place.

' I am the grub-man. Such gentlemen as have friends here, hire me to provide them with something good to eat.'

' Is this so ? ' said I, turning to the turnkey.

He said it was.

' Well, then,' said I, slipping some silver into the grub-man's hands (for so they called him), ' I want you to give particular attention to my friend there ; let him have the best dinner you can get. And you must be as polite to him as possible.'

' Introduce me, will you ? ' said the grub-man, looking at me with an expression which seemed to say he was all impatience for an opportunity to give a specimen of his breeding.

Thinking it would prove of benefit to the scrivener, I acquiesced ; and, asking the grub-man his name, went up with him to Bartleby.

' Bartleby, this is a friend ; you will find him very useful to you.'

' Your sarvant, sir, your sarvant,' said the grub-man, making a low salutation behind his apron. ' Hope you find it pleasant here, sir; nice grounds—cool apartments—hope you'll stay with us some time—try to make it agreeable. What will you have for dinner to-day?'

'I prefer not to dine to-day,' said Bartleby, turning away. 'It would disagree with me; I am unused to dinners.' So saying, he slowly moved to the other side of the enclosure, and took up a position fronting the dead-wall.

'How's this?' said the grub-man, addressing me with a stare of astonishment. 'He's odd, ain't he?'

'I think he is a little deranged,' said I sadly.

'Deranged? deranged is it? Well, now, upon my word, I thought that friend of yourn was a gentleman forger; they are always pale and genteel-like, them forgers. I can't help pity 'em—can't help it, sir. Did you know Monroe Edwards?' he added touchingly, and paused. Then, laying his hand piteously on my shoulder, sighed, 'he died of consumption at Sing-Sing. So you weren't acquainted with Monroe?'

'No, I was never socially acquainted with any forgers. But I cannot stop longer. Look to my friend yonder. You will not lose by it. I will see you again.'

Some few days after this, I again obtained admission to the Tombs, and went through the corridors in quest of Bartleby; but without finding him.

'I saw him coming from his cell not long ago,' said a turnkey, 'maybe he's gone to loiter in the yards.'

So I went in that direction.

'Are you looking for the silent man?' said another turnkey, passing me. 'Yonder he lies—sleeping in the yard there. 'Tis not twenty minutes since I saw him lie down.'

The yard was entirely quiet. It was not accessible to the common prisoners. The surrounding walls, of

amazing thickness, kept off all sounds behind them.
The Egyptian character of the masonry weighed upon
me with its gloom. But a soft imprisoned turf grew under
foot. The heart of the eternal pyramids, it seemed,
wherein, by some strange magic, through the clefts,
grass-seed, dropped by birds, had sprung.

Strangely huddled at the base of the wall, his knees
drawn up, and lying on his side, his head touching the
cold stones, I saw the wasted Bartleby. But nothing
stirred. I paused; then went close up to him; stooped
over, and saw that his dim eyes were open; otherwise
he seemed profoundly sleeping. Something prompted
me to touch him. I felt his hand, when a tingling shiver
ran up my arm and down my spine to my feet.

The round face of the grub-man peered upon me now.
' His dinner is ready. Won't he dine to-day, either ?
Or does he live without dining ? '

' Lives without dining,' said I, and closed the eyes.

' Eh !—He 's asleep, ain't he ? '

' With kings and counsellors,' murmured I.

* * * * * * *

There would seem little need for proceeding further in
this history. Imagination will readily supply the meagre
recital of poor Bartleby's interment. But, ere parting
with the reader, let me say, that if this little narrative
has sufficiently interested him, to awaken curiosity as
to who Bartleby was, and what manner of life he led
prior to the present narrator's making his acquaintance, I can only reply, that in such curiosity I fully
share, but am wholly unable to gratify it. Yet here
I hardly know whether I should divulge one little item
of rumour, which came to my ear a few months after
the scrivener's decease. Upon what basis it rested I
could never ascertain; and hence, how true it is I
cannot now tell. But, inasmuch as this vague report

has not been without a certain suggestive interest to me, however sad, it may prove the same with some others ; and so I will briefly mention it. The report was this : that Bartleby had been a subordinate clerk in the Dead Letter Office at Washington, from which he had been suddenly removed by a change in the administration. When I think over this rumour, hardly can I express the emotions which seize me. Dead letters ! does it not sound like dead men ? Conceive a man by nature and misfortune prone to a pallid hopelessness, can any business seem more fitted to heighten it than that of continually handling these dead letters, and assorting them for the flames ? For by the cartload they are annually burned. Sometimes from out the folded paper the pale clerk takes a ring—the finger it was meant for, perhaps, moulders in the grave ; a bank-note sent in swiftest charity—he whom it would relieve, nor eats nor hungers any more ; pardon for those who died despairing ; hope for those who died unhoping ; good tidings for those who died stifled by unrelieved calamities. On errands of life, these letters speed to death.

Ah, Bartleby ! Ah, humanity !

E

BENITO CERENO

In the year 1799, Captain Amasa Delano, of Duxbury, in Massachusetts, commanding a large sealer and general trader, lay at anchor with a valuable cargo, in the harbour of St. Maria—a small, desert, uninhabited island toward the southern extremity of the long coast of Chili. There he had touched for water.

On the second day, not long after dawn, while lying in his berth, his mate came below, informing him that a strange sail was coming into the bay. Ships were then not so plenty in those waters as now. He rose, dressed, and went on deck.

The morning was one peculiar to that coast. Everything was mute and calm ; everything gray. The sea, though undulated into long roods of swells, seemed fixed, and was sleeked at the surface like waved lead that has cooled and set in the smelter's mould. The sky seemed a gray surtout. Flights of troubled gray fowl, kith and kin with flights of troubled gray vapours among which they were mixed, skimmed low and fitfully over the waters, as swallows over meadows before storms. Shadows present, foreshadowing deeper shadows to come.

To Captain Delano's surprise, the stranger, viewed through the glass, showed no colours ; though to do so upon entering a haven, however uninhabited in its shores, where but a single other ship might be lying, was the custom among peaceful seamen of all nations. Considering the lawlessness and loneliness of the spot, and

the sort of stories, at that day, associated with those
seas, Captain Delano's surprise might have deepened
into some uneasiness had he not been a person of a
singularly undistrustful good-nature, not liable, except
on extraordinary and repeated incentives, and hardly
then, to indulge in personal alarms, any way involving
the imputation of malign evil in man. Whether, in
view of what humanity is capable, such a trait implies,
along with a benevolent heart, more than ordinary
quickness and accuracy of intellectual perception, may
be left to the wise to determine.

But whatever misgivings might have obtruded on first
seeing the stranger, would almost, in any seaman's
mind, have been dissipated by observing that the ship,
in navigating into the harbour, was drawing too near
the land ; a sunken reef making out off her bow. This
seemed to prove her a stranger, indeed, not only to the
sealer, but the island ; consequently, she could be no
wonted freebooter on that ocean. With no small
interest, Captain Delano continued to watch her—a
proceeding not much facilitated by the vapours partly
mantling the hull, through which the far matin light
from her cabin streamed equivocally enough ; much
like the sun—by this time hemisphered on the rim of
the horizon, and, apparently, in company with the
strange ship entering the harbour—which, wimpled by
the same low, creeping clouds, showed not unlike a
Lima intriguante's one sinister eye peering across the
Plaza from the Indian loop-hole of her dusk *saya-y-
manta*.

It might have been but a deception of the vapours,
but the longer the stranger was watched the more
singular appeared her manœuvres. Ere long it seemed
hard to decide whether she meant to come in or no—
what she wanted, or what she was about. The wind,

which had breezed up a little during the night, was
now extremely light and baffling, which the more increased the apparent uncertainty of her movements.

Surmising, at last, that it might be a ship in distress,
Captain Delano ordered his whale-boat to be dropped,
and, much to the wary opposition of his mate, prepared
to board her, and, at the least, pilot her in. On the night
previous, a fishing - party of the seamen had gone a
long distance to some detached rocks out of sight from
the sealer, and, an hour or two before daybreak, had
returned, having met with no small success. Presuming
that the stranger might have been long off soundings,
the good captain put several baskets of the fish, for
presents, into his boat, and so pulled away. From her
continuing too near the sunken reef, deeming her in
danger, calling to his men, he made all haste to apprise
those on board of their situation. But, some time ere
the boat came up, the wind, light though it was, having
shifted, had headed the vessel off, as well as partly
broken the vapours from about her.

Upon gaining a less remote view, the ship, when made
signally visible on the verge of the leaden-hued swells,
with the shreds of fog here and there raggedly furring
her, appeared like a whitewashed monastery after a
thunder-storm, seen perched upon some dun cliff among
the Pyrenees. But it was no purely fanciful resemblance
which now, for a moment, almost led Captain Delano
to think that nothing less than a ship-load of monks was
before him. Peering over the bulwarks were what really
seemed, in the hazy distance, throngs of dark cowls;
while, fitfully revealed through the open port-holes, other
dark moving figures were dimly descried, as of Black
Friars pacing the cloisters.

Upon a still nigher approach, this appearance was
modified, and the true character of the vessel was plain—

a Spanish merchantman of the first class, carrying negro slaves, amongst other valuable freight, from one colonial port to another. A very large, and, in its time, a very fine vessel, such as in those days were at intervals encountered along that main ; sometimes superseded Acapulco treasure-ships, or retired frigates of the Spanish king's navy, which, like superannuated Italian palaces, still, under a decline of masters, preserved signs of former state.

As the whale-boat drew more and more nigh, the cause of the peculiar pipe-clayed aspect of the stranger was seen in the slovenly neglect pervading her. The spars, ropes, and great part of the bulwarks, looked woolly, from long unacquaintance with the scraper, tar, and the brush. Her keel seemed laid, her ribs put together, and she launched, from Ezekiel's Valley of Dry Bones.

In the present business in which she was engaged, the ship's general model and rig appeared to have undergone no material change from their original warlike and Froissart pattern. However, no guns were seen.

The tops were large, and were railed about with what had once been octagonal net-work, all now in sad disrepair. These tops hung overhead like three ruinous aviaries, in one of which was seen perched, on a rattlin, a white noddy, a strange fowl, so called from its lethargic, somnambulistic character, being frequently caught by hand at sea. Battered and mouldy, the castellated forecastle seemed some ancient turret, long ago taken by assault, and then left to decay. Toward the stern, two high-raised quarter-galleries—the balustrades here and there covered with dry, tindery sea-moss—opening out from the unoccupied state-cabin, whose dead-lights, for all the mild weather, were hermetically closed and caulked—these tenantless balconies hung over the sea as

if it were the grand Venetian canal. But the principal
relic of faded grandeur was the ample oval of the
shield-like stern-piece, intricately carved with the arms
of Castile and Leon, medallioned about by groups of
mythological or symbolical devices; uppermost and
central of which was a dark satyr in a mask, holding
his foot on the prostrate neck of a writhing figure, likewise masked.

Whether the ship had a figure-head, or only a plain
beak, was not quite certain, owing to canvas wrapped
about that part, either to protect it while undergoing
a refurbishing, or else decently to hide its decay. Rudely
painted or chalked, as in a sailor freak, along the forward
side of a sort of pedestal below the canvas, was the
sentence, '*Seguid vuestro jefe*' (follow your leader);
while upon the tarnished head-boards, near by, appeared,
in stately capitals, once gilt, the ship's name, 'SAN
DOMINICK,' each letter streakingly corroded with
tricklings of copper-spike rust; while, like mourning
weeds, dark festoons of sea-grass slimily swept to and
fro over the name, with every hearse-like roll of the
hull.

As, at last, the boat was hooked from the bow along
toward the gangway amidship, its keel, while yet some
inches separated from the hull, harshly grated as on a
sunken coral reef. It proved a huge bunch of con-
globated barnacles adhering below the water to the
side like a wen—a token of baffling airs and long calms
passed somewhere in those seas.

Climbing the side, the visitor was at once surrounded
by a clamorous throng of whites and blacks, but the latter
outnumbering the former more than could have been
expected, negro transportation-ship as the stranger in
port was. But, in one language, and as with one voice,
all poured out a common tale of suffering; in which

the negresses, of whom there were not a few, exceeded
the others in their dolorous vehemence. The scurvy,
together with the fever, had swept off a great part of
their number, more especially the Spaniards. Off Cape
Horn they had narrowly escaped shipwreck ; then, for
days together, they had lain tranced without wind ;
their provisions were low ; their water next to none ;
their lips that moment were baked.

While Captain Delano was thus made the mark of all
eager tongues, his one eager glance took in all faces,
with every other object about him.

Always upon first boarding a large and populous ship
at sea, especially a foreign one, with a nondescript crew
such as Lascars or Manilla men, the impression varies
in a peculiar way from that produced by first entering
a strange house with strange inmates in a strange land.
Both house and ship—the one by its walls and blinds,
the other by its high bulwarks like ramparts—hoard
from view their interiors till the last moment ; but in
the case of the ship there is this addition : that the
living spectacle it contains, upon its sudden and complete disclosure, has, in contrast with the blank ocean
which zones it, something of the effect of enchantment.
The ship seems unreal ; these strange costumes, gestures,
and faces, but a shadowy tableau just emerged from the
deep, which directly must receive back what it gave.

Perhaps it was some such influence, as above is
attempted to be described, which, in Captain Delano's
mind, heightened whatever, upon a staid scrutiny, might
have seemed unusual ; especially the conspicuous figures
of four elderly grizzled negroes, their heads like black,
doddered willow-tops, who, in venerable contrast to the
tumult below them, were couched, sphinx-like, one on
the starboard cat-head, another on the larboard, and the
remaining pair face to face on the opposite bulwarks

above the main-chains. They each had bits of un-stranded old junk in their hands, and, with a sort of stoical self-content, were picking the junk into oakum, a small heap of which lay by their sides. They accompanied the task with a continuous, low, monotonous chant ; droning and druling away like so many gray-headed bagpipers playing a funeral march.

The quarter-deck rose into an ample elevated poop, upon the forward verge of which, lifted, like the oakum-pickers, some eight feet above the general throng, sat along in a row, separated by regular spaces, the cross-legged figures of six other blacks ; each with a rusty hatchet in his hand, which, with a bit of brick and a rag, he was engaged like a scullion in scouring ; while between each two was a small stack of hatchets, their rusted edges turned forward awaiting a like operation. Though occasionally the four oakum-pickers would briefly address some person or persons in the crowd below, yet the six hatchet-polishers neither spoke to others, nor breathed a whisper among themselves, but sat intent upon their task, except at intervals, when, with the peculiar love in negroes of uniting industry with pastime, two and two they sideways clashed their hatchets together, like cymbals, with a barbarous din. All six, unlike the generality, had the raw aspect of unsophisticated Africans.

But that first comprehensive glance which took in those ten figures, with scores less conspicuous, rested but an instant upon them, as, impatient of the hubbub of voices, the visitor turned in quest of whomsoever it might be that commanded the ship.

But as if not unwilling to let nature make known her own case among his suffering charge, or else in despair of restraining it for the time, the Spanish captain, a gentlemanly, reserved-looking, and rather young man

to a stranger's eye, dressed with singular richness, but
bearing plain traces of recent sleepless cares and dis-
quietudes, stood passively by, leaning against the mainmast, at one moment casting a dreary, spiritless look
upon his excited people, at the next an unhappy glance
toward his visitor. By his side stood a black of small
stature, in whose rude face, as occasionally, like a
shepherd's dog, he mutely turned it up into the Spaniard's,
sorrow and affection were equally blended.

Struggling through the throng, the American advanced
to the Spaniard, assuring him of his sympathies, and
offering to render whatever assistance might be in his
power. To which the Spaniard returned for the present
but grave and ceremonious acknowledgments, his national
formality dusked by the saturnine mood of ill-health.

But losing no time in mere compliments, Captain
Delano, returning to the gangway, had his basket of fish
brought up ; and as the wind still continued light, so
that some hours at least must elapse ere the ship could
be brought to the anchorage, he bade his men return
to the sealer, and fetch back as much water as the
whale-boat could carry, with whatever soft bread the
steward might have, all the remaining pumpkins on
board, with a box of sugar, and a dozen of his private
bottles of cider.

Not many minutes after the boat's pushing off, to
the vexation of all, the wind entirely died away, and the
tide turning, began drifting back the ship helplessly
seaward. But trusting this would not last long, Captain
Delano sought, with good hopes, to cheer up the strangers,
feeling no small satisfaction that, with persons in their
condition, he could—thanks to his frequent voyages
along the Spanish main—converse with some freedom
in their native tongue.

While left alone with them, he was not long in observing

some things tending to heighten his first impressions ;
but surprise was lost in pity, both for the Spaniards and
blacks, alike evidently reduced from scarcity of water
and provisions ; while long-continued suffering seemed
to have brought out the less good-natured qualities of
the negroes, besides, at the same time, impairing the
Spaniard's authority over them. But, under the circumstances, precisely this condition of things was to have
been anticipated. In armies, navies, cities, or families,
in nature herself, nothing more relaxes good order than
misery. Still, Captain Delano was not without the idea,
that had Benito Cereno been a man of greater energy,
misrule would hardly have come to the present pass.
But the debility, constitutional or induced by hardships, bodily and mental, of the Spanish captain, was
too obvious to be overlooked. A prey to settled de-
jection, as if long mocked with hope he would not now
indulge it, even when it had ceased to be a mock, the
prospect of that day, or evening at furthest, lying at
anchor, with plenty of water for his people, and a brother
captain to counsel and befriend, seemed in no perceptible
degree to encourage him. His mind appeared unstrung,
if not still more seriously affected. Shut up in these
oaken walls, chained to one dull round of command,
whose unconditionality cloyed him, like some hypochondriac abbot he moved slowly about, at times suddenly
pausing, starting, or staring, biting his lip, biting his
finger-nail, flushing, paling, twitching his beard, with
other symptoms of an absent or moody mind. This
distempered spirit was lodged, as before hinted, in as
distempered a frame. He was rather tall, but seemed
never to have been robust, and now with nervous suffering was almost worn to a skeleton. A tendency to some
pulmonary complaint appeared to have been lately
confirmed. His voice was like that of one with lungs

half gone—hoarsely suppressed, a husky whisper. No
wonder that, as in this state he tottered about, his
private servant apprehensively followed him. Sometimes the negro gave his master his arm, or took his
handkerchief out of his pocket for him ; performing
these and similar offices with that affectionate zeal
which transmutes into something filial or fraternal acts
in themselves but menial ; and which has gained for the
negro the repute of making the most pleasing body-
servant in the world ; one, too, whom a master need be
on no stiffly superior terms with, but may treat with
familiar trust ; less a servant than a devoted companion.
    Marking the noisy indocility of the blacks in general,
as well as what seemed the sullen inefficiency of the
whites, it was not without humane satisfaction that
Captain Delano witnessed the steady good conduct of
Babo.
    But the good conduct of Babo, hardly more than the
ill-behaviour of others, seemed to withdraw the half-
lunatic Don Benito from his cloudy languor. Not that
such precisely was the impression made by the Spaniard
on the mind of his visitor. The Spaniard's individual
unrest was, for the present, but noted as a conspicuous
feature in the ship's general affliction. Still, Captain
Delano was not a little concerned at what he could not
help taking for the time to be Don Benito's unfriendly
indifference toward himself. The Spaniard's manner,
too, conveyed a sort of sour and gloomy disdain, which
he seemed at no pains to disguise. But this the American
in charity ascribed to the harassing effects of sickness,
since, in former instances, he had noted that there are
peculiar natures on whom prolonged physical suffering
seems to cancel every social instinct of kindness ; as if,
forced to black bread themselves, they deemed it but
equity that each person coming nigh them should,

indirectly, by some slight or affront, be made to partake
of their fare.

But ere long Captain Delano bethought him that,
indulgent as he was at the first, in judging the Spaniard,
he might not, after all, have exercised charity enough.
At bottom it was Don Benito's reserve which displeased
him ; but the same reserve was shown toward all but his
faithful personal attendant. Even the formal reports
which, according to sea-usage, were, at stated times,
made to him by some petty underling, either a white,
mulatto, or black, he hardly had patience enough to
listen to, without betraying contemptuous aversion. His
manner upon such occasions was, in its degree, not
unlike that which might be supposed to have been his
imperial countryman's, Charles v., just previous to the
anchoritish retirement of that monarch from the throne.

This splenetic disrelish of his place was evinced in
almost every function pertaining to it. Proud as he
was moody, he condescended to no personal mandate.
Whatever special orders were necessary, their delivery
was delegated to his body-servant, who in turn transferred them to their ultimate destination, through
runners, alert Spanish boys or slave-boys, like pages or
pilot-fish within easy call continually hovering round
Don Benito. So that to have beheld this undemon-
strative invalid gliding about, apathetic and mute, no
landsman could have dreamed that in him was lodged
a dictatorship beyond which, while at sea, there was no
earthly appeal.

Thus, the Spaniard, regarded in his reserve, seemed
the involuntary victim of mental disorder. But, in fact,
his reserve might, in some degree, have proceeded from
design. If so, then here was evinced the unhealthy
climax of that icy though conscientious policy, more or
less adopted by all commanders of large ships, which,

except in signal emergencies, obliterates alike the manifestation of sway with every trace of sociality; transforming the man into a block, or rather into a loaded cannon, which, until there is call for thunder, has nothing to say.

Viewing him in this light, it seemed but a natural token of the perverse habit induced by a long course of such hard self-restraint, that, notwithstanding the present condition of his ship, the Spaniard should still persist in a demeanour, which, however harmless, or, it may be, appropriate, in a well-appointed vessel, such as the *San Dominick* might have been at the outset of the voyage, was anything but judicious now. But the Spaniard, perhaps, thought that it was with captains as with gods: reserve, under all events, must still be their cue. But probably this appearance of slumbering dominion might have been but an attempted disguise to conscious imbecility—not deep policy, but shallow device. But be all this as it might, whether Don Benito's manner was designed or not, the more Captain Delano noted its pervading reserve, the less he felt uneasiness at any particular manifestation of that reserve toward himself.

Neither were his thoughts taken up by the captain alone. Wonted to the quiet orderliness of the sealer's comfortable family of a crew, the noisy confusion of the *San Dominick*'s suffering host repeatedly challenged his eye. Some prominent breaches, not only of discipline but of decency, were observed. These Captain Delano could not but ascribe, in the main, to the absence of those subordinate deck-officers to whom, along with higher duties, is entrusted what may be styled the police department of a populous ship. True, the old oakum-pickers appeared at times to act the part of monitorial constables to their countrymen, the blacks; but though occasionally succeeding in allaying trifling

outbreaks now and then between man and man, they
could do little or nothing toward establishing general
quiet. The *San Dominick* was in the condition of a
transatlantic emigrant ship, among whose multitude of
living freight are some individuals, doubtless, as little
troublesome as crates and bales; but the friendly
remonstrances of such with their ruder companions are
of not so much avail as the unfriendly arm of the mate.
What the *San Dominick* wanted was, what the emigrant
ship has, stern superior officers. But on these decks not
so much as a fourth mate was to be seen.

The visitor's curiosity was roused to learn the particulars of those mishaps which had brought about such
absenteeism, with its consequences; because, though
deriving some inkling of the voyage from the wails which
at the first moment had greeted him, yet of the details
no clear understanding had been had. The best account
would, doubtless, be given by the captain. Yet at first
the visitor was loth to ask it, unwilling to provoke some
distant rebuff. But plucking up courage, he at last
accosted Don Benito, renewing the expression of his
benevolent interest, adding, that did he (Captain Delano)
but know the particulars of the ship's misfortunes, he
would, perhaps, be better able in the end to relieve
them. Would Don Benito favour him with the whole
story.

Don Benito faltered; then, like some somnambulist
suddenly interfered with, vacantly stared at his visitor,
and ended by looking down on the deck. He main-
tained this posture so long, that Captain Delano, almost
equally disconcerted, and involuntarily almost as rude,
turned suddenly from him, walking forward to accost
one of the Spanish seamen for the desired information.
But he had hardly gone five paces, when, with a sort of
eagerness, Don Benito invited him back, regretting his

momentary absence of mind, and professing readiness to gratify him.

While most part of the story was being given, the two captains stood on the after part of the main-deck, a privileged spot, no one being near but the servant.

'It is now a hundred and ninety days,' began the Spaniard, in his husky whisper, 'that this ship, well officered and well manned, with several cabin passengers—some fifty Spaniards in all—sailed from Buenos Ayres bound to Lima, with a general cargo, hardware, Paraguay tea and the like—and,' pointing forward, 'that parcel of negroes, now not more than a hundred and fifty, as you see, but then numbering over three hundred souls. Off Cape Horn we had heavy gales. In one moment, by night, three of my best officers, with fifteen sailors, were lost, with the main-yard ; the spar snapping under them in the slings, as they sought, with heavers, to beat down the icy sail. To lighten the hull, the heavier sacks of mata were thrown into the sea, with most of the water-pipes lashed on deck at the time. And this last necessity it was, combined with the prolonged detentions afterward experienced, which eventually brought about our chief causes of suffering. When——'

Here there was a sudden fainting attack of his cough, brought on, no doubt, by his mental distress. His servant sustained him, and drawing a cordial from his pocket placed it to his lips. He a little revived. But unwilling to leave him unsupported while yet imperfectly restored, the black with one arm still encircled his master, at the same time keeping his eye fixed on his face, as if to watch for the first sign of complete restoration, or relapse, as the event might prove.

The Spaniard proceeded, but brokenly and obscurely, as one in a dream.

—' Oh, my God ! rather than pass through what I have, with joy I would have hailed the most terrible gales ; but——'

His cough returned and with increased violence ; this subsiding, with reddened lips and closed eyes he fell heavily against his supporter.

' His mind wanders. He was thinking of the plague that followed the gales,' plaintively sighed the servant ; ' my poor, poor master ! ' wringing one hand, and with the other wiping the mouth. ' But be patient, señor,' again turning to Captain Delano, ' these fits do not last long ; master will soon be himself.'

Don Benito reviving, went on ; but as this portion of the story was very brokenly delivered, the substance only will here be set down.

It appeared that after the ship had been many days tossed in storms off the Cape, the scurvy broke out, carrying off numbers of the whites and blacks. When at last they had worked round into the Pacific, their spars and sails were so damaged, and so inadequately handled by the surviving mariners, most of whom were become invalids, that, unable to lay her northerly course by the wind, which was powerful, the unmanageable ship, for successive days and nights, was blown north-westward, where the breeze suddenly deserted her, in unknown waters, to sultry calms. The absence of the water-pipes now proved as fatal to life as before their presence had menaced it. Induced, or at least aggravated, by the more than scanty allowance of water, a malignant fever followed the scurvy ; with the excessive heat of the lengthened calm, making such short work of it as to sweep away, as by billows, whole families of the Africans, and a yet larger number, proportionably, of the Spaniards, including, by a luckless fatality, every remaining officer on board. Consequently, in the smart west winds eventually following the calm, the already rent sails, having to be simply dropped, not furled, at need, had been gradually reduced to the beggars' rags they were now. To procure substitutes for his lost sailors, as well as supplies of water and sails, the captain, at the earliest opportunity, had made for Baldivia, the southernmost civilised port of Chili and South America ; but upon nearing the coast the thick weather had prevented him from so much as sighting that harbour. Since which period, almost without a crew, and almost without canvas, and almost without water, and, at intervals, giving its added dead to the sea, the *San Dominick* had been battledored about by contrary winds, inveigled by currents, or grown weedy in calms. Like a man lost in woods, more than once she had doubled upon her own track.

' But throughout these calamities,' huskily continued Don Benito, painfully turning in the half-embrace of his servant, ' I have to thank those negroes you see, who, though to your inexperienced eyes appearing unruly, have, indeed, conducted themselves with less of restlessness than even their owner could have thought possible under such circumstances.'

Here he again fell faintly back. Again his mind wandered ; but he rallied, and less obscurely proceeded.

' Yes, their owner was quite right in assuring me that no fetters would be needed with his blacks ; so that while, as is wont in this transportation, these negroes have always remained upon deck—not thrust below, as in the Guinea-men—they have, also, from the beginning, been freely permitted to range within given bounds at their pleasure.'

Once more the faintness returned—his mind roved— but, recovering, he resumed.

' But it is Babo here to whom, under God, I owe not

F

only my own preservation, but likewise to him, chiefly, the merit is due, of pacifying his more ignorant brethren, when at intervals tempted to murmurings.'

' Ah, master,' sighed the black, bowing his face, ' don't speak of me ; Babo is nothing ; what Babo has done was but duty.'

' Faithful fellow ! ' cried Captain Delano. ' Don Benito, I envy you such a friend ; slave I cannot call him.'

As master and man stood before him, the black upholding the white, Captain Delano could not but bethink him of the beauty of that relationship which could present such a spectacle of fidelity on the one hand and confidence on the other. The scene was heightened by the contrast in dress, denoting their relative positions. The Spaniard wore a loose Chili jacket of dark velvet ; white small-clothes and stockings, with silver buckles at the knee and instep ; a high-crowned sombrero, of fine grass ; a slender sword, silver mounted, hung from a knot in his sash—the last being an almost invariable adjunct, more for utility than ornament, of a South American gentleman's dress to this hour. Excepting when his occasional nervous contortions brought about disarray, there was a certain precision in his attire curiously at variance with the unsightly disorder around ; especially in the belittered ghetto, forward of the mainmast, wholly occupied by the blacks.

The servant wore nothing but wide trowsers, apparently, from their coarseness and patches, made out of some old topsail ; they were clean, and confined at the waist by a bit of unstranded rope, which, with his composed, deprecatory air at times, made him look something like a begging friar of St. Francis.

However unsuitable for the time and place, at least in the blunt-thinking American's eyes, and however strangely surviving in the midst of all his afflictions, the toilet of Don Benito might not, in fashion at least, have gone beyond the style of the day among South Americans of his class. Though on the present voyage sailing from Buenos Ayres, he had avowed himself a native and resident of Chili, whose inhabitants had not so generally adopted the plain coat and once plebeian pantaloons ; but, with a becoming modification, adhered to their provincial costume, picturesque as any in the world. Still, relatively to the pale history of the voyage, and his own pale face, there seemed something so incongruous in the Spaniard's apparel, as almost to suggest the image of an invalid courtier tottering about London streets in the time of the plague.

The portion of the narrative which, perhaps, most excited interest, as well as some surprise, considering the latitudes in question, was the long calms spoken of, and more particularly the ship's so long drifting about. Without communicating the opinion, of course, the American could not but impute at least part of the detentions both to clumsy seamanship and faulty navigation. Eyeing Don Benito's small, yellow hands, he easily inferred that the young captain had not got into command at the hawse-hole, but the cabin window ; and if so, why wonder at incompetence, in youth, sickness, and gentility united ?

But drowning criticism in compassion, after a fresh repetition of his sympathies, Captain Delano, having heard out his story, not only engaged, as in the first place, to see Don Benito and his people supplied in their immediate bodily needs, but, also, now further promised to assist him in procuring a large permanent supply of water, as well as some sails and rigging ; and, though it would involve no small embarrassment to himself, yet he would spare three of his best seamen for temporary deck officers ; so that without delay the

ship might proceed to Conception, there fully to refit
for Lima, her destined port.

Such generosity was not without its effect, even upon
the invalid. His face lighted up ; eager and hectic, he
met the honest glance of his visitor. With gratitude he
seemed overcome.

'This excitement is bad for master,' whispered the
servant, taking his arm, and with soothing words gently
drawing him aside.

When Don Benito returned, the American was pained
to observe that his hopefulness, like the sudden kindling
in his cheek, was but febrile and transient.

Ere long, with a joyless mien, looking up toward the
poop, the host invited his guest to accompany him there,
for the benefit of what little breath of wind might be stirring.

As, during the telling of the story, Captain Delano
had once or twice started at the occasional cymballing
of the hatchet-polishers, wondering why such an inter-
ruption should be allowed, especially in that part of
the ship, and in the ears of an invalid ; and moreover,
as the hatchets had anything but an attractive look,
and the handlers of them still less so, it was, therefore,
to tell the truth, not without some lurking reluctance,
or even shrinking, it may be, that Captain Delano, with
apparent complaisance, acquiesced in his host's invitation. The more so, since, with an untimely caprice of
punctilio, rendered distressing by his cadaverous aspect,
Don Benito, with Castilian bows, solemnly insisted upon
his guest's preceding him up the ladder leading to the
elevation ; where, one on each side of the last step,
sat for armorial supporters and sentries two of the
ominous file. Gingerly enough stepped good Captain
Delano between them, and in the instant of leaving
them behind, like one running the gauntlet, he felt an
apprehensive twitch in the calves of his legs.

But when, facing about, he saw the whole file, like so many organ-grinders, still stupidly intent on their work, unmindful of everything besides, he could not but smile at his late fidgety panic.

Presently, while standing with his host, looking forward upon the decks below, he was struck by one of those instances of insubordination previously alluded to. Three black boys, with two Spanish boys, were sitting together on the hatches, scraping a rude wooden platter, in which some scanty mess had recently been cooked. Suddenly, one of the black boys, enraged at a word dropped by one of his white companions, seized a knife, and, though called to forbear by one of the oakum-pickers, struck the lad over the head, inflicting a gash from which blood flowed.

In amazement, Captain Delano inquired what this meant. To which the pale Don Benito dully muttered, that it was merely the sport of the lad.

' Pretty serious sport, truly,' rejoined Captain Delano. '·Had such a thing happened on board the *Bachelor's Delight*, instant punishment would have followed.'

At these words the Spaniard turned upon the American one of his sudden, staring, half-lunatic looks ; then, relapsing into his torpor, answered, ' Doubtless, doubtless, señor.'

Is it, thought Captain Delano, that this hapless man is one of those paper captains I 've known, who by policy wink at what by power they cannot put down ? I know no sadder sight than a commander who has little of command but the name.

' I should think, Don Benito,' he now said, glancing toward the oakum-picker who had sought to interfere with the boys, ' that you would find it advantageous to keep all your blacks employed, especially the younger ones, no matter at what useless task, and no matter what

happens to the ship. Why, even with my little band,
I find such a course indispensable. I once kept a crew
on my quarter-deck thrumming mats for my cabin,
when, for three days, I had given up my ship—mats,
men, and all—for a speedy loss, owing to the violence
of a gale, in which we could do nothing but helplessly
drive before it.'

'Doubtless, doubtless,' muttered Don Benito.

'But,' continued Captain Delano, again glancing upon
the oakum-pickers and then at the hatchet-polishers,
near by, 'I see you keep some, at least, of your host
employed.'

'Yes,' was again the vacant response.

'Those old men there, shaking their pows from their
pulpits,' continued Captain Delano, pointing to the
oakum-pickers, 'seem to act the part of old dominies to
the rest, little heeded as their admonitions are at times.
Is this voluntary on their part, Don Benito, or have you
appointed them shepherds to your flock of black sheep?'

'What posts they fill, I appointed them,' rejoined
the Spaniard, in an acrid tone, as if resenting some
supposed satiric reflection.

'And these others, these Ashantee conjurers here,'
continued Captain Delano, rather uneasily eyeing the
brandished steel of the hatchet-polishers, where, in spots,
it had been brought to a shine, 'this seems a curious
business they are at, Don Benito?'

'In the gales we met,' answered the Spaniard, 'what
of our general cargo was not thrown overboard was
much damaged by the brine. Since coming into calm
weather, I have had several cases of knives and hatchets
daily brought up for overhauling and cleaning.'

'A prudent idea, Don Benito. You are part owner
of ship and cargo, I presume; but none of the slaves,
perhaps?'

'I am owner of all you see,' impatiently returned Don Benito, 'except the main company of blacks, who belonged to my late friend, Alexandro Aranda.'

As he mentioned this name, his air was heart-broken ; his knees shook ; his servant supported him.

Thinking he divined the cause of such unusual emotion, to confirm his surmise, Captain Delano, after a pause, said : 'And may I ask, Don Benito, whether—since a while ago you spoke of some cabin passengers—the friend, whose loss so afflicts you, at the outset of the voyage accompanied his blacks ? '

' Yes.'

' But died of the fever ? '

' Died of the fever. Oh, could I but——'

Again quivering, the Spaniard paused.

'Pardon me,' said Captain Delano lowly, ' but I think that, by a sympathetic experience, I conjecture, Don Benito, what it is that gives the keener edge to your grief. It was once my hard fortune to lose, at sea, a dear friend, my own brother, then supercargo. Assured of the welfare of his spirit, its departure I could have borne like a man ; but that honest eye, that honest hand—both of which had so often met mine—and that warm heart ; all, all—like scraps to the dogs—to throw all to the sharks ! It was then I vowed never to have for fellow-voyager a man I loved, unless, unbeknown to him, I had provided every requisite, in case of a fatality, for embalming his mortal part for interment on shore. Were your friend's remains now on board this ship, Don Benito, not thus strangely would the mention of his name affect you.'

' On board this ship ? ' echoed the Spaniard. Then, with horrified gestures, as directed against some spectre, he unconsciously fell into the ready arms of his attendant, who, with a silent appeal toward Captain Delano, seemed

beseeching him not again to broach a theme so un-
speakably distressing to his master.

This poor fellow now, thought the pained American,
is the victim of that sad superstition which associates
goblins with the deserted body of man, as ghosts with
an abandoned house.   How unlike are we made !   What
to me, in like case, would have been a solemn satisfaction,
the bare suggestion, even, terrifies the Spaniard into
this trance.   Poor Alexandro Aranda !   what would you
say could you here see your friend—who, on former
voyages, when you, for months, were left behind, has,
I dare say, often longed, and longed, for one peep at
you—now transported with terror at the least thought
of having you any way nigh him.

At this moment, with a dreary graveyard toll, be-
tokening a flaw, the ship's forecastle bell, smote by one
of the grizzled oakum-pickers, proclaimed ten o'clock
through the leaden calm ;   when Captain Delano's attention was caught by the moving figure of a gigantic
black, emerging from the general crowd below, and
slowly advancing toward the elevated poop.   An iron
collar was about his neck, from which depended a chain,
thrice wound round his body ;   the terminating links
padlocked together at a broad band of iron, his girdle.

' How like a mute Atufal moves,' murmured the
servant.

The black mounted the steps of the poop, and, like
a brave prisoner, brought up to receive sentence, stood
in unquailing muteness before Don Benito, now recovered from his attack.

At the first glimpse of his approach, Don Benito had
started, a resentful shadow swept over his face ;   and, as
with the sudden memory of bootless rage, his white lips
glued together.

This is some mulish mutineer, thought Captain Delano,

surveying, not without a mixture of admiration, the colossal form of the negro.

'See, he waits your question, master,' said the servant.

Thus reminded, Don Benito, nervously averting his glance, as if shunning, by anticipation, some rebellious response, in a disconcerted voice, thus spoke :

'Atufal, will you ask my pardon now ? '

The black was silent.

'Again, master,' murmured the servant, with bitter upbraiding eyeing his countryman, 'again, master ; he will bend to master yet.'

'Answer,' said Don Benito, still averting his glance, 'say but the one word, *pardon*, and your chains shall be off.'

Upon this, the black, slowly raising both arms, let them lifelessly fall, his links clanking, his head bowed ; as much as to say, 'No, I am content.'

'Go,' said Don Benito, with inkept and unknown emotion.

Deliberately as he had come, the black obeyed.

'Excuse me, Don Benito,' said Captain Delano, 'but this scene surprises me ; what means it, pray ? '

'It means that that negro alone, of all the band, has given me peculiar cause of offence. I have put him in chains ; I——'

Here he paused ; his hand to his head, as if there were a swimming there, or a sudden bewilderment of memory had come over him ; but meeting his servant's kindly glance seemed reassured, and proceeded :

'I could not scourge such a form. But I told him he must ask my pardon. As yet he has not. At my command, every two hours he stands before me.'

'And how long has this been ? '

'Some sixty days.'

'And obedient in all else ? And respectful ? '

' Yes.'

' Upon my conscience, then,' exclaimed Captain Delano impulsively, ' he has a royal spirit in him, this fellow.'

' He may have some right to it,' bitterly returned Don Benito, ' he says he was king in his own land.'

' Yes,' said the servant, entering a word, ' those slits in Atufal's ears once held wedges of gold ; but poor Babo here, in his own land, was only a poor slave ; a black man's slave was Babo, who now is the white's.'

Somewhat annoyed by these conversational familiarities, Captain Delano turned curiously upon the attendant, then glanced inquiringly at his master ; but, as if long wonted to these little informalities, neither master nor man seemed to understand him.

' What, pray, was Atufal's offence, Don Benito ? ' asked Captain Delano ; ' if it was not something very serious, take a fool's advice, and, in view of his general docility, as well as in some natural respect for his spirit, remit him his penalty.'

' No, no, master never will do that,' here murmured the servant to himself, ' proud Atufal must first ask master's pardon. The slave there carries the padlock, but master here carries the key.'

His attention thus directed, Captain Delano now noticed for the first, that, suspended by a slender silken cord from Don Benito's neck, hung a key. At once, from the servant's muttered syllables, divining the key's purpose, he smiled and said :—' So, Don Benito—padlock and key—significant symbols, truly.'

Biting his lip, Don Benito faltered.

Though the remark of Captain Delano, a man of such native simplicity as to be incapable of satire or irony, had been dropped in playful allusion to the Spaniard's singularly evidenced lordship over the black ; yet the hypochondriac seemed some way to have taken it as a malicious reflection upon his confessed inability thus far to break down, at least, on a verbal summons, the entrenched will of the slave. Deploring this supposed misconception, yet despairing of correcting it, Captain Delano shifted the subject; but finding his companion more than ever withdrawn, as if still sourly digesting the lees of the presumed affront above mentioned, by and by Captain Delano likewise became less talkative, oppressed, against his own will, by what seemed the secret vindictiveness of the morbidly sensitive Spaniard. But the good sailor, himself of a quite contrary disposition, refrained, on his part, alike from the appearance as from the feeling of resentment, and if silent, was only so from contagion.

Presently the Spaniard, assisted by his servant, somewhat discourteously crossed over from his guest; a procedure which, sensibly enough, might have been allowed to pass for idle caprice of ill-humour, had not master and man, lingering round the corner of the elevated skylight, began whispering together in low voices. This was unpleasing. And more; the moody air of the Spaniard, which at times had not been without a sort of valetudinarian stateliness, now seemed anything but dignified; while the menial familiarity of the servant lost its original charm of simple-hearted attachment.

In his embarrassment, the visitor turned his face to the other side of the ship. By so doing, his glance accidentally fell on a young Spanish sailor, a coil of rope in his hand, just stepped from the deck to the first round of the mizen-rigging. Perhaps the man would not have been particularly noticed, were it not that, during his ascent to one of the yards, he, with a sort of covert intentness, kept his eye fixed on Captain Delano, from whom, presently, it passed, as if by a natural sequence, to the two whisperers.

His own attention thus redirected to that quarter, Captain Delano gave a slight start. From something in Don Benito's manner just then, it seemed as if the visitor had, at least partly, been the subject of the withdrawn consultation going on—a conjecture as little agreeable to the guest as it was little flattering to the host.

The singular alternations of courtesy and ill-breeding in the Spanish captain were unaccountable, except on one of two suppositions—innocent lunacy, or wicked imposture.

But the first idea, though it might naturally have occurred to an indifferent observer, and, in some respect, had not hitherto been wholly a stranger to Captain Delano's mind, yet, now that, in an incipient way, he began to regard the stranger's conduct something in the light of an intentional affront, of course the idea of lunacy was virtually vacated. But if not a lunatic, what then ? Under the circumstances, would a gentleman, nay, any honest boor, act the part now acted by his host ? The man was an impostor. Some low-born adventurer, masquerading as an oceanic grandee ; yet so ignorant of the first requisites of mere gentlemanhood as to be betrayed into the present remarkable indecorum. That strange ceremoniousness, too, at other times evinced, seemed not uncharacteristic of one playing a part above his real level. Benito Cereno—Don Benito Cereno—a sounding name. One, too, at that period, not unknown, in the surname, to supercargoes and sea-captains trading along the Spanish Main, as belonging to one of the most enterprising and extensive mercantile families in all those provinces ; several members of it having titles ; a sort of Castilian Rothschild, with a noble brother, or cousin, in every great trading town of South America. The alleged Don Benito was in early manhood, about twenty-nine or thirty. To assume a

sort of roving cadetship in the maritime affairs of such
a house, what more likely scheme for a young knave of
talent and spirit ? But the Spaniard was a pale invalid.
Never mind. For even to the degree of simulating
mortal disease, the craft of some tricksters had been
known to attain. To think that, under the aspect of
infantile weakness, the most savage energies might be
couched—those velvets of the Spaniard but the silky
paw to his fangs.

From no train of thought did these fancies come ; not
from within, but from without ; suddenly, too, and in
one throng, like hoar frost ; yet as soon to vanish as
the mild sun of Captain Delano's good-nature regained
its meridian.

Glancing over once more toward his host—whose side-
face, revealed above the skylight, was now turned
toward him—he was struck by the profile, whose clearness of cut was refined by the thinness, incident to ill-
health, as well as ennobled about the chin by the beard.
Away with suspicion. He was a true off-shoot of a true
hidalgo Cereno.

Relieved by these and other better thoughts, the
visitor, lightly humming a tune, now began indifferently
pacing the poop, so as not to betray to Don Benito that
he had at all mistrusted incivility, much less duplicity ;
for such mistrust would yet be proved illusory, and by
the event ; though, for the present, the circumstance
which had provoked that distrust remained unexplained.
But when that little mystery should have been cleared
up, Captain Delano thought he might extremely regret
it, did he allow Don Benito to become aware that he
had indulged in ungenerous surmises. In short, to the
Spaniard's black-letter text, it was best, for a while, to
leave open margin.

Presently, his pale face twitching and overcast, the

Spaniard, still supported by his attendant, moved over
toward his guest, when, with even more than his usual
embarrassment, and a strange sort of intriguing intona-
tion in his husky whisper, the following conversation
began :—

'Señor, may I ask how long you have lain at this
isle ? '

'Oh, but a day or two, Don Benito.'

'And from what port are you last ? '

'Canton.'

'And there, señor, you exchanged your seal-skins for
teas and silks, I think you said ? '

'Yes. Silks, mostly.'

'And the balance you took in specie, perhaps ? '

Captain Delano, fidgeting a little, answered :

'Yes ; some silver ; not a very great deal, though.'

'Ah—well. May I ask how many men have you,
señor ? '

Captain Delano slightly started, but answered :

'About five-and-twenty, all told.'

'And at present, señor, all on board, I suppose ? '

'All on board, Don Benito,' replied the captain, now
with satisfaction.

'And will be to-night, señor ? '

At this last question, following so many pertinacious
ones, for the soul of him Captain Delano could not but
look very earnestly at the questioner, who, instead of
meeting the glance, with every token of craven dis-
composure dropped his eyes to the deck ; presenting an
unworthy contrast to his servant, who, just then, was
kneeling at his feet, adjusting a loose shoe-buckle ; his
disengaged face meantime, with humble curiosity, turned
openly up into his master's downcast one.

The Spaniard, still with a guilty shuffle, repeated his
question :

'And—and will be to-night, señor ? '

'Yes, for aught I know,' returned Captain Delano—
'but nay,' rallying himself into fearless truth, 'some of
them talked of going off on another fishing party about
midnight.'

'Your ships generally go—go more or less armed, I
believe, señor ? '

'Oh, a six-pounder or two, in case of emergency,' was
the intrepidly indifferent reply, 'with a small stock of
muskets, sealing-spears, and cutlasses, you know.'

As he thus responded, Captain Delano again glanced
at Don Benito, but the latter's eyes were averted ; while
abruptly and awkwardly shifting the subject, he made
some peevish allusion to the calm, and then, without
apology, once more, with his attendant, withdrew to
the opposite bulwarks, where the whispering was resumed.

At this moment, and ere Captain Delano could cast
a cool thought upon what had just passed, the young
Spanish sailor, before mentioned, was seen descending
from the rigging. In act of stooping over to spring inboard to the deck, his voluminous, unconfined frock, or
shirt, of coarse woollen, much spotted with tar, opened
out far down the chest, revealing a soiled under-garment
of what seemed the finest linen, edged, about the neck,
with a narrow blue ribbon, sadly faded and worn. At
this moment the young sailor's eye was again fixed on
the whisperers, and Captain Delano thought he observed
a lurking significance in it, as if silent signs, of some
Freemason sort, had that instant been interchanged.

This once more impelled his own glance in the direction
of Don Benito, and, as before, he could not but infer
that himself formed the subject of the conference. He
paused. The sound of the hatchet-polishing fell on his
ears. He cast another swift side-look at the two. They

had the air of conspirators. In connection with the late questionings, and the incident of the young sailor, these things now begat such return of involuntary suspicion, that the singular guilelessness of the American could not endure it. Plucking up a gay and humorous expression, he crossed over to the two rapidly, saying : ' Ha, Don Benito, your black here seems high in your trust ; a sort of privy-counsellor, in fact.'

Upon this, the servant looked up with a good-natured grin, but the master started as from a venomous bite. It was a moment or two before the Spaniard sufficiently recovered himself to reply ; which he did, at last, with cold constraint : ' Yes, señor, I have trust in Babo.'

Here Babo, changing his previous grin of mere animal humour into an intelligent smile, not ungratefully eyed his master.

Finding that the Spaniard now stood silent and reserved, as if involuntarily, or purposely giving hint that his guest's proximity was inconvenient just then, Captain Delano, unwilling to appear uncivil even to incivility itself, made some trivial remark and moved off ; again and again turning over in his mind the mysterious demeanour of Don Benito Cereno.

He had descended from the poop, and, wrapped in thought, was passing near a dark hatchway, leading down into the steerage, when, perceiving motion there, he looked to see what moved. The same instant there was a sparkle in the shadowy hatchway, and he saw one of the Spanish sailors, prowling there, hurriedly placing his hand in the bosom of his frock, as if hiding something. Before the man could have been certain who it was that was passing, he slunk below out of sight. But enough was seen of him to make it sure that he was the same young sailor before noticed in the rigging.

What was that which so sparkled ? thought Captain

Delano. It was no lamp—no match—no live coal.
Could it have been a jewel ?   But how come sailors with
jewels ?—or with silk-trimmed under-shirts either ?   Has
he been robbing the trunks of the dead cabin passengers ?
But if so, he would hardly wear one of the stolen articles
on board ship here.   Ah, ah—if, now, that was, indeed,
a secret sign I saw passing between this suspicious
fellow and his captain a while since ; if I could only be
certain that, in my uneasiness, my senses did not deceive
me, then——

Here, passing from one suspicious thing to another,
his mind revolved the strange questions put to him
concerning his ship.

By a curious coincidence, as each point was recalled,
the black wizards of Ashantee would strike up with their
hatchets, as in ominous comment on the white stranger's
thoughts.   Pressed by such enigmas and portents, it
would have been almost against nature, had not, even
into the least distrustful heart, some ugly misgivings
obtruded.

Observing the ship, now helplessly fallen into a current,
with enchanted sails, drifting with increased rapidity
seaward ; and noting that, from a lately intercepted
projection of the land, the sealer was hidden, the stout
mariner began to quake at thoughts which he barely
durst confess to himself.   Above all, he began to feel a
ghostly dread of Don Benito.   And yet, when he roused
himself, dilated his chest, felt himself strong on his legs,
and coolly considered it—what did all these phantoms
amount to ?

Had the Spaniard any sinister scheme, it must have
reference not so much to him (Captain Delano) as to his
ship (the *Bachelor's Delight*).   Hence the present drifting
away of the one ship from the other, instead of favouring
any such possible scheme, was, for the time, at least,

G

opposed to it. Clearly any suspicion, combining such contradictions, must needs be delusive. Besides, was it not absurd to think of a vessel in distress—a vessel by sickness almost dismanned of her crew—a vessel whose inmates were parched for water—was it not a thousand times absurd that such a craft should, at present, be of a piratical character; or her commander, either for himself or those under him, cherish any desire but for speedy relief and refreshment? But then, might not general distress, and thirst in particular, be affected? And might not that same undiminished Spanish crew, alleged to have perished off to a remnant, be at that very moment lurking in the hold? On heart-broken pretence of entreating a cup of cold water, fiends in human form had got into lonely dwellings, nor retired until a dark deed had been done. And among the Malay pirates, it was no unusual thing to lure ships after them into their treacherous harbours, or entice boarders from a declared enemy at sea, by the spectacle of thinly manned or vacant decks, beneath which prowled a hundred spears with yellow arms ready to upthrust them through the mats. Not that Captain Delano had entirely credited such things. He had heard of them—and now, as stories, they recurred. The present destination of the ship was the anchorage. There she would be near his own vessel. Upon gaining that vicinity, might not the *San Dominick*, like a slumbering volcano, suddenly let loose energies now hid?

He recalled the Spaniard's manner while telling his story. There was a gloomy hesitancy and subterfuge about it. It was just the manner of one making up his tale for evil purposes as he goes. But if that story was not true, what was the truth? That the ship had unlawfully come into the Spaniard's possession? But in many of its details, especially in reference to the

more calamitous parts, such as the fatalities among the
seamen, the consequent prolonged beating about, the
past sufferings from obstinate calms, and still continued
suffering from thirst; in all these points, as well as
others, Don Benito's story had corroborated not only
the wailing ejaculations of the indiscriminate multitude,
white and black, but likewise—what seemed impossible
to be counterfeit—by the very expression and play of
every human feature, which Captain Delano saw. If
Don Benito's story was, throughout, an invention, then
every soul on board, down to the youngest negress, was
his carefully drilled recruit in the plot : an incredible
inference. And yet, if there was ground for mistrusting
his veracity, that inference was a legitimate one.

But those questions of the Spaniard. There, indeed,
one might pause. Did they not seem put with much
the same object with which the burglar or assassin, by
day-time, reconnoitres the walls of a house ? But, with
ill purposes, to solicit such information openly of the
chief person endangered, and so, in effect, setting him on
his guard ; how unlikely a procedure was that. Absurd,
then, to suppose that those questions had been prompted
by evil designs. Thus, the same conduct, which, in this
instance, had raised the alarm, served to dispel it. In
short, scarce any suspicion or uneasiness, however
apparently reasonable at the time, which was not now,
with equal apparent reason, dismissed.

At last he began to laugh at his former forebodings ;
and laugh at the strange ship for, in its aspect, some
way siding with them, as it were ; and laugh, too, at the
odd-looking blacks, particularly those old scissors-
grinders, the Ashantees ; and those bedridden old
knitting women, the oakum-pickers ; and almost at the
dark Spaniard himself, the central hobgoblin of all.

For the rest, whatever in a serious way seemed

enigmatical, was now good-naturedly explained away by
the thought that, for the most part, the poor invalid
scarcely knew what he was about ; either sulking in
black vapours, or putting idle questions without sense
or object. Evidently, for the present, the man was not
fit to be entrusted with the ship. On some benevolent
plea withdrawing the command from him, Captain
Delano would yet have to send her to Conception, in
charge of his second mate, a worthy person and good
navigator—a plan not more convenient for the *San
Dominick* than for Don Benito ; for, relieved from all
anxiety, keeping wholly to his cabin, the sick man,
under the good nursing of his servant, would, probably,
by the end of the passage, be in a measure restored to
health, and with that he should also be restored to
authority.

Such were the American's thoughts. They were
tranquillising. There was a difference between the idea
of Don Benito's darkly preordaining Captain Delano's
fate, and Captain Delano's lightly arranging Don Benito's.
Nevertheless, it was not without something of relief that
the good seaman presently perceived his whale-boat in
the distance. Its absence had been prolonged by unexpected detention at the sealer's side, as well as its
returning trip lengthened by the continual recession of
the goal.

The advancing speck was observed by the blacks.
Their shouts attracted the attention of Don Benito, who,
with a return of courtesy, approaching Captain Delano,
expressed satisfaction at the coming of some supplies,
slight and temporary as they must necessarily prove.

Captain Delano responded ; but while doing so, his
attention was drawn to something passing on the deck
below : among the crowd climbing the landward bulwarks, anxiously watching the coming boat, two blacks,

to all appearances accidentally incommoded by one of the sailors, violently pushed him aside, which the sailor some way resenting, they dashed him to the deck, despite the earnest cries of the oakum-pickers.

'Don Benito,' said Captain Delano quickly, 'do you see what is going on there? Look!'

But, seized by his cough, the Spaniard staggered, with both hands to his face, on the point of falling. Captain Delano would have supported him, but the servant was more alert, who, with ono hand sustaining his master, with the other applied the cordial. Don Benito restored, the black withdrew his support, slipping aside a little, but dutifully remaining within call of a whisper. Such discretion was here evinced as quite wiped away, in the visitor's eyes, any blemish of impropriety which might have attached to the attendant from the indecorous conferences before mentioned; showing, too, that if the servant were to blame, it might be more the master's fault than his own, since, when left to himself, he could conduct thus well.

His glance called away from the spectacle of disorder to the more pleasing one before him, Captain Delano could not avoid again congratulating his host upon possessing such a servant, who, though perhaps a little too forward now and then, must upon the whole be invaluable to one in the invalid's situation.

'Tell me, Don Benito,' he added, with a smile—'I should like to have your man here, myself—what will you take for him? Would fifty doubloons be any object?'

'Master wouldn't part with Babo for a thousand doubloons,' murmured the black, overhearing the offer, and taking it in earnest, and, with the strange vanity of a faithful slave, appreciated by his master, scorning to hear so paltry a valuation put upon him by a stranger.

But Don Benito, apparently hardly yet completely re-stored, and again interrupted by his cough, made but some broken reply.

Soon his physical distress became so great, affecting his mind, too, apparently, that, as if to screen the sad spectacle, the servant gently conducted his master below.

Left to himself, the American, to while away the time till his boat should arrive, would have pleasantly accosted some one of the few Spanish seamen he saw ; but recalling something that Don Benito had said touch-ing their ill conduct, he refrained ; as a shipmaster indisposed to countenance cowardice or unfaithfulness in seamen.

While, with these thoughts, standing with eye directed forward toward that handful of sailors, suddenly he thought that one or two of them returned the glance and with a sort of meaning. He rubbed his eyes, and looked again ; but again seemed to see the same thing. Under a new form, but more obscure than any previous one, the old suspicions recurred, but, in the absence of Don Benito, with less of panic than before. Despite the bad account given of the sailors, Captain Delano resolved forthwith to accost one of them. Descending the poop, he made his way through the blacks, his movement drawing a queer cry from the oakum-pickers, prompted by whom, the negroes, twitching each other aside, divided before him ; but, as if curious to see what was the object of this deliberate visit to their ghetto, closing in behind, in tolerable order, followed the white stranger up. His progress thus proclaimed as by mounted kings-at-arms, and escorted as by a Caffre guard of honour, Captain Delano, assuming a good-humoured, off-handed air, continued to advance ; now and then saying a blithe word to the negroes, and his eye curiously surveying the white faces, here and there sparsely mixed in with the blacks, like stray white pawns venturously involved in the ranks of the chessmen opposed.

While thinking which of them to select for his purpose, he chanced to observe a sailor seated on the deck engaged in tarring the strap of a large block, a circle of blacks squatted round him inquisitively eyeing the process.

The mean employment of the man was in contrast with something superior in his figure. His hand, black with continually thrusting it into the tar-pot held for him by a negro, seemed not naturally allied to his face, a face which would have been a very fine one but for its haggardness. Whether this haggardness had aught to do with criminality, could not be determined; since, as intense heat and cold, though unlike, produce like sensations, so innocence and guilt, when, through casual association with mental pain, stamping any visible impress, use one seal—a hacked one.

Not again that this reflection occurred to Captain Delano at the time, charitable man as he was. Rather another idea. Because observing so singular a haggardness combined with a dark eye, averted as in trouble and shame, and then again recalling Don Benito's confessed ill opinion of his crew, insensibly he was operated upon by certain general notions which, while disconnecting pain and abashment from virtue, invariably link them with vice.

If, indeed, there be any wickedness on board this ship, thought Captain Delano, be sure that man there has fouled his hand in it, even as now he fouls it in the pitch. I don't like to accost him. I will speak to this other, this old Jack here on the windlass.

He advanced to an old Barcelona tar, in ragged red breeches and dirty night-cap, cheeks trenched and bronzed, whiskers dense as thorn hedges. Seated be-

tween two sleepy-looking Africans, this mariner, like
his younger shipmate, was employed upon some rigging—
splicing a cable—the sleepy-looking blacks performing
the inferior function of holding the outer parts of the
ropes for him.

Upon Captain Delano's approach, the man at once
hung his head below its previous level ; the one necessary
for business. It appeared as if he desired to be thought
absorbed, with more than common fidelity, in his task.
Being addressed, he glanced up, but with what seemed
a furtive, diffident air, which sat strangely enough on
his weather-beaten visage, much as if a grizzly bear,
instead of growling and biting, should simper and cast
sheep's eyes. He was asked several questions concerning
the voyage—questions purposely referring to several
particulars in Don Benito's narrative, not previously
corroborated by those impulsive cries greeting the
visitor on first coming on board. The questions were
briefly answered, confirming all that remained to be
confirmed of the story. The negroes about the windlass
joined in with the old sailor ; but, as they became talkative, he by degrees became mute, and at length quite
glum, seemed morosely unwilling to answer more questions, and yet, all the while, this ursine air was somehow
mixed with his sheepish one.

Despairing of getting into unembarrassed talk with
such a centaur, Captain Delano, after glancing round
for a more promising countenance, but seeing none,
spoke pleasantly to the blacks to make way for him ;
and so, amid various grins and grimaces, returned to
the poop, feeling a little strange at first, he could hardly
tell why, but upon the whole with regained confidence in
Benito Cereno.

How plainly, thought he, did that old whiskerando
yonder betray a consciousness of ill desert. No doubt,

when he saw me coming, he dreaded lest I, apprised by his captain of the crew's general misbehaviour, came with sharp words for him, and so down with his head. And yet—and yet, now that I think of it, that very old fellow, if I err not, was one of those who seemed so earnestly eyeing me here a while since. Ah, these currents spin one's head round almost as much as they do the ship. Ha, there now's a pleasant sort of sunny sight; quite sociable, too.

His attention had been drawn to a slumbering negress, partly disclosed through the lacework of some rigging, lying, with youthful limbs carelessly disposed, under the lee of the bulwarks, like a doe in the shade of a woodland rock. Sprawling at her lapped breasts was her wide-awake fawn, stark naked, its black little body half lifted from the deck, crosswise with its dam's; its hands, like two paws, clambering upon her; its mouth and nose ineffectually rooting to get at the mark; and meantime giving a vexatious half-grunt, blending with the composed snore of the negress.

The uncommon vigour of the child at length roused the mother. She started up, at a distance facing Captain Delano. But as if not at all concerned at the attitude in which she had been caught, delightedly she caught the child up, with maternal transports, covering it with kisses.

There's naked nature, now; pure tenderness and love, thought Captain Delano, well pleased.

This incident prompted him to remark the other negresses more particularly than before. He was gratified with their manners : like most uncivilised women, they seemed at once tender of heart and tough of constitution ; equally ready to die for their infants or fight for them. Unsophisticated as leopardesses ; loving as doves. Ah! thought Captain Delano, these, perhaps, are some of the very women whom Ledyard saw in Africa, and gave such a noble account of.

These natural sights somehow insensibly deepened his confidence and ease. At last he looked to see how his boat was getting on; but it was still pretty remote. He turned to see if Don Benito had returned; but he had not.

To change the scene, as well as to please himself with a leisurely observation of the coming boat, stepping over into the mizen-chains, he clambered his way into the starboard quarter-gallery—one of those abandoned Venetian-looking water-balconies previously mentioned—retreats cut off from the deck. As his foot pressed the half-damp, half-dry sea-mosses matting the place, and a chance phantom cat's-paw—an islet of breeze, unheralded, unfollowed—as this ghostly cat's-paw came fanning his cheek; as his glance fell upon the row of small, round dead-lights—all closed like coppered eyes of the coffined—and the state-cabin door, once connecting with the gallery, even as the dead-lights had once looked out upon it, but now caulked fast like a sarcophagus lid; and to a purple-black, tarred-over panel, threshold, and post; and he bethought him of the time, when that state-cabin and this state-balcony had heard the voices of the Spanish king's officers, and the forms of the Lima viceroy's daughters had perhaps leaned where he stood—as these and other images flitted through his mind, as the cat's-paw through the calm, gradually he felt rising a dreamy inquietude, like that of one who alone on the prairie feels unrest from the repose of the noon.

He leaned against the carved balustrade, again looking off toward his boat; but found his eye falling upon the ribbon grass, trailing along the ship's water-line, straight as a border of green box; and parterres of seaweed,

broad ovals and crescents, floating nigh and far, with
what seemed long formal alleys between, crossing the
terraces of swells, and sweeping round as if leading to
the grottoes below. And overhanging all was the
balustrade by his arm, which, partly stained with pitch
and partly embossed with moss, seemed the charred ruin
of some summer-house in a grand garden long running
to waste.

Trying to break one charm, he was but becharmed
anew. Though upon the wide sea, he seemed in some
far inland country ; prisoner in some deserted château,
left to stare at empty grounds, and peer out at vague
roads, where never wagon or wayfarer passed.

But these enchantments were a little disenchanted as
his eye fell on the corroded main-chains. Of an ancient
style, massy and rusty in link, shackle, and bolt, they
seemed even more fit for the ship's present business
than the one for which she had been built.

Presently he thought something moved nigh the
chains. He rubbed his eyes, and looked hard. Groves
of rigging were about the chains ; and there, peering
from behind a great stay, like an Indian from behind a
hemlock, a Spanish sailor, a marling-spike in his hand,
was seen, who made what seemed an imperfect gesture
toward the balcony, but immediately, as if alarmed by
some advancing step along the deck within, vanished
into the recesses of the hempen forest, like a poacher.

What meant this ? Something the man had sought
to communicate, unbeknown to anyone, even to his
captain. Did the secret involve aught unfavourable to
his captain ? Were those previous misgivings of Captain
Delano's about to be verified ? Or, in his haunted mood
at the moment, had some random, unintentional motion
of the man, while busy with the stay, as if repairing
it, been mistaken for a significant beckoning ?

Not unbewildered, again he gazed off for his boat.
But it was temporarily hidden by a rocky spur of the
isle. As with some eagerness he bent forward, watching for the first shooting view of its beak, the balustrade
gave way before him like charcoal. Had he not clutched
an outreaching rope he would have fallen into the sea.
The crash, though feeble, and the fall, though hollow,
of the rotten fragments, must have been overheard.
He glanced up. With sober curiosity peering down
upon him was one of the old oakum-pickers, slipped
from his perch to an outside boom ; while below the
old negro, and, invisible to him, reconnoitring from a
port-hole like a fox from the mouth of its den, crouched
the Spanish sailor again. From something suddenly
suggested by the man's air, the mad idea now darted
into Captain Delano's mind, that Don Benito's plea of
indisposition, in withdrawing below, was but a pretence :
that he was engaged there maturing his plot, of which
the sailor, by some means gaining an inkling, had a
mind to warn the stranger against ; incited, it may be,
by gratitude for a kind word on first boarding the ship.
Was it from foreseeing some possible interference like
this, that Don Benito had, beforehand, given such a
bad character of his sailors, while praising the negroes ;
though, indeed, the former seemed as docile as the
latter the contrary ? The whites, too, by nature, were
the shrewder race. A man with some evil design, would
he not be likely to speak well of that stupidity which
was blind to his depravity, and malign that intelligence
from which it might not be hidden ? Not unlikely,
perhaps. But if the whites had dark secrets concerning
Don Benito, could then Don Benito be any way in com-
plicity with the blacks ? But they were too stupid.
Besides, who ever heard of a white so far a renegade as
to apostatise from his very species almost, by leaguing

in against it with negroes ? These difficulties recalled former ones. Lost in their mazes, Captain Delano, who had now regained the deck, was uneasily advancing along it, when he observed a new face ; an aged sailor seated cross-legged near the main hatchway. His skin was shrunk up with wrinkles like a pelican's empty pouch ; his hair frosted ; his countenance grave and composed. His hands were full of ropes, which he was working into a large knot. Some blacks were about him obligingly dipping the strands for him, here and there, as the exigencies of the operation demanded.

Captain Delano crossed over to him, and stood in silence surveying the knot ; his mind, by a not uncongenial transition, passing from its own entanglements to those of the hemp. For intricacy, such a knot he had never seen in an American ship, nor indeed any other. The old man looked like an Egyptian priest, making Gordian knots for the temple of Ammon. The knot seemed a combination of double-bowline-knot, treble-crown-knot, back-handed-well-knot, knot-in-and-out-knot, and jamming-knot.

At last, puzzled to comprehend the meaning of such a knot, Captain Delano addressed the knotter :—

' What are you knotting there, my man ? '

' The knot,' was the brief reply, without looking up.

' So it seems ; but what is it for ? '

' For someone else to undo,' muttered back the old man, plying his fingers harder than ever, the knot being now nearly completed.

While Captain Delano stood watching him, suddenly the old man threw the knot toward him, saying in broken English—the first heard in the ship—something to this effect : ' Undo it, cut it, quick.' It was said lowly, but with such condensation of rapidity that the long, slow words in Spanish, which had preceded and followed, almost operated as covers to the brief English between.

For a moment, knot in hand, and knot in head, Captain Delano stood mute ; while, without further heeding him, the old man was now intent upon other ropes. Presently there was a slight stir behind Captain Delano. Turning, he saw the chained negro, Atufal, standing quietly there. The next moment the old sailor rose, muttering, and, followed by his subordinate negroes, removed to the forward part of the ship, where in the crowd he disappeared.

An elderly negro, in a clout like an infant's, and with a pepper-and-salt head, and a kind of attorney air, now approached Captain Delano. In tolerable Spanish, and with a good-natured, knowing wink, he informed him that the old knotter was simple-witted, but harmless ; often playing his odd tricks. The negro concluded by begging the knot, for of course the stranger would not care to be troubled with it. Unconsciously, it was handed to him. With a sort of *congé*, the negro received it, and, turning his back, ferreted into it like a detective custom-house officer after smuggled laces. Soon, with some African word, equivalent to pshaw, he tossed the knot overboard.

All this is very queer now, thought Captain Delano, with a qualmish sort of emotion ; but, as one feeling incipient sea-sickness, he strove, by ignoring the symptoms, to get rid of the malady. Once more he looked off for his boat. To his delight, it was now again in view, leaving the rocky spur astern.

The sensation here experienced, after at first relieving his uneasiness, with unforeseen efficacy soon began to remove it. The less distant sight of that well-known boat—showing it, not as before, half blended with the haze, but with outline defined, so that its individuality, like a man's, was manifest; that boat, *Rover* by name, which, though now in strange seas, had often pressed the beach of Captain Delano's home, and, brought to its threshold for repairs, had familiarly lain there, as a Newfoundland dog; the sight of that household boat evoked a thousand trustful associations, which, contrasted with previous suspicions, filled him not only with lightsome confidence, but somehow with half-humorous self-reproaches at his former lack of it.

'What, I, Amasa Delano—Jack of the Beach, as they called me when a lad—I, Amasa; the same that, duck-satchel in hand, used to paddle along the water-side to the school-house made from the old hulk—I, little Jack of the Beach, that used to go berrying with cousin Nat and the rest; I to be murdered here at the ends of the earth, on board a haunted pirate-ship by a horrible Spaniard? Too nonsensical to think of! Who would murder Amasa Delano? His conscience is clean. There is someone above. Fie, fie, Jack of the Beach! you are a child indeed; a child of the second childhood, old boy; you are beginning to dote and drule, I'm afraid.'

Light of heart and foot, he stepped aft, and there was met by Don Benito's servant, who, with a pleasing expression, responsive to his own present feelings, informed him that his master had recovered from the effects of his coughing fit, and had just ordered him to go present his compliments to his good guest, Don Amasa, and say that he (Don Benito) would soon have the happiness to rejoin him.

There now, do you mark that? again thought Captain Delano, walking the poop. What a donkey I was. This kind gentleman who here sends me his kind compliments, he, but ten minutes ago, dark-lantern in hand, was dodging round some old grindstone in the hold,

sharpening a hatchet for me, I thought. Well, well ;
these long calms have a morbid effect on the mind, I 've
often heard, though I never believed it before. Ha !
glancing toward the boat ; there 's *Rover* ; good dog ;
a white bone in her mouth. A pretty big bone though,
seems to me.—What ? Yes, she has fallen afoul of the
bubbling tide-rip there. It sets her the other way, too,
for the time. Patience.

It was now about noon, though, from the grayness of
everything, it seemed to be getting toward dusk.

The calm was confirmed. In the far distance, away
from the influence of land, the leaden ocean seemed laid
out and leaded up, its course finished, soul gone, defunct. But the current from landward, where the ship
was, increased ; silently sweeping her further and further
toward the tranced waters beyond.

Still, from his knowledge of those latitudes, cherishing
hopes of a breeze, and a fair and fresh one, at any
moment, Captain Delano, despite present prospects,
buoyantly counted upon bringing the *San Dominick*
safely to anchor ere night. The distance swept over
was nothing ; since, with a good wind, ten minutes'
sailing would retrace more than sixty minutes' drifting.
Meantime, one moment turning to mark *Rover* fighting
the tide-rip, and the next to see Don Benito approaching,
he continued walking the poop.

Gradually he felt a vexation arising from the delay
of his boat ; this soon merged into uneasiness ; and at
last—his eye falling continually, as from a stage-box
into the pit, upon the strange crowd before and below
him, and, by and by, recognising there the face—now
composed to indifference—of the Spanish sailor who had
seemed to beckon from the main-chains—something of
his old trepidations returned.

Ah, thought he—gravely enough—this is like the ague :

because it went off, it follows not that it won't come
back.

Though ashamed of the relapse, he could not altogether
subdue it ; and so, exerting his good-nature to the
utmost, insensibly he came to a compromise.

Yes, this is a strange craft ; a strange history, too, and
strange folks on board.   But—nothing more.

By way of keeping his mind out of mischief till the
boat should arrive, he tried to occupy it with turning
over and over, in a purely speculative sort of way, some
lesser peculiarities of the captain and crew.   Among
others, four curious points recurred :—

First, the affair of the Spanish lad assailed with a
knife by the slave-boy ; an act winked at by Don Benito.
Second, the tyranny in Don Benito's treatment of
Atufal, the black ; as if a child should lead a bull of
the Nile by the ring in his nose.   Third, the trampling
of the sailor by the two negroes ; a piece of insolence
passed over without so much as a reprimand.   Fourth,
the cringing submission to their master of all the ship's
underlings, mostly blacks ; as if by the least inadvertence they feared to draw down his despotic displeasure.

Coupling these points, they seemed somewhat contra-
dictory.   But what then, thought Captain Delano,
glancing toward his now nearing boat—what then ?
Why, Don Benito is a very capricious commander.
But he is not the first of the sort I have seen ; though
it 's true he rather exceeds any other.   But as a nation—
continued he in his reveries—these Spaniards are all an
odd set ; the very word Spaniard has a curious, con-
spirator, Guy-Fawkish twang to it.   And yet, I dare
say, Spaniards in the main are as good folks as any in
Duxbury, Massachusetts.   Ah, good !   At last *Rover* has
come.

As, with its welcome freight, the boat touched the

H

side, the oakum-pickers, with venerable gestures, sought
to restrain the blacks, who, at the sight of three gurried
water-casks in its bottom, and a pile of wilted pumpkins
in its bow, hung over the bulwarks in disorderly
raptures.

Don Benito, with his servant, now appeared; his
coming, perhaps, hastened by hearing the noise. Of
him Captain Delano sought permission to serve out the
water, so that all might share alike, and none injure
themselves by unfair excess. But sensible, and, on Don
Benito's account, kind as this offer was, it was received
with what seemed impatience; as if aware that he
lacked energy as a commander, Don Benito, with the
true jealousy of weakness, resented as an affront any
interference. So, at least, Captain Delano inferred.

In another moment the casks were being hoisted in,
when some of the eager negroes accidentally jostled
Captain Delano, where he stood by the gangway; so
that, unmindful of Don Benito, yielding to the impulse
of the moment, with good-natured authority he bade
the blacks stand back; to enforce his words making
use of a half-mirthful, half-menacing gesture. Instantly
the blacks paused, just where they were, each negro
and negress suspended in his or her posture, exactly
as the word had found them—for a few seconds continuing
so—while, as between the responsive posts of a telegraph, an unknown syllable ran from man to man among
the perched oakum-pickers. While the visitor's attention was fixed by this scene, suddenly the hatchet-
polishers half rose, and a rapid cry came from Don
Benito.

Thinking that at the signal of the Spaniard he was
about to be massacred, Captain Delano would have
sprung for his boat, but paused, as the oakum-pickers,
dropping down into the crowd with earnest exclamations,

forced every white and every negro back, at the same
moment, with gestures friendly and familiar, almost
jocose, bidding him, in substance, not be a fool. Simul-
taneously the hatchet-polishers resumed their seats,
quietly as so many tailors, and at once, as if nothing had
happened, the work of hoisting in the casks was resumed,
whites and blacks singing at the tackle.

Captain Delano glanced toward Don Benito. As he
saw his meagre form in the act of recovering itself
from reclining in the servant's arms, into which the
agitated invalid had fallen, he could not but marvel at
the panic by which himself had been surprised, on the
darting supposition that such a commander, who, upon
a legitimate occasion, so trivial, too, as it now appeared,
could lose all self-command, was, with energetic iniquity,
going to bring about his murder.

The casks being on deck, Captain Delano was handed
a number of jars and cups by one of the steward's aids,
who, in the name of his captain, entreated him to do
as he had proposed—dole out the water. He complied,
with republican impartiality as to this republican element,
which always seeks one level, serving the oldest white
no better than the youngest black; excepting, indeed,
poor Don Benito, whose condition, if not rank, demanded
an extra allowance. To him, in the first place, Captain
Delano presented a fair pitcher of the fluid; but, thirst-
ing as he was for it, the Spaniard quaffed not a drop
until after several grave bows and salutes. A reciproca-
tion of courtesies which the sight-loving Africans hailed
with clapping of hands.

Two of the less wilted pumpkins being reserved for
the cabin table, the residue were minced up on the
spot for the general regalement. But the soft bread,
sugar, and bottled cider, Captain Delano would have
given the whites alone, and in chief Don Benito; but

the latter objected ; which disinterestedness not a little pleased the American ; and so mouthfuls all around were given alike to whites and blacks ; excepting one bottle of cider, which Babo insisted upon setting aside for his master.

Here it may be observed that as on the first visit of the boat, the American had not permitted his men to board the ship, neither did he now ; being unwilling to add to the confusion of the decks.

Not uninfluenced by the peculiar good-humour at present prevailing, and for the time oblivious of any but benevolent thoughts, Captain Delano, who, from recent indications, counted upon a breeze within an hour or two at furthest, dispatched the boat back to the sealer, with orders for all the hands that could be spared immediately to set about rafting casks to the watering-place and filling them.   Likewise he bade word be carried to his chief officer, that if, against present expectation, the ship was not brought to anchor by sunset, he need be under no concern ; for as there was to be a full moon that night, he (Captain Delano) would remain on board ready to play the pilot, come the wind soon or late.

As the two captains stood together, observing the departing boat—the servant, as it happened, having just spied a spot on his master's velvet sleeve, and silently engaged rubbing it out—the American expressed his regrets that the *San Dominick* had no boats ; none, at least, but the unseaworthy old hulk of the long-boat, which, warped as a camel's skeleton in the desert, and almost as bleached, lay pot-wise inverted amidships, one side a little tipped, furnishing a subterraneous sort of den for family groups of the blacks, mostly women and small children ; who, squatting on old mats below, or perched above in the dark dome, on the elevated seats, were descried, some distance within, like a social circle of bats, sheltering in some friendly cave ; at intervals, ebon flights of naked boys and girls, three or four years old, darting in and out of the den's mouth.

' Had you three or four boats now, Don Benito,' said Captain Delano, ' I think that, by tugging at the oars, your negroes here might help along matters some. Did you sail from port without boats, Don Benito ? '

' They were stove in the gales, señor.'

' That was bad. Many men, too, you lost then. Boats and men. Those must have been hard gales, Don Benito.'

' Past all speech,' cringed the Spaniard.

' Tell me, Don Benito,' continued his companion with increased interest, ' tell me, were these gales immediately off the pitch of Cape Horn ? '

' Cape Horn ?—who spoke of Cape Horn ? '

' Yourself did, when giving me an account of your voyage,' answered Captain Delano, with almost equal astonishment at this eating of his own words, even as he ever seemed eating his own heart, on the part of the Spaniard. ' You yourself, Don Benito, spoke of Cape Horn,' he emphatically repeated.

The Spaniard turned, in a sort of stooping posture, pausing an instant, as one about to make a plunging exchange of elements, as from air to water.

At this moment a messenger-boy, a white, hurried by, in the regular performance of his function carrying the last expired half-hour forward to the forecastle, from the cabin time-piece, to have it struck at the ship's large bell.

' Master,' said the servant, discontinuing his work on the coat sleeve, and addressing the rapt Spaniard with a sort of timid apprehensiveness, as one charged with a duty, the discharge of which, it was foreseen, would

prove irksome to the very person who had imposed it,
and for whose benefit it was intended, ' master told me
never mind where he was, or how engaged, always to
remind him, to a minute, when shaving-time comes.
Miguel has gone to strike the half-hour afternoon.   It
is *now*, master.   Will master go into the cuddy ? '

' Ah—yes,' answered the Spaniard, starting, as from
dreams into realities ; then turning upon Captain Delano,
he said that ere long he would resume the conversation.

' Then if master means to talk more to Don Amasa,'
said the servant, ' why not let Don Amasa sit by master
in the cuddy, and master can talk, and Don Amasa can
listen, while Babo here lathers and strops.'

' Yes,' said Captain Delano, not unpleased with this
sociable plan, ' yes, Don Benito, unless you had rather
not, I will go with you.'

' Be it so, señor.'

As the three passed aft, the American could not but
think it another strange instance of his host's capriciousness, this being shaved with such uncommon punctuality
in the middle of the day.   But he deemed it more than
likely that the servant's anxious fidelity had something
to do with the matter ; inasmuch as the timely interrup-
tion served to rally his master from the mood which had
evidently been coming upon him.

The place called the cuddy was a light deck-cabin
formed by the poop, a sort of attic to the large cabin
below.   Part of it had formerly been the quarters of the
officers ; but since their death all the partitionings had
been thrown down, and the whole interior converted
into one spacious and airy marine hall ; for absence of
fine furniture and picturesque disarray of odd appurtenances, somewhat answering to the wide, cluttered hall
of some eccentric bachelor-squire in the country, who
hangs his shooting-jacket and tobacco-pouch on deer

antlers, and keeps his fishing-rod, tongs, and walking-stick in the same corner.

The similitude was heightened, if not originally suggested, by glimpses of the surrounding sea; since, in one aspect, the country and the ocean seem cousins-german.

The floor of the cuddy was matted. Overhead, four or five old muskets were stuck into horizontal holes along the beams. On one side was a claw-footed old table lashed to the deck; a thumbed missal on it, and over it a small, meagre crucifix attached to the bulk-head. Under the table lay a dented cutlass or two, with a hacked harpoon, among some melancholy old rigging, like a heap of poor friars' girdles. There were also two long, sharp-ribbed settees of Malacca cane, black with age, and uncomfortable to look at as inquisitors' racks, with a large, misshapen arm-chair, which, furnished with a rude barber's crotch at the back, working with a screw, seemed some grotesque engine of torment. A flag locker was in one corner, open, exposing various coloured bunting, some rolled up, others half unrolled, still others tumbled. Opposite was a cumbrous washstand, of black mahogany, all of one block, with a pedestal, like a font, and over it a railed shelf, containing combs, brushes, and other implements of the toilet. A torn hammock of stained grass swung near; the sheets tossed, and the pillow wrinkled up like a brow, as if whoever slept here slept but illy, with alternate visitations of sad thoughts and bad dreams.

The further extremity of the cuddy, overhanging the ship's stern, was pierced with three openings, windows or port-holes, according as men or cannon might peer, socially or unsocially, out of them. At present neither men nor cannon were seen, though huge ring-bolts and other rusty iron fixtures of the woodwork hinted of twenty-four-pounders.

Glancing toward the hammock as he entered, Captain Delano said, ' You sleep here, Don Benito ? '

' Yes, señor, since we got into mild weather.'

' This seems a sort of dormitory, sitting-room, sail-loft, chapel, armoury, and private closet all together, Don Benito,' added Captain Delano, looking round.

' Yes, señor ; events have not been favourable to much order in my arrangements.'

Here the servant, napkin on arm, made a motion as if waiting his master's good pleasure. Don Benito signified his readiness, when, seating him in the Malacca arm-chair, and for the guest's convenience drawing opposite one of the settees, the servant commenced operations by throwing back his master's collar and loosening his cravat.

There is something in the negro which, in a peculiar way, fits him for avocations about one's person. Most negroes are natural valets and hair-dressers ; taking to the comb and brush congenially as to the castanets, and flourishing them apparently with almost equal satis-faction. There is, too, a smooth tact about them in this employment, with a marvellous, noiseless, gliding briskness, not ungraceful in its way, singularly pleasing to behold, and still more so to be the manipulated subject of. And above all is the great gift of good-humour. Not the mere grin or laugh is here meant. Those were unsuitable. But a certain easy cheerful-ness, harmonious in every glance and gesture ; as though God had set the whole negro to some pleasant tune.

When to this is added the docility arising from the unaspiring contentment of a limited mind, and that susceptibility of blind attachment sometimes inhering in indisputable inferiors, one readily perceives why those hypochondriacs, Johnson and Byron—it may be, something like the hypochondriac Benito Cereno—took to their hearts, almost to the exclusion of the entire white race, their serving-men, the negroes, Barber and Fletcher. But if there be that in the negro which exempts him from the inflicted sourness of the morbid or cynical mind, how, in his most prepossessing aspects, must he appear to a benevolent one ? When at ease with respect to exterior things, Captain Delano's nature was not only benign, but familiarly and humorously so. At home, he had often taken rare satisfaction in sitting in his door, watching some free man of colour at his work or play. If on a voyage he chanced to have a black sailor, invariably he was on chatty and half-gamesome terms with him. In fact, like most men of a good, blithe heart, Captain Delano took to negroes, not philanthropically, but genially, just as other men to Newfoundland dogs.

Hitherto, the circumstances in which he found the *San Dominick* had repressed the tendency. But in the cuddy, relieved from his former uneasiness, and, for various reasons, more sociably inclined than at any previous period of the day, and seeing the coloured servant, napkin on arm, so debonnaire about his master, in a business so familiar as that of shaving, too, all his old weakness for negroes returned.

Among other things, he was amused with an odd instance of the African love of bright colours and fine shows, in the black's informally taking from the flag-locker a great piece of bunting of all hues, and lavishly tucking it under his master's chin for an apron.

The mode of shaving among the Spaniards is a little different from what it is with other nations. They have a basin, specifically called a barber's basin, which on one side is scooped out, so as accurately to receive the chin, against which it is closely held in lathering ; which is done, not with a brush, but with soap dipped in the water of the basin and rubbed on the face.

In the present instance salt-water was used for lack of better ; and the parts lathered were only the upper lip, and low down under the throat, all the rest being cultivated beard.

The preliminaries being somewhat novel to Captain Delano, he sat curiously eyeing them, so that no conversation took place, nor, for the present, did Don Benito appear disposed to renew any.

Setting down his basin, the negro searched among the razors, as for the sharpest, and having found it, gave it an additional edge by expertly stropping it on the firm, smooth, oily skin of his open palm ; he then made a gesture as if to begin, but midway stood suspended for an instant, one hand elevating the razor, the other professionally dabbling among the bubbling suds on the Spaniard's lank neck. Not unaffected by the close sight of the gleaming steel, Don Benito nervously shuddered ; his usual ghastliness was heightened by the lather, which lather, again, was intensified in its hue by the contrasting sootiness of the negro's body. Altogether the scene was somewhat peculiar, at least to Captain Delano, nor, as he saw the two thus postured, could he resist the vagary, that in the black he saw a headsman, and in the white a man at the block. But this was one of those antic conceits, appearing and vanishing in a breath, from which, perhaps, the best regulated mind is not always free.

Meantime the agitation of the Spaniard had a little loosened the bunting from around him, so that one broad fold swept curtain-like over the chair-arm to the floor, revealing, amid a profusion of armorial bars and ground-colours—black, blue and yellow—a closed castle in a blood-red field diagonal with a lion rampant in a white.

'The castle and the lion,' exclaimed Captain Delano— 'why, Don Benito, this is the flag of Spain you use here. It's well it's only I, and not the king, that sees this,' he added, with a smile, 'but'—turning toward the black—'it's all one, I suppose, so the colours be gay'; which playful remark did not fail somewhat to tickle the negro.

'Now, master,' he said, readjusting the flag, and pressing the head gently further back into the crotch of the chair; 'now, master,' and the steel glanced nigh the throat.

Again Don Benito faintly shuddered.

'You must not shake so, master. See, Don Amasa, master always shakes when I shave him. And yet master knows I never yet have drawn blood, though it's true, if master will shake so, I may some of these times. Now, master,' he continued. 'And now, Don Amasa, please go on with your talk about the gale, and all that; master can hear, and, between times, master can answer.'

'Ah yes, these gales,' said Captain Delano; 'but the more I think of your voyage, Don Benito, the more I wonder, not at the gales, terrible as they must have been, but at the disastrous interval following them. For here, by your account, have you been these two months and more getting from Cape Horn to St. Maria, a distance which I myself, with a good wind, have sailed in a few days. True, you had calms, and long ones, but to be becalmed for two months, that is, at least, unusual. Why, Don Benito, had almost any other gentleman told me such a story, I should have been half disposed to a little incredulity.'

Here an involuntary expression came over the Spaniard,

similar to that just before on the deck, and whether it
was the start he gave, or a sudden gawky roll of the
hull in the calm, or a momentary unsteadiness of the
servant's hand, however it was, just then the razor drew
blood, spots of which stained the creamy lather under
the throat : immediately the black barber drew back
his steel, and, remaining in his professional attitude,
back to Captain Delano, and face to Don Benito, held
up the trickling razor, saying, with a sort of half-humorous sorrow, ' See, master—you shook so—here 's Babo's
first blood.'

No sword drawn before James the First of England,
no assassination in that timid king's presence, could
have produced a more terrified aspect than was now
presented by Don Benito.

Poor fellow, thought Captain Delano, so nervous he
can't even bear the sight of barber's blood ; and this
unstrung, sick man, is it credible that I should have
imagined he meant to spill all my blood, who can't
endure the sight of one little drop of his own ? Surely,
Amasa Delano, you have been beside yourself this day.
Tell it not when you get home, sappy Amasa. Well,
well, he looks like a murderer, doesn't he ? More like
as if himself were to be done for. Well, well, this day's
experience shall be a good lesson.

Meantime, while these things were running through
the honest seaman's mind, the servant had taken the
napkin from his arm, and to Don Benito had said :
' But answer Don Amasa, please, master, while I wipe
this ugly stuff off the razor, and strop it again.'

As he said the words, his face was turned half round,
so as to be alike visible to the Spaniard and the American,
and seemed, by its expression, to hint, that he was
desirous, by getting his master to go on with the conversation, considerately to withdraw his attention from

the recent annoying accident. As if glad to snatch the
offered relief, Don Benito resumed, rehearsing to Captain
Delano, that not only were the calms of unusual duration,
but the ship had fallen in with obstinate currents ;
and other things he added, some of which were but
repetitions of former statements, to explain how it came
to pass that the passage from Cape Horn to St. Maria
had been so exceedingly long ; now and then mingling
with his words incidental praises, less qualified than
before, to the blacks, for their general good conduct.
These particulars were not given consecutively, the
servant, at convenient times, using his razor, and so,
between the intervals of shaving, the story and panegyric
went on with more than usual huskiness.

To Captain Delano's imagination, now again not wholly
at rest, there was something so hollow in the Spaniard's
manner, with apparently some reciprocal hollowness in
the servant's dusky comment of silence, that the idea
flashed across him, that possibly master and man, for
some unknown purpose, were acting out, both in word
and deed, nay, to the very tremor of Don Benito's
limbs, some juggling play before him. Neither did the
suspicion of collusion lack apparent support, from the
fact of those whispered conferences before mentioned.
But then, what could be the object of enacting this
play of the barber before him ? At last, regarding the
notion as a whimsy, insensibly suggested, perhaps, by
the theatrical aspect of Don Benito in his harlequin
ensign, Captain Delano speedily banished it.

The shaving over, the servant bestirred himself with
a small bottle of scented waters, pouring a few drops
on the head, and then diligently rubbing ; the vehemence
of the exercise causing the muscles of his face to twitch
rather strangely.

His next operation was with comb, scissors, and

brush ; going round and round, smoothing a curl here, clipping an unruly whisker-hair there, giving a graceful sweep to the temple-lock, with other impromptu touches evincing the hand of a master ; while, like any resigned gentleman in barber's hands, Don Benito bore all, much less uneasily, at least, than he had done the razoring ; indeed, he sat so pale and rigid now, that the negro seemed a Nubian sculptor finishing off a white statue-head.

All being over at last, the standard of Spain removed, tumbled up, and tossed back into the flag-locker, the negro's warm breath blowing away any stray hair which might have lodged down his master's neck ; collar and cravat readjusted ; a speck of lint whisked off the velvet lapel ; all this being done ; backing off a little space, and pausing with an expression of subdued self-complacency, the servant for a moment surveyed his master, as, in toilet at least, the creature of his own tasteful hands.

Captain Delano playfully complimented him upon his achievement ; at the same time congratulating Don Benito.

But neither sweet waters, nor shampooing, nor fidelity, nor sociality, delighted the Spaniard. Seeing him relapsing into forbidding gloom, and still remaining seated, Captain Delano, thinking that his presence was undesired just then, withdrew, on pretence of seeing whether, as he had prophesied, any signs of a breeze were visible.

Walking forward to the mainmast, he stood a while thinking over the scene, and not without some undefined misgivings, when he heard a noise near the cuddy, and turning, saw the negro, his hand to his cheek. Advancing, Captain Delano perceived that the cheek was bleeding. He was about to ask the cause, when the negro's wailing soliloquy enlightened him.

' Ah, when will master get better from his sickness ;
only the sour heart that sour sickness breeds made him
serve Babo so ; cutting Babo with the razor, because,
only by accident, Babo had given master one little
scratch ; and for the first time in so many a day, too.
Ah, ah, ah,' holding his hand to his face.

Is it possible, thought Captain Delano ; was it to
wreak in private his Spanish spite against this poor
friend of his, that Don Benito, by his sullen manner,
impelled me to withdraw ?   Ah, this slavery breeds ugly
passions in man.—Poor fellow !

He was about to speak in sympathy to the negro, but
with a timid reluctance he now re-entered the cuddy.

Presently master and man came forth ; Don Benito
leaning on his servant as if nothing had happened.

But a sort of love-quarrel, after all, thought Captain
Delano.

He accosted Don Benito, and they slowly walked
together. They had gone but a few paces, when the
steward—a tall, rajah-looking mulatto, orientally set off
with a pagoda turban formed by three or four Madras
handkerchiefs wound about his head, tier on tier—
approaching with a salaam, announced lunch in the
cabin.

On their way thither, the two captains were preceded
by the mulatto, who, turning round as he advanced,
with continual smiles and bows, ushered them on, a
display of elegance which quite completed the insignifi-
cance of the small bare-headed Babo, who, as if not
unconscious of inferiority, eyed askance the graceful
steward. But in part, Captain Delano imputed his
jealous watchfulness to that peculiar feeling which the
full-blooded African entertains for the adulterated one.
As for the steward, his manner, if not bespeaking much
dignity of self-respect, yet evidenced his extreme desire

to please ; which is doubly meritorious, as at once Christian and Chesterfieldian.

Captain Delano observed with interest that while the complexion of the mulatto was hybrid, his physiognomy was European—classically so.

' Don Benito,' whispered he, ' I am glad to see this usher-of-the-golden-rod of yours ; the sight refutes an ugly remark once made to me by a Barbados planter ; that when a mulatto has a regular European face, look out for him ; he is a devil. But see, your steward here has features more regular than King George's of England ; and yet there he nods, and bows, and smiles ; a king, indeed—the king of kind hearts and polite fellows. What a pleasant voice he has, too ! '

' He has, señor.'

' But tell me, has he not, so far as you have known him, always proved a good, worthy fellow ? ' said Captain Delano, pausing, while with a final genuflection the steward disappeared into the cabin ; ' come, for the reason just mentioned, I am curious to know.'

' Francesco is a good man,' a sort of sluggishly responded Don Benito, like a phlegmatic appreciator, who would neither find fault nor flatter.

' Ah, I thought so. For it were strange, indeed, and not very creditable to us white-skins, if a little of our blood mixed with the African's should, far from improving the latter's quality, have the sad effect of pouring vitriolic acid into black broth ; improving the hue, perhaps, but not the wholesomeness.'

' Doubtless, doubtless, señor, but '—glancing at Babo— ' not to speak of negroes, your planter's remark I have heard applied to the Spanish and Indian intermixtures in our provinces. But I know nothing about the matter,' he listlessly added.

And here they entered the cabin.

The lunch was a frugal one. Some of Captain Delano's fresh fish and pumpkins, biscuit and salt beef, the reserved bottle of cider, and the *San Dominick's* last bottle of Canary.

As they entered, Francesco, with two or three coloured aids, was hovering over the table giving the last adjustments. Upon perceiving their master they withdrew, Francesco making a smiling *congé*, and the Spaniard, without condescending to notice it, fastidiously remarking to his companion that he relished not superfluous attendance.

Without companions, host and guest sat down, like a childless married couple, at opposite ends of the table, Don Benito waving Captain Delano to his place, and, weak as he was, insisting upon that gentleman being seated before himself.

The negro placed a rug under Don Benito's feet, and a cushion behind his back, and then stood behind, not his master's chair, but Captain Delano's. At first, this a little surprised the latter. But it was soon evident that, in taking his position, the black was still true to his master; since by facing him he could the more readily anticipate his slightest want.

'This is an uncommonly intelligent fellow of yours, Don Benito,' whispered Captain Delano across the table.

'You say true, señor.'

During the repast, the guest again reverted to parts of Don Benito's story, begging further particulars here and there. He inquired how it was that the scurvy and fever should have committed such wholesale havoc upon the whites, while destroying less than half of the blacks. As if this question reproduced the whole scene of plague before the Spaniard's eyes, miserably reminding him of his solitude in a cabin where before he had had so many friends and officers round him, his hand shook, his face became hueless, broken words escaped ; but directly the sane memory of the past seemed replaced by insane terrors of the present. With starting eyes he stared before him at vacancy. For nothing was to be seen but the hand of his servant pushing the Canary over toward him. At length a few sips served partially to restore him. He made random reference to the different constitution of races, enabling one to offer more resistance to certain maladies than another. The thought was new to his companion.

Presently Captain Delano, intending to say something to his host concerning the pecuniary part of the business he had undertaken for him, especially—since he was strictly accountable to his owners—with reference to the new suit of sails, and other things of that sort ; and naturally preferring to conduct such affairs in private, was desirous that the servant should withdraw ; imagining that Don Benito for a few minutes could dispense with his attendance. He, however, waited a while ; thinking that, as the conversation proceeded, Don Benito, without being prompted, would perceive the propriety of the step.

But it was otherwise. At last catching his host's eye, Captain Delano, with a slight backward gesture of his thumb, whispered, ' Don Benito, pardon me, but there is an interference with the full expression of what I have to say to you.'

Upon this the Spaniard changed countenance ; which was imputed to his resenting the hint, as in some way a reflection upon his servant. After a moment's pause, he assured his guest that the black's remaining with them could be of no disservice ; because since losing his officers he had made Babo (whose original office, it now appeared, had been captain of the slaves) not

only his constant attendant and companion, but in all
things his confidant.

After this, nothing more could be said ; though,
indeed, Captain Delano could hardly avoid some little
tinge of irritation upon being left ungratified in so inconsiderable a wish, by one, too, for whom he intended
such solid services. But it is only his querulousness,
thought he ; and so filling his glass he proceeded to
business.

The price of the sails and other matters was fixed
upon. But while this was being done, the American
observed that, though his original offer of assistance
had been hailed with hectic animation, yet now when
it was reduced to a business transaction, indifference
and apathy were betrayed. Don Benito, in fact,
appeared to submit to hearing the details more out of
regard to common propriety than from any impression
that weighty benefit to himself and his voyage was
involved.

Soon, his manner became still more reserved. The
effort was vain to seek to draw him into social talk.
Gnawed by his splenetic mood, he sat twitching his
beard, while to little purpose the hand of his servant,
mute as that on the wall, slowly pushed over the
Canary.

Lunch being over, they sat down on the cushioned
transom ; the servant placing a pillow behind his master.
The long continuance of the calm had now affected the
atmosphere. Don Benito sighed heavily, as if for
breath.

' Why not adjourn to the cuddy,' said Captain Delano ;
' there is more air there.' But the host sat silent and
motionless.

Meantime his servant knelt before him, with a large
fan of feathers. And Francesco, coming in on tiptoes,

handed the negro a little cup of aromatic waters, with which at intervals he chafed his master's brow ; smoothing the hair along the temples as a nurse does a child's. He spoke no word. He only rested his eye on his master's, as if, amid all Don Benito's distress, a little to refresh his spirit by the silent sight of fidelity.

Presently the ship's bell sounded two o'clock ; and through the cabin windows a slight rippling of the sea was discerned ; and from the desired direction.

'There,' exclaimed Captain Delano, 'I told you so, Don Benito, look ! '

He had risen to his feet, speaking in a very animated tone, with a view the more to rouse his companion. But though the crimson curtain of the stern window near him that moment fluttered against his pale cheek, Don Benito seemed to have even less welcome for the breeze than the calm.

Poor fellow, thought Captain Delano, bitter experience has taught him that one ripple does not make a wind, any more than one swallow a summer. But he is mistaken for once. I will get his ship in for him, and prove it.

Briefly alluding to his weak condition, he urged his host to remain quietly where he was, since he (Captain Delano) would with pleasure take upon himself the responsibility of making the best use of the wind.

Upon gaining the deck, Captain Delano started at the unexpected figure of Atufal, monumentally fixed at the threshold, like one of those sculptured porters of black marble guarding the porches of Egyptian tombs.

But this time the start was, perhaps, purely physical. Atufal's presence, singularly attesting docility even in sullenness, was contrasted with that of the hatchet-polishers, who in patience evinced their industry ; while both spectacles showed, that lax as Don Benito's general authority might be, still, whenever he chose to exert it, no man so savage or colossal but must, more or less, bow.

Snatching a trumpet which hung from the bulwarks, with a free step Captain Delano advanced to the forward edge of the poop, issuing his orders in his best Spanish. The few sailors and many negroes, all equally pleased, obediently set about heading the ship toward the harbour.

While giving some directions about setting a lower stun'-sail, suddenly Captain Delano heard a voice faithfully repeating his orders. Turning, he saw Babo, now for the time acting, under the pilot, his original part of captain of the slaves. This assistance proved valuable. Tattered sails and warped yards were soon brought into some trim. And no brace or halyard was pulled but to the blithe songs of the inspirited negroes.

Good fellows, thought Captain Delano, a little training would make fine sailors of them. Why, see, the very women pull and sing too. These must be some of those Ashantee negresses that make such capital soldiers, I 've heard. But who 's at the helm ? I must have a good hand there.

He went to see.

The *San Dominick* steered with a cumbrous tiller, with large horizontal pulleys attached. At each pulley-end stood a subordinate black, and between them, at the tiller-head, the responsible post, a Spanish seaman, whose countenance evinced his due share in the general hopefulness and confidence at the coming of the breeze.

He proved the same man who had behaved with so shamefaced an air on the windlass.

' Ah—it is you, my man,' exclaimed Captain Delano— ' well, no more sheep's-eyes now ;—look straight forward and keep the ship so. Good hand, I trust ? And want to get into the harbour, don't you ? '

The man assented with an inward chuckle, grasping the tiller-head firmly. Upon this, unperceived by the American, the two blacks eyed the sailor intently.

Finding all right at the helm, the pilot went forward to the forecastle, to see how matters stood there.

The ship now had way enough to breast the current. With the approach of evening, the breeze would be sure to freshen.

Having done all that was needed for the present, Captain Delano, giving his last orders to the sailors, turned aft to report affairs to Don Benito in the cabin ; perhaps additionally incited to rejoin him by the hope of snatching a moment's private chat while the servant was engaged upon deck.

From opposite sides, there were, beneath the poop, two approaches to the cabin ; one further forward than the other, and consequently communicating with a longer passage.   Marking the servant still above, Captain Delano, taking the nighest entrance—the one last named, and at whose porch Atufal still stood—hurried on his way, till, arrived at the cabin threshold, he paused an instant, a little to recover from his eagerness.   Then, with the words of his intended business upon his lips, he entered. As he advanced toward the seated Spaniard, he heard another footstep, keeping time with his. From the opposite door, a salver in hand, the servant was likewise advancing.

' Confound the faithful fellow,' thought Captain Delano ; ' what a vexatious coincidence.'

Possibly the vexation might have been something different, were it not for the brisk confidence inspired by the breeze. But even as it was, he felt a slight twinge, from a sudden indefinite association in his mind of Babo with Atufal.

' Don Benito,' said he ' I give you joy ; the breeze

will hold, and will increase. By the way, your tall man and time-piece, Atufal, stands without. By your order, of course ? '

Don Benito recoiled, as if at some bland satirical touch, delivered with such adroit garnish of apparent good breeding as to present no handle for retort.

He is like one flayed alive, thought Captain Delano ; where may one touch him without causing a shrink ?

The servant moved before his master, adjusting a cushion ; recalled to civility, the Spaniard stiffly replied : ' You are right. The slave appears where you saw him, according to my command ; which is, that if at the given hour I am below, he must take his stand and abide my coming.'

' Ah now, pardon me, but that is treating the poor fellow like an ex-king indeed. Ah, Don Benito,' smiling, ' for all the licence you permit in some things, I fear lest, at bottom, you are a bitter hard master.'

Again Don Benito shrank ; and this time, as the good sailor thought, from a genuine twinge of his conscience.

Again conversation became constrained. In vain Captain Delano called attention to the now perceptible motion of the keel gently cleaving the sea ; with lacklustre eye, Don Benito returned words few and reserved.

By and by, the wind having steadily risen, and still blowing right into the harbour, bore the *San Dominick* swiftly on. Rounding a point of land, the sealer at distance came into open view.

Meantime Captain Delano had again repaired to the deck, remaining there some time. Having at last altered the ship's course, so as to give the reef a wide berth, he returned for a few moments below.

I will cheer up my poor friend this time, thought he.

' Better and better, Don Benito,' he cried as he blithely re-entered : ' there will soon be an end to your cares, at least for a while. For when, after a long, sad voyage, you know, the anchor drops into the haven, all its vast weight seems lifted from the captain's heart. We are getting on famously, Don Benito. My ship is in sight. Look through this side-light here ; there she is ; all a-taunt-o ! The *Bachelor's Delight*, my good friend. Ah, how this wind braces one up. Come, you must take a cup of coffee with me this evening. My old steward will give you as fine a cup as ever any sultan tasted. What say you, Don Benito, will you ? '

At first, the Spaniard glanced feverishly up, casting a longing look toward the sealer, while with mute concern his servant gazed into his face. Suddenly the old ague of coldness returned, and dropping back to his cushions he was silent.

' You do not answer. Come, all day you have been my host ; would you have hospitality all on one side ? '

' I cannot go,' was the response.

' What ? it will not fatigue you. The ships will lie together as near as they can, without swinging foul. It will be little more than stepping from deck to deck ; which is but as from room to room. Come, come, you must not refuse me.'

' I cannot go,' decisively and repulsively repeated Don Benito.

Renouncing all but the last appearance of courtesy, with a sort of cadaverous sullenness, and biting his thin nails to the quick, he glanced, almost glared, at his guest, as if impatient that a stranger's presence should interfere with the full indulgence of his morbid hour. Meantime the sound of the parted waters came more and more gurglingly and merrily in at the windows ; as reproaching him for his dark spleen ; as telling him that, sulk as he might, and go mad with it, nature cared not a jot ; since, whose fault was it, pray ?

But the foul mood was now at its depth, as the fair wind at its height.

There was something in the man so far beyond any mere unsociality or sourness previously evinced, that even the forbearing good-nature of his guest could no longer endure it. Wholly at a loss to account for such demeanour, and deeming sickness with eccentricity, however extreme, no adequate excuse, well satisfied, too, that nothing in his own conduct could justify it, Captain Delano's pride began to be roused. Himself became reserved. But all seemed one to the Spaniard. Quitting him, therefore, Captain Delano once more went to the deck.

The ship was now within less than two miles of the sealer. The whale-boat was seen darting over the interval.

To be brief, the two vessels, thanks to the pilot's skill, ere long in neighbourly style lay anchored together.

Before returning to his own vessel, Captain Delano had intended communicating to Don Benito the smaller details of the proposed services to be rendered. But, as it was, unwilling anew to subject himself to rebuffs, he resolved, now that he had seen the *San Dominick* safely moored, immediately to quit her, without further allusion to hospitality or business. Indefinitely postponing his ulterior plans, he would regulate his future actions according to future circumstances. His boat was ready to receive him; but his host still tarried below. Well, thought Captain Delano, if he has little breeding, the more need to show mine. He descended to the cabin to bid a ceremonious, and, it may be, tacitly rebukeful adieu. But to his great satisfaction, Don Benito, as if he began to feel the weight of that treatment with which his slighted guest had, not indecorously, retaliated upon him, now supported by his servant, rose to his feet, and grasping Captain Delano's hand, stood tremulous ; too much agitated to speak. But the good augury hence drawn was suddenly dashed, by his resuming all his previous reserve, with augmented gloom, as, with half-averted eyes, he silently reseated himself on his cushions. With a corresponding return of his own chilled feelings, Captain Delano bowed and withdrew.

He was hardly midway in the narrow corridor, dim as a tunnel, leading from the cabin to the stairs, when a sound, as of the tolling for execution in some jail-yard, fell on his ears. It was the echo of the ship's flawed bell, striking the hour, drearily reverberated in this subterranean vault. Instantly, by a fatality not to be withstood, his mind, responsive to the portent, swarmed with superstitious suspicions. He paused. In images far swifter than these sentences, the minutest details of all his former distrusts swept through him.

Hitherto, credulous good-nature had been too ready to furnish excuses for reasonable fears. Why was the Spaniard, so superfluously punctilious at times, now heedless of common propriety in not accompanying to the side his departing guest ? Did indisposition forbid ? Indisposition had not forbidden more irksome exertion that day. His last equivocal demeanour recurred. He had risen to his feet, grasped his guest's hand, motioned toward his hat ; then, in an instant, all was eclipsed in sinister muteness and gloom. Did this imply one brief, repentant relenting at the final moment, from some iniquitous plot, followed by remorseless return to it ? His last glance seemed to express a calamitous, yet acquiescent farewell to Captain Delano forever. Why decline the invitation to visit the sealer that evening ? Or was the Spaniard less hardened than the Jew, who refrained not from supping at the board of him whom

the same night he meant to betray ?   What imported
all those day-long enigmas and contradictions, except
they were intended to mystify, preliminary to some
stealthy blow ?   Atufal, the pretended rebel, but punctual
shadow, that moment lurked by the threshold without.
He seemed a sentry, and more. Who, by his own
confession, had stationed him there ?   Was the negro
now lying in wait ?

The Spaniard behind—his creature before : to rush
from darkness to light was the involuntary choice.

The next moment, with clenched jaw and hand, he
passed Atufal, and stood unharmed in the light.   As he
saw his trim ship lying peacefully at anchor, and almost
within ordinary call ; as he saw his household boat,
with familiar faces in it, patiently rising and falling on
the short waves by the *San Dominick*'s side ; and then,
glancing about the decks where he stood, saw the oakum-
pickers still gravely plying their fingers ; and heard the
low, buzzing whistle and industrious hum of the hatchet-
polishers, still bestirring themselves over their endless
occupation ; and more than all, as he saw the benign
aspect of nature, taking her innocent repose in the
evening ; the screened sun in the quiet camp of the
west shining out like the mild light from Abraham's
tent ; as charmed eye and ear took in all these, with
the chained figure of the black, clenched jaw and hand
relaxed.   Once again he smiled at the phantoms which
had mocked him, and felt something like a tinge of
remorse, that, by harbouring them even for a moment,
he should, by implication, have betrayed an atheist
doubt of the ever-watchful Providence above.

There was a few minutes' delay, while, in obedience
to his orders, the boat was being hooked along to the
gangway. During this interval, a sort of saddened
satisfaction stole over Captain Delano, at thinking of

the kindly offices he had that day discharged for a stranger. Ah, thought he, after good actions one's conscience is never ungrateful, however much so the benefited party may be.

Presently, his foot, in the first act of descent into the boat, pressed the first round of the side-ladder, his face presented inward upon the deck. In the same moment, he heard his name courteously sounded; and, to his pleased surprise, saw Don Benito advancing—an unwonted energy in his air, as if, at the last moment, intent upon making amends for his recent discourtesy. With instinctive good feeling, Captain Delano, withdrawing his foot, turned and reciprocally advanced. As he did so, the Spaniard's nervous eagerness increased, but his vital energy failed; so that, the better to support him, the servant, placing his master's hand on his naked shoulder, and gently holding it there, formed himself into a sort of crutch.

When the two captains met, the Spaniard again fervently took the hand of the American, at the same time casting an earnest glance into his eyes, but, as before, too much overcome to speak.

I have done him wrong, self-reproachfully thought Captain Delano; his apparent coldness has deceived me; in no instance has he meant to offend.

Meantime, as if fearful that the continuance of the scene might too much unstring his master, the servant seemed anxious to terminate it. And so, still presenting himself as a crutch, and walking between the two captains, he advanced with them toward the gangway; while still, as if full of kindly contrition, Don Benito would not let go the hand of Captain Delano, but retained it in his, across the black's body.

Soon they were standing by the side, looking over into the boat, whose crew turned up their curious eyes.

Waiting a moment for the Spaniard to relinquish his hold, the now embarrassed Captain Delano lifted his foot, to overstep the threshold of the open gangway ; but still Don Benito would not let go his hand. And yet, with an agitated tone, he said, ' I can go no further ; here I must bid you adieu. Adieu, my dear, dear Don Amasa. Go—go ! ' suddenly tearing his hand loose, ' go, and God guard you better than me, my best friend.'

Not unaffected, Captain Delano would now have lingered ; but catching the meekly admonitory eye of the servant, with a hasty farewell he descended into his boat, followed by the continual adieus of Don Benito, standing rooted in the gangway.

Seating himself in the stern, Captain Delano, making a last salute, ordered the boat shoved off. The crew had their oars on end. The bowsmen pushed the boat a sufficient distance for the oars to be lengthwise dropped. The instant that was done, Don Benito sprang over the bulwarks, falling at the feet of Captain Delano ; at the same time calling toward his ship, but in tones so frenzied, that none in the boat could understand him. But, as if not equally obtuse, three sailors, from three different and distant parts of the ship, splashed into the sea, swimming after their captain, as if intent upon his rescue.

The dismayed officer of the boat eagerly asked what this meant. To which, Captain Delano, turning a disdainful smile upon the unaccountable Spaniard, answered that, for his part, he neither knew nor cared ; but it seemed as if Don Benito had taken it into his head to produce the impression among his people that the boat wanted to kidnap him. ' Or else—give way for your lives,' he wildly added, starting at a clattering hubbub in the ship, above which rang the tocsin of the hatchet-polishers; and seizing Don Benito by the throat he added, 'this plotting pirate means murder!' Here, in apparent verification of the words, the servant, a dagger in his hand, was seen on the rail overhead, poised, in the act of leaping, as if with desperate fidelity to befriend his master to the last; while, seemingly to aid the black, the three white sailors were trying to clamber into the hampered bow. Meantime, the whole host of negroes, as if inflamed at the sight of their jeopardised captain, impended in one sooty avalanche over the bulwarks.

All this, with what preceded, and what followed, occurred with such involutions of rapidity, that past, present, and future seemed one.

Seeing the negro coming, Captain Delano had flung the Spaniard aside, almost in the very act of clutching him, and, by the unconscious recoil, shifting his place, with arms thrown up, so promptly grappled the servant in his descent, that with dagger presented at Captain Delano's heart, the black seemed of purpose to have leaped there as to his mark. But the weapon was wrenched away, and the assailant dashed down into the bottom of the boat, which now, with disentangled oars, began to speed through the sea.

At this juncture, the left hand of Captain Delano, on one side, again clutched the half-reclined Don Benito, heedless that he was in a speechless faint, while his right foot, on the other side, ground the prostrate negro; and his right arm pressed for added speed on the after-oar, his eye bent forward, encouraging his men to their utmost.

But here, the officer of the boat, who had at last succeeded in beating off the towing sailors, and was now, with face turned aft, assisting the bowsman at his oar, suddenly called to Captain Delano, to see what the

black was about ; while a Portuguese oarsman shouted
to him to give heed to what the Spaniard was saying.

Glancing down at his feet, Captain Delano saw the
freed hand of the servant aiming with a second dagger—
a small one, before concealed in his wool—with this he
was snakishly writhing up from the boat's bottom, at
the heart of his master, his countenance lividly vindictive, expressing the centred purpose of his soul ;
while the Spaniard, half choked, was vainly shrinking
away, with husky words, incoherent to all but the
Portuguese.

That moment, across the long-benighted mind of
Captain Delano, a flash of revelation swept, illuminating,
in unanticipated clearness, his host's whole mysterious
demeanour, with every enigmatic event of the day, as
well as the entire past voyage of the *San Dominick*.
He smote Babo's hand down, but his own heart smote
him harder. With infinite pity he withdrew his hold
from Don Benito. Not Captain Delano, but Don Benito,
the black, in leaping into the boat, had intended to
stab.

Both the black's hands were held, as, glancing up
toward the *San Dominick*, Captain Delano, now with
scales dropped from his eyes, saw the negroes, not in
misrule, not in tumult, not as if frantically concerned
for Don Benito, but with mask torn away, flourishing
hatchets and knives, in ferocious piratical revolt. Like
delirious black dervishes, the six Ashantees danced on
the poop. Prevented by their foes from springing into
the water, the Spanish boys were hurrying up to the
topmost spars, while such of the few Spanish sailors,
not already in the sea, less alert, were descried, helplessly mixed in, on deck, with the blacks.

Meantime Captain Delano hailed his own vessel,
ordering the ports up, and the guns run out. But by

this time the cable of the *San Dominick* had been cut;
and the fag-end, in lashing out, whipped away the
canvas shroud about the beak, suddenly revealing, as
the bleached hull swung round toward the open ocean,
death for the figure-head, in a human skeleton; chalky
comment on the chalked words below, '*Follow your
leader.*'

At the sight, Don Benito, covering his face, wailed
out: ''Tis he, Aranda! my murdered, unburied
friend!'

Upon reaching the sealer, calling for ropes, Captain
Delano bound the negro, who made no resistance, and
had him hoisted to the deck. He would then have
assisted the now almost helpless Don Benito up the
side; but Don Benito, wan as he was, refused to move,
or be moved, until the negro should have been first put
below out of view. When, presently assured that it
was done, he no more shrank from the ascent.

The boat was immediately dispatched back to pick
up the three swimming sailors. Meantime, the guns
were in readiness, though, owing to the *San Dominick*
having glided somewhat astern of the sealer, only the
aftermost one could be brought to bear. With this,
they fired six times; thinking to cripple the fugitive
ship by bringing down her spars. But only a few
inconsiderable ropes were shot away. Soon the ship
was beyond the gun's range, steering broad out of the
bay; the blacks thickly clustering round the bowsprit,
one moment with taunting cries toward the whites, the
next with upthrown gestures hailing the now dusky
moors of ocean—cawing crows escaped from the hand
of the fowler.

The first impulse was to slip the cables and give chase.
But, upon second thoughts, to pursue with whale-boat
and yawl seemed more promising.

Upon inquiring of Don Benito what firearms they had on board the *San Dominick*, Captain Delano was answered that they had none that could be used ; because, in the earlier stages of the mutiny, a cabin passenger, since dead, had secretly put out of order the locks of what few muskets there were. But with all his remaining strength, Don Benito entreated the American not to give chase, either with ship or boat ; for the negroes had already proved themselves such desperadoes, that, in case of a present assault, nothing but a total massacre of the whites could be looked for. But, regarding this warning as coming from one whose spirit had been crushed by misery, the American did not give up his design.

The boats were got ready and armed. Captain Delano ordered his men into them. He was going himself when Don Benito grasped his arm.

' What ! have you saved my life, señor, and are you now going to throw away your own ? '

The officers also, for reasons connected with their interests and those of the voyage, and a duty owing to the owners, strongly objected against their commander's going. Weighing their remonstrances a moment, Captain Delano felt bound to remain ; appointing his chief mate—an athletic and resolute man, who had been a privateer's-man—to head the party. The more to encourage the sailors, they were told, that the Spanish captain considered his ship good as lost ; that she and her cargo, including some gold and silver, were worth more than a thousand doubloons. Take her, and no small part should be theirs. The sailors replied with a shout.

The fugitives had now almost gained an offing. It was nearly night ; but the moon was rising. After hard, prolonged pulling, the boats came up on the ship's

quarters, at a suitable distance laying upon their oars
to discharge their muskets. Having no bullets to return,
the negroes sent their yells. But, upon the second
volley, Indian-like, they hurtled their hatchets. One
took off a sailor's fingers. Another struck the whale-
boat's bow, cutting off the rope there, and remaining
stuck in the gunwale like a woodman's axe. Snatching
it, quivering from its lodgment, the mate hurled it back.
The returned gauntlet now stuck in the ship's broken
quarter-gallery, and so remained.

The negroes giving too hot a reception, the whites
kept a more respectful distance. Hovering now just
out of reach of the hurtling hatchets, they, with a view
to the close encounter which must soon come, sought
to decoy the blacks into entirely disarming themselves
of their most murderous weapons in a hand-to-hand
fight, by foolishly flinging them, as missiles, short of the
mark, into the sea. But, ere long, perceiving the
stratagem, the negroes desisted, though not before many
of them had to replace their lost hatchets with handspikes ; an exchange which, as counted upon, proved,
in the end, favourable to the assailants.

Meantime, with a strong wind, the ship still clove the
water ; the boats alternately falling behind, and pulling
up, to discharge fresh volleys.

The fire was mostly directed toward the stern, since
there, chiefly, the negroes, at present, were clustering.
But to kill or maim the negroes was not the object.
To take them, with the ship, was the object. To do it,
the ship must be boarded ; which could not be done
by boats while she was sailing so fast.

A thought now struck the mate. Observing the
Spanish boys still aloft, high as they could get, he called
to them to descend to the yards, and cut adrift the
sails. It was done. About this time, owing to causes

hereafter to be shown, two Spaniards, in the dress of sailors, and conspicuously showing themselves, were killed ; not by volleys, but by deliberate marksman's shots ; while, as it afterward appeared, by one of the general discharges, Atufal, the black, and the Spaniard at the helm likewise were killed. What now with the loss of the sails, and loss of leaders, the ship became unmanageable to the negroes.

With creaking masts, she came heavily round to the wind ; the prow slowly swinging into view of the boats, its skeleton gleaming in the horizontal moonlight, and casting a gigantic ribbed shadow upon the water. One extended arm of the ghost seemed beckoning the whites to avenge it.

' Follow your leader ! ' cried the mate ; and, one on each bow, the boats boarded. Sealing-spears and cutlasses crossed hatchets and handspikes. Huddled upon the long-boat amidships, the negresses raised a wailing chant, whose chorus was the clash of the steel.

For a time, the attack wavered ; the negroes wedging themselves to beat it back ; the half-repelled sailors, as yet unable to gain a footing, fighting as troopers in the saddle, one leg sideways flung over the bulwarks, and one without, plying their cutlasses like carters' whips. But in vain. They were almost overborne, when, rallying themselves into a squad as one man, with a huzza, they sprang inboard, where, entangled, they involuntarily separated again. For a few breaths' space, there was a vague, muffled, inner sound, as of submerged sword-fish rushing hither and thither through shoals of black-fish. Soon, in a reunited band, and joined by the Spanish seamen, the whites came to the surface, irresistibly driving the negroes toward the stern. But a barricade of casks and sacks, from side to side, had been thrown up by the mainmast. Here the negroes faced

about, and though scorning peace or truce, yet fain
would have had respite. But, without pause, over-
leaping the barrier, the unflagging sailors again closed.
Exhausted, the blacks now fought in despair. Their
red tongues lolled, wolf-like, from their black mouths.
But the pale sailors' teeth were set ; not a word was
spoken ; and, in five minutes more, the ship was won.

Nearly a score of the negroes were killed. Exclusive
of those by the balls, many were mangled ; their wounds
—mostly inflicted by the long-edged sealing-spears—re-
sembling those shaven ones of the English at Preston-
pans, made by the poled scythes of the Highlanders.
On the other side, none were killed, though several were
wounded ; some severely, including the mate. The
surviving negroes were temporarily secured, and the
ship, towed back into the harbour at midnight, once
more lay anchored.

Omitting the incidents and arrangements ensuing,
suffice it that, after two days spent in refitting, the ships
sailed in company for Conception, in Chili, and thence
for Lima, in Peru ; where, before the vice-regal courts,
the whole affair, from the beginning, underwent in-
vestigation.

Though, midway on the passage, the ill-fated Spaniard,
relaxed from constraint, showed some signs of regaining
health with free-will ; yet, agreeably to his own foreboding, shortly before arriving at Lima, he relapsed,
finally becoming so reduced as to be carried ashore in
arms. Hearing of his story and plight, one of the
many religious institutions of the City of Kings opened
an hospitable refuge to him, where both physician and
priest were his nurses, and a member of the order volunteered to be his one special guardian and consoler, by
night and by day.

The following extracts, translated from one of the

official Spanish documents, will, it is hoped, shed light
on the preceding narrative, as well as, in the first place,
reveal the true port of departure and true history of the
San Dominick's voyage, down to the time of her touching
at the island of St. Maria.

But, ere the extracts come, it may be well to preface
them with a remark.

The document selected, from among many others, for
partial translation, contains the deposition of Benito
Cereno ; the first taken in the case. Some disclosures
therein were, at the time, held dubious for both learned
and natural reasons. The tribunal inclined to the
opinion that the deponent, not undisturbed in his mind
by recent events, raved of some things which could never
have happened. But subsequent depositions of the
surviving sailors, bearing out the revelations of their
captain in several of the strangest particulars, gave
credence to the rest. So that the tribunal, in its final
decision, rested its capital sentences upon statements
which, had they lacked confirmation, it would have
deemed it but duty to reject.

I, DON JOSÉ DE ABOS AND PADILLA, His Majesty's
Notary for the Royal Revenue, and Register of this
Province, and Notary Public of the Holy Crusade of this
Bishopric, etc.

Do certify and declare, as much as is requisite in law,
that, in the criminal cause commenced the twenty-
fourth of the month of September, in the year seventeen
hundred and ninety-nine, against the negroes of the ship
San Dominick, the following declaration before me was
made :—

Declaration of the first witness, DON BENITO CERENO.

The same day, and month, and year, His Honour,

Doctor Juan Martinez de Rozas, Councillor of the Royal
Audience of this Kingdom, and learned in the law of
this Intendency, ordered the captain of the ship *San
Dominick*, Don Benito Cereno, to appear ; which he did
in his litter, attended by the monk Infelez ; of whom he
received the oath, which he took by God, our Lord, and
a sign of the Cross ; under which he promised to tell
the truth of whatever he should know and should be
asked ;—and being interrogated agreeably to the tenor
of the act commencing the process, he said, that on the
twentieth of May last, he set sail with his ship from the
port of Valparaiso, bound to that of Callao ; loaded
with the produce of the country besides thirty cases of
hardware and one hundred and sixty blacks, of both
sexes, mostly belonging to Don Alexandro Aranda,
gentleman, of the city of Mendoza ; that the crew of
the ship consisted of thirty-six men, besides the persons
who went as passengers ; that the negroes were in part
as follows :—

[*Here, in the original, follows a list of some fifty names,
descriptions, and ages, compiled from certain recovered
documents of Aranda's, and also from recollections of the
deponent, from which portions only are extracted.*]

—One, from about eighteen to nineteen years, named
José, and this was the man that waited upon his master,
Don Alexandro, and who speaks well the Spanish, having
served him four or five years ; * * * a mulatto, named
Francesco, the cabin steward, of a good person and
voice, having sung in the Valparaiso churches, native
of the province of Buenos Ayres, aged about thirty-five
years. * * * A smart negro, named Dago, who had been
for many years a gravedigger among the Spaniards,
aged forty-six years. * * * Four old negroes, born in
Africa, from sixty to seventy, but sound, caulkers by

trade, whose names are as follows :—the first was named
Muri, and he was killed (as was also his son named
Diamelo) ; the second, Nacta ; the third, Yola, likewise
killed ; the fourth, Ghofan ; and six full-grown negroes,
aged from thirty to forty-five, all raw, and born among
the Ashantees—Matiluqui, Yan, Lecbe, Mapenda, Yam-
baio, Akim ; four of whom were killed ; * * * a powerful
negro named Atufal, who being supposed to have been
a chief in Africa, his owner set great store by him. * * *
And a small negro of Senegal, but some years among the
Spaniards, aged about thirty, which negro's name was
Babo ; * * * that he does not remember the names of
the others, but that still expecting the residue of Don
Alexandro's papers will be found, will then take due
account of them all, and remit to the court ; * * * and
thirty-nine women and children of all ages.

[The catalogue over, the deposition goes on :]

* * * That all the negroes slept upon deck, as is
customary in this navigation, and none wore fetters,
because the owner, his friend Aranda, told him that
they were all tractable ; * * * that on the seventh day
after leaving port, at three o'clock in the morning, all
the Spaniards being asleep except the two officers on
the watch, who were the boatswain, Juan Robles, and
the carpenter, Juan Bautista Gayete, and the helmsman
and his boy, the negroes revolted suddenly, wounded
dangerously the boatswain and the carpenter, and suc-
cessively killed eighteen men of those who were sleeping
upon deck, some with handspikes and hatchets, and
others by throwing them alive overboard, after tying
them ; that of the Spaniards upon deck, they left about
seven, as he thinks, alive and tied, to manoeuvre the
ship, and three or four more, who hid themselves,
remained also alive. Although in the act of revolt

the negroes made themselves masters of the hatchway, six or seven wounded went through it to the
cockpit, without any hindrance on their part ; that
during the act of revolt, the mate and another person,
whose name he does not recollect, attempted to come
up through the hatchway, but being quickly wounded,
were obliged to return to the cabin ; that the deponent
resolved at break of day to come up the companion-way,
where the negro Babo was, being the ringleader, and
Atufal, who assisted him, and having spoken to them,
exhorted them to cease committing such atrocities,
asking them, at the same time, what they wanted and
intended to do, offering, himself, to obey their commands;
that notwithstanding this, they threw, in his presence,
three men, alive and tied, overboard ; that they told
the deponent to come up, and that they would not kill
him ; which having done, the negro Babo asked him
whether there were in these seas any negro countries
where they might be carried, and he answered them,
No ; that the negro Babo afterward told him to carry
them to Senegal, or to the neighbouring islands of St.
Nicholas ; and he answered, that this was impossible,
on account of the great distance, the necessity involved
of rounding Cape Horn, the bad condition of the vessel,
the want of provisions, sails, and water ; but that the
negro Babo replied to him he must carry them in any
way ; that they would do and conform themselves to
everything the deponent should require as to eating
and drinking ; that after a long conference, being absolutely compelled to please them, for they threatened to
kill all the whites if they were not, at all events, carried
to Senegal, he told them that what was most wanting
for the voyage was water ; that they would go near the
coast to take it, and thence they would proceed on
their course ; that the negro Babo agreed to it ; and the

deponent steered toward the intermediate ports, hoping to meet some Spanish or foreign vessel that would save them ; that within ten or eleven days they saw the land, and continued their course by it in the vicinity of Nasca ; that the deponent observed that the negroes were now restless and mutinous, because he did not effect the taking in of water, the negro Babo having required, with threats, that it should be done, without fail, the following day ; he told him he saw plainly that the coast was steep, and the rivers designated in the maps were not to be found, with other reasons suitable to the circumstances ; that the best way would be to go to the island of Santa Maria, where they might water easily, it being a solitary island, as the foreigners did ; that the deponent did not go to Pisco, that was near, nor make any other port of the coast, because the negro Babo had intimated to him several times, that he would kill all the whites the very moment he should perceive any city, town, or settlement of any kind on the shores to which they should be carried : that having determined to go to the island of Santa Maria, as the deponent had planned, for the purpose of trying whether, on the passage or near the island itself, they could find any vessel that should favour them, or whether he could escape from it in a boat to the neighbouring coast of Arruco, to adopt the necessary means he immediately changed his course, steering for the island ; that the negroes Babo and Atufal held daily conferences, in which they discussed what was necessary for their design of returning to Senegal, whether they were to kill all the Spaniards, and particularly the deponent ; that eight days after parting with the coast of Nasca, the deponent being on the watch a little after daybreak, and soon after the negroes had their meeting, the negro Babo came to the place where the deponent was, and told

him that he had determined to kill his master, Don
Alexandro Aranda, both because he and his companions
could not otherwise be sure of their liberty, and that to
keep the seamen in subjection, he wanted to prepare
a warning of what road they should be made to take
did they or any of them oppose him ; and that, by
means of the death of Don Alexandro, that warning
would best be given ; but, that what this last meant,
the deponent did not at the time comprehend, nor
could not, further than that the death of Don Alexandro
was intended ; and moreover the negro Babo proposed
to the deponent to call the mate Raneds, who was
sleeping in the cabin, before the thing was done, for
fear, as the deponent understood it, that the mate,
who was a good navigator, should be killed with Don
Alexandro and the rest ; that the deponent, who was
the friend, from youth, of Don Alexandro, prayed and
conjured, but all was useless ; for the negro Babo
answered him that the thing could not be prevented,
and that all the Spaniards risked their death if they
should attempt to frustrate his will in this matter, or
any other ; that, in this conflict, the deponent called
the mate, Raneds, who was forced to go apart, and
immediately the negro Babo commanded the Ashantee
Matiluqui and the Ashantee Lecbe to go and commit
the murder ; that those two went down with hatchets
to the berth of Don Alexandro ; that, yet half alive and
mangled, they dragged him on deck ; that they were
going to throw him overboard in that state, but the
negro Babo stopped them, bidding the murder be completed on the deck before him, which was done, when,
by his orders, the body was carried below, forward ;
that nothing more was seen of it by the deponent for
three days ; * * * that Don Alonzo Sidonia, an old man,
long resident at Valparaiso, and lately appointed to a

civil office in Peru, whither he had taken passage, was at the time sleeping in the berth opposite Don Alexandro's; that awakening at his cries, surprised by them, and at the sight of the negroes with their bloody hatchets in their hands, he threw himself into the sea through a window which was near him, and was drowned, without it being in the power of the deponent to assist or take him up; * * * that a short time after killing Aranda, they brought upon deck his german-cousin, of middle-age, Don Francisco Masa, of Mendoza, and the young Don Joaquin, Marques de Aramboalaza, then lately from Spain, with his Spanish servant Ponce, and the three young clerks of Aranda, José Mozairi, Lorenzo Bargas, and Hermenegildo Gandix, all of Cadiz; that Don Joaquin and Hermenegildo Gandix, the negro Babo, for purposes hereafter to appear, preserved alive; but Don Francisco Masa José Mozairi, and Lorenzo Bargas, with Ponce the servant, besides the boatswain, Juan Robles, the boatswain's mates, Manuel Viscaya and Roderigo Hurta, and four of the sailors, the negro Babo ordered to be thrown alive into the sea, although they made no resistance, nor begged for anything else but mercy; that the boatswain, Juan Robles, who knew how to swim, kept the longest above water, making acts of contrition, and, in the last words he uttered, charged this deponent to cause mass to be said for his soul to our Lady of Succour : * * * that, during the three days which followed, the deponent, uncertain what fate had befallen the remains of Don Alexandro, frequently asked the negro Babo where they were, and, if still on board, whether they were to be preserved for interment ashore, entreating him so to order it; that the negro Babo answered nothing till the fourth day, when at sunrise, the deponent coming on deck, the negro Babo showed him a skeleton, which had been substituted for the

ship's proper figure-head—the image of Christopher
Colon, the discoverer of the New World; that the
negro Babo asked him whose skeleton that was, and
whether, from its whiteness, he should not think it a
white's; that, upon discovering his face, the negro
Babo, coming close, said words to this effect : ' Keep
faith with the blacks from here to Senegal, or you shall
in spirit, as now in body, follow your leader,' pointing
to the prow; * * * that the same morning the negro
Babo took by succession each Spaniard forward, and
asked him whose skeleton that was, and whether, from
its whiteness, he should not think it a white's; that
each Spaniard covered his face; that then to each the
negro Babo repeated the words in the first place said
to the deponent ; * * * that they (the Spaniards), being
then assembled aft, the negro Babo harangued them,
saying that he had now done all ; that the deponent
(as navigator for the negroes) might pursue his course,
warning him and all of them that they should, soul and
body, go the way of Don Alexandro, if he saw them
(the Spaniards) speak or plot anything against them
(the negroes)—a threat which was repeated every day ;
that, before the events last mentioned, they had tied
the cook to throw him overboard, for it is not known
what thing they heard him speak, but finally the negro
Babo spared his life, at the request of the deponent ;
that a few days after, the deponent, endeavouring not
to omit any means to preserve the lives of the remaining
whites, spoke to the negroes peace and tranquillity,
and agreed to draw up a paper, signed by the deponent
and the sailors who could write, as also by the negro
Babo, for himself and all the blacks, in which the deponent
obliged himself to carry them to Senegal, and they not
to kill any more, and he formally to make over to them
the ship, with the cargo, with which they were for that

time satisfied and quieted. * * * But the next day, the
more surely to guard against the sailors' escape, the
negro Babo commanded all the boats to be destroyed
but the long-boat, which was unseaworthy, and another,
a cutter in good condition, which knowing it would yet
be wanted for towing the water-casks, he had it lowered
down into the hold.

*   *   *   *   *   *   *

[*Various particulars of the prolonged and perplexed
navigation ensuing here follow, with incidents of a calamitous
calm, from which portion one passage is extracted, to
wit :*]

—That on the fifth day of the calm, all on board
suffering much from the heat, and want of water, and
five having died in fits, and mad, the negroes became
irritable, and for a chance gesture, which they deemed
suspicious—though it was harmless—made by the mate,
Raneds, to the deponent in the act of handing a quadrant,
they killed him ; but that for this they afterward were
sorry, the mate being the only remaining navigator on
board, except the deponent.

*   *   *   *   *   *   *

—That omitting other events, which daily happened,
and which can only serve uselessly to recall past misfortunes and conflicts, after seventy-three days' navigation, reckoned from the time they sailed from Nasca,
during which they navigated under a scanty allowance
of water, and were afflicted with the calms before-
mentioned, they at last arrived at the island of Santa
Maria, on the seventeenth of the month of August, at
about six o'clock in the afternoon, at which hour they
cast anchor very near the American ship, *Bachelor's
Delight*, which lay in the same bay, commanded by the
generous Captain Amasa Delano ; but at six o'clock in

the morning, they had already descried the port, and
the negroes became uneasy, as soon as at distance they
saw the ship, not having expected to see one there ;
that the negro Babo pacified them, assuring them that
no fear need be had ; that straightway he ordered the
figure on the bow to be covered with canvas, as for
repairs, and had the decks a little set in order ; that for
a time the negro Babo and the negro Atufal conferred ;
that the negro Atufal was for sailing away, but the
negro Babo would not, and, by himself, cast about
what to do ; that at last he came to the deponent, pro-
posing to him to say and do all that the deponent declares to have said and done to the American captain ;
* * * that the negro Babo warned him that if he varied
in the least, or uttered any word, or gave any look
that should give the least intimation of the past events
or present state, he would instantly kill him, with all
his companions, showing a dagger, which he carried
hid, saying something which, as he understood it, meant
that that dagger would be alert as his eye ; that the
negro Babo then announced the plan to all his companions, which pleased them ; that he then, the better
to disguise the truth, devised many expedients, in some
of them uniting deceit and defence ; that of this sort
was the device of the six Ashantees before-named, who
were his bravos ; that them he stationed on the break
of the poop, as if to clean certain hatchets (in cases,
which were part of the cargo), but in reality to use
them, and distribute them at need, and at a given word
he told them ; that, among other devices, was the
device of presenting Atufal, his right-hand man, as
chained, though in a moment the chains could be
dropped ; that in every particular he informed the
deponent what part he was expected to enact in every
device, and what story he was to tell on every occasion,

always threatening him with instant death if he varied
in the least ; that, conscious that many of the negroes
would be turbulent, the negro Babo appointed the four
aged negroes, who were caulkers, to keep what domestic
order they could on the decks ; that again and again he
harangued the Spaniards and his companions, informing
them of his intent, and of his devices, and of the invented
story that this deponent was to tell ; charging them
lest any of them varied from that story ; that these
arrangements were made and matured during the interval
of two or three hours, between their first sighting the
ship and the arrival on board of Captain Amasa Delano ;
that this happened about half-past seven o'clock in the
morning, Captain Amasa Delano coming in his boat,
and all gladly receiving him ; that the deponent, as well
as he could force himself, acting then the part of principal owner, and a free captain of the ship, told Captain
Amasa Delano, when called upon, that he came from
Buenos Ayres, bound to Lima, with three hundred
negroes ; that off Cape Horn, and in a subsequent
fever, many negroes had died ; that also, by similar
casualties, all the sea-officers and the greatest part of
the crew had died.

* * * * * * *

[*And so the deposition goes on, circumstantially re-
counting the fictitious story dictated to the deponent by
Babo, and through the deponent imposed upon Captain
Delano ; and also recounting the friendly offers of Captain
Delano, with other things, but all of which is here omitted.
After the fictitious story, etc., the deposition proceeds :*]

* * * * * * *

—that the generous Captain Amasa Delano remained
on board all the day, till he left the ship anchored at
six o'clock in the evening, deponent speaking to him

always of his pretended misfortunes, under the fore-
mentioned principles, without having had it in his power
to tell a single word, or give him the least hint, that he
might know the truth and state of things ; because the
negro Babo, performing the office of an officious servant
with all the appearance of submission of the humble
slave, did not leave the deponent one moment ; that
this was in order to observe the deponent's actions and
words, for the negro Babo understands well the Spanish ;
and besides, there were thereabout some others who were
constantly on the watch, and likewise understood the
Spanish ; * * * that upon one occasion, while deponent
was standing on the deck conversing with Amasa Delano,
by a secret sign the negro Babo drew him (the deponent)
aside, the act appearing as if originating with the deponent ; that then, he being drawn aside, the negro
Babo proposed to him to gain from Amasa Delano full
particulars about his ship, and crew, and arms ; that
the deponent asked ' For what ? ' that the negro Babo
answered he might conceive ; that, grieved at the
prospect of what might overtake the generous Captain
Amasa Delano, the deponent at first refused to ask the
desired questions, and used every argument to induce
the negro Babo to give up this new design ; that the
negro Babo showed the point of his dagger ; that, after
the information had been obtained, the negro Babo
again drew him aside, telling him that that very night
he (the deponent) would be captain of two ships, instead
of one, for that, great part of the American's ship's crew
being to be absent fishing, the six Ashantees, without
anyone else, would easily take it ; that at this time he
said other things to the same purpose ; that no entreaties
availed ; that, before Amasa Delano's coming on board,
no hint had been given touching the capture of the
American ship : that to prevent this project the deponent

was powerless ; * * * —that in some things his memory
is confused, he cannot distinctly recall every event ; * * *
—that as soon as they had cast anchor at six of the
clock in the evening, as has before been stated, the
American captain took leave, to return to his vessel ;
that upon a sudden impulse, which the deponent believes
to have come from God and his angels, he, after the
farewell had been said, followed the generous Captain
Amasa Delano as far as the gunwale, where he stayed,
under pretence of taking leave, until Amasa Delano
should have been seated in his boat ; that on shoving
off, the deponent sprang from the gunwale into the
boat, and fell into it, he knows not how, God guarding
him ; that——

    *   *   *   *   *   *   *

*[Here, in the original, follows the account of what further
happened at the escape, and how the San Dominick was
retaken, and of the passage to the coast ; including in the
recital many expressions of ' eternal gratitude ' to the
' generous Captain Amasa Delano.' The deposition then
proceeds with recapitulatory remarks, and a partial re-
numeration of the negroes, making record of their individual
part in the past events, with a view to furnishing, according
to command of the court, the data whereon to found the
criminal sentences to be pronounced. From this portion
is the following :]*

—That he believes that all the negroes, though not
in the first place knowing to the design of revolt, when
it was accomplished, approved it. * * * That the negro,
José, eighteen years old, and in the personal service
of Don Alexandro, was the one who communicated the
information to the negro Babo, about the state of things
in the cabin, before the revolt ; that this is known,
because, in the preceding midnight, he used to come from

his berth, which was under his master's, in the cabin, to the deck where the ringleader and his associates were, and had secret conversations with the negro Babo, in which he was several times seen by the mate ; that, one night, the mate drove him away twice ; * * * that this same negro José was the one who, without being commanded to do so by the negro Babo, as Lecbe and Matiluqui were, stabbed his master, Don Alexandro, after he had been dragged half-lifeless to the deck ; * * * that the mulatto steward, Francesco, was of the first band of revolters, that he was, in all things, the creature and tool of the negro Babo ; that, to make his court, he, just before a repast in the cabin, proposed, to the negro Babo, poisoning a dish for the generous Captain Amasa Delano ; this is known and believed, because the negroes have said it ; but that the negro Babo, having another design, forbade Francesco ; * * * that the Ashantee Lecbe was one of the worst of them ; for that, on the day the ship was retaken, he assisted in the defence of her, with a hatchet in each hand, with one of which he wounded, in the breast, the chief mate of Amasa Delano, in the first act of boarding ; this all knew ; that, in sight of the deponent, Lecbe struck, with a hatchet, Don Francisco Masa, when, by the negro Babo's orders, he was carrying him to throw him overboard, alive, besides participating in the murder, before mentioned, of Don Alexandro Aranda, and others of the cabin passengers ; that, owing to the fury with which the Ashantees fought in the engagement with the boats, but this Lecbe and Yan survived ; that Yan was bad as Lecbe ; that Yan was the man who, by Babo's command, willingly prepared the skeleton of Don Alexandro, in a way the negroes afterward told the deponent, but which he, so long as reason is left him, can never divulge ; that Yan and Lecbe were the

two who, in a calm by night, riveted the skeleton to the
bow ; this also the negroes told him ; that the negro
Babo was he who traced the inscription below it ; that
the negro Babo was the plotter from first to last ; he
ordered every murder, and was the helm and keel of the
revolt ; that Atufal was his lieutenant in all ; but
Atufal, with his own hand, committed no murder ; nor
did the negro Babo ; * * * that Atufal was shot, being
killed in the fight with the boats, ere boarding ; * * *
that the negresses, of age, were knowing to the revolt,
and testified themselves satisfied at the death of their
master, Don Alexandro ; that, had the negroes not
restrained them, they would have tortured to death,
instead of simply killing, the Spaniards slain by command of the negro Babo ; that the negresses used their
utmost influence to have the deponent made away
with ; that, in the various acts of murder, they sang
songs and danced—not gaily, but solemnly ; and before
the engagement with the boats, as well as during the
action, they sang melancholy songs to the negroes, and
that this melancholy tone was more inflaming than a
different one would have been, and was so intended; that
all this is believed, because the negroes have said it.

—That of the thirty-six men of the crew, exclusive
of the passengers (all of whom are now dead), which
the deponent had knowledge of, six only remained alive,
with four cabin-boys and ship-boys, not included with the
crew ; * * * —that the negroes broke an arm of one of
the cabin-boys and gave him strokes with hatchets.

[*Then follow various random disclosures referring to
various periods of time. The following are extracted :*]

—That during the presence of Captain Amasa Delano
on board, some attempts were made by the sailors, and
one by Hermenegildo Gandix, to convey hints to him

of the true state of affairs ; but that these attempts
were ineffectual, owing to fear of incurring death, and,
furthermore, owing to the devices which offered contradictions to the true state of affairs, as well as owing
to the generosity and piety of Amasa Delano incapable
of sounding such wickedness ; * * * that Luys Galgo, a
sailor about sixty years of age, and formerly of the
king's navy, was one of those who sought to convey
tokens to Captain Amasa Delano ; but his intent, though
undiscovered, being suspected, he was, on a pretence,
made to retire out of sight, and at last into the hold,
and there was made away with. This the negroes have
since said ; * * * that one of the ship-boys feeling, from
Captain Amasa Delano's presence, some hopes of release,
and not having enough prudence, dropped some chance
word respecting his expectations, which being overheard and understood by a slave-boy with whom he
was eating at the time, the latter struck him on the
head with a knife, inflicting a bad wound, but of which
the boy is now healing ; that likewise, not long before
the ship was brought to anchor, one of the seamen,
steering at the time, endangered himself by letting the
blacks remark some expression in his countenance,
arising from a cause similar to the above ; but this
sailor, by his heedful after conduct, escaped ; * * * that
these statements are made to show the court that from
the beginning to the end of the revolt, it was impossible
for the deponent and his men to act otherwise than
they did ; * * * —that the third clerk, Hermenegildo
Gandix, who before had been forced to live among the
seamen, wearing a seaman's habit, and in all respects
appearing to be one for the time, he, Gandix, was killed
by a musket-ball fired through mistake from the boats
before boarding ; having in his fright run up the mizen-
rigging, calling to the boats—' don't board,' lest upon

their boarding the negroes should kill him ; that this inducing the Americans to believe he some way favoured the cause of the negroes, they fired two balls at him, so that he fell wounded from the rigging, and was drowned in the sea ; * * * —that the young Don Joaquin, Marques de Aramboalaza, like Hermenegildo Gandix, the third clerk, was degraded to the office and appearance of a common seaman ; that upon one occasion when Don Joaquin shrank, the negro Babo commanded the Ashantee Lecbe to take tar and heat it, and pour it upon Don Joaquin's hands ; * * * —that Don Joaquin was killed owing to another mistake of the Americans, but one impossible to be avoided, as upon the approach of the boats, Don Joaquin, with a hatchet tied edge out and upright to his hand, was made by the negroes to appear on the bulwarks ; whereupon, seen with arms in his hands and in a questionable attitude, he was shot for a renegade seaman ; * * * —that on the person of Don Joaquin was found secreted a jewel, which, by papers that were discovered, proved to have been meant for the shrine of our Lady of Mercy in Lima ; a votive offering, beforehand prepared and guarded, to attest his gratitude, when he should have landed in Peru, his last destination, for the safe conclusion of his entire voyage from Spain ; * * * —that the jewel, with the other effects of the late Don Joaquin, is in the custody of the brethren of the Hospital de Sacerdotes, awaiting the disposition of the honourable court ; * * * —that, owing to the condition of the deponent, as well as the haste in which the boats departed for the attack, the Americans were not forewarned that there were, among the apparent crew, a passenger and one of the clerks disguised by the negro Babo ; * * * —that, besides the negroes killed in the action, some were killed after the capture and re-anchoring at night, when shackled to the ring-bolts on deck ; that these deaths were committed by the sailors, ere they could be prevented. That so soon as informed of it, Captain Amasa Delano used all his authority, and, in particular with his own hand, struck down Martinez Gola, who, having found a razor in the pocket of an old jacket of his, which one of the shackled negroes had on, was aiming it at the negro's throat ; that the noble Captain Amasa Delano also wrenched from the hand of Bartholomew Barlo a dagger, secreted at the time of the massacre of the whites, with which he was in the act of stabbing a shackled negro, who, the same day, with another negro, had thrown him down and jumped upon him ; * * * —that, for all the events, befalling through so long a time, during which the ship was in the hands of the negro Babo, he cannot here give account ; but that, what he has said is the most substantial of what occurs to him at present, and is the truth under the oath which he has taken ; which declaration he affirmed and ratified, after hearing it read to him.

He said that he is twenty-nine years of age, and broken in body and mind ; that when finally dismissed by the court, he shall not return home to Chili, but betake himself to the monastery on Mount Agonia without ; and signed with his honour, and crossed himself, and, for the time, departed as he came, in his litter, with the monk Infelez, to the Hospital de Sacerdotes.

BENITO CERENO.

DOCTOR ROZAS.

If the Deposition have served as the key to fit into the lock of the complications which precede it, then, as a vault whose door has been flung back, the *San Dominick*'s hull lies open to-day.

Hitherto the nature of this narrative, besides rendering the intricacies in the beginning unavoidable, has more or less required that many things, instead of being set down in the order of occurrence, should be retrospectively, or irregularly given ; this last is the case with the following passages, which will conclude the account :—

During the long, mild voyage to Lima, there was, as before hinted, a period during which the sufferer a little recovered his health, or, at least in some degree, his tranquillity. Ere the decided relapse which came, the two captains had many cordial conversations—their fraternal unreserve in singular contrast with former withdrawments.

Again and again it was repeated, how hard it had been to enact the part forced on the Spaniard by Babo.

' Ah, my dear friend,' Don Benito once said, ' at those very times when you thought me so morose and ungrateful, nay, when, as you now admit, you half thought me plotting your murder, at those very times my heart was frozen ; I could not look at you, thinking of what, both on board this ship and your own, hung, from other hands, over my kind benefactor. And as God lives, Don Amasa, I know not whether desire for my own safety alone could have nerved me to that leap into your boat, had it not been for the thought that, did you, unenlightened, return to your ship, you, my best friend, with all who might be with you, stolen upon, that night, in your hammocks, would never in this world have wakened again. Do but think how you walked this deck, how you sat in this cabin, every inch of ground mined into honeycombs under you. Had I dropped the least hint, made the least advance toward an understanding between us, death, explosive death—yours as mine—would have ended the scene.'

' True, true,' cried Captain Delano, starting, ' you have saved my life, Don Benito, more than I yours ; saved it, too, against my knowledge and will.'

'Nay, my friend,' rejoined the Spaniard, courteous even to the point of religion, 'God charmed your life, but you saved mine. To think of some things you did— those smilings and chattings, rash pointings and ges-turings. For less than these, they slew my mate, Raneds; but you had the Prince of Heaven's safe-conduct through all ambuscades.'

'Yes, all is owing to Providence, I know : but the temper of my mind that morning was more than com-monly pleasant, while the sight of so much suffering, more apparent than real, added to my good-nature, compassion, and charity, happily interweaving the three. Had it been otherwise, doubtless, as you hint, some of my interferences might have ended unhappily enough. Besides, those feelings I spoke of enabled me to get the better of momentary distrust, at times when acuteness might have cost me my life, without saving another's. Only at the end did my suspicions get the better of me, and you know how wide of the mark they then proved.'

'Wide, indeed,' said Don Benito sadly ; 'you were with me all day ; stood with me, sat with me, talked with me, looked at me, ate with me, drank with me ; and yet, your last act was to clutch for a monster, not only an innocent man, but the most pitiable of all men. To such degree may malign machinatiqns and decep-tions impose. So far may even the best man err, in judging the conduct of one with the recesses of whose condition he is not acquainted. But you were forced to it ; and you were in time undeceived. Would that, in both respects, it was so ever, and with all men.'

'You generalise, Don Benito ; and mournfully enough. But the past is past ; why moralise upon it ? Forget it. See, yon bright sun has forgotten it all, and the blue sea, and the blue sky ; these have turned over new leaves.'

'Because they have no memory,' he dejectedly replied; 'because they are not human.'

'But these mild Trades that now fan your cheek, do they not come with a human-like healing to you? Warm friends, steadfast friends are the Trades.'

'With their steadfastness they but waft me to my tomb, señor,' was the foreboding response.

'You are saved,' cried Captain Delano, more and more astonished and pained; 'you are saved: what has cast such a shadow upon you?'

'The negro.'

There was silence, while the moody man sat, slowly and unconsciously gathering his mantle about him, as if it were a pall.

There was no more conversation that day.

But if the Spaniard's melancholy sometimes ended in muteness upon topics like the above, there were others upon which he never spoke at all; on which, indeed, all his old reserves were piled. Pass over the worst, and, only to elucidate, let an item or two of these be cited. The dress, so precise and costly, worn by him on the day whose events have been narrated, had not willingly been put on. And that silver-mounted sword, apparent symbol of despotic command, was not, indeed, a sword, but the ghost of one. The scabbard, artificially stiffened, was empty.

As for the black—whose brain, not body, had schemed and led the revolt, with the plot—his slight frame, inadequate to that which it held, had at once yielded to the superior muscular strength of his captor, in the boat. Seeing all was over, he uttered no sound, and could not be forced to. His aspect seemed to say, since I cannot do deeds, I will not speak words. Put in irons in the hold, with the rest, he was carried to Lima. During the passage, Don Benito did not visit him. Nor then, nor at any time after, would he look at him. Before the tribunal he refused. When pressed by the judges he fainted. On the testimony of the sailors alone rested the legal identity of Babo.

Some months after, dragged to the gibbet at the tail of a mule, the black met his voiceless end. The body was burned to ashes; but for many days the head, that hive of subtlety, fixed on a pole in the Plaza, met, unabashed, the gaze of the whites; and across the Plaza looked toward St. Bartholomew's church, in whose vaults slept then, as now, the recovered bones of Aranda: and across the Rimac bridge looked toward the monastery, on Mount Agonia without; where, three months after being dismissed by the court, Benito Cereno, borne on the bier, did, indeed, follow his leader.

THE LIGHTNING-ROD MAN

WHAT grand irregular thunder, thought I, standing on my hearth-stone among the Acroceraunian hills, as the scattered bolts boomed overhead, and crashed down among the valleys, every bolt followed by zigzag irradiations, and swift slants of sharp rain, which audibly rang, like a charge of spear-points, on my low shingled roof. I suppose, though, that the mountains hereabouts break and churn up the thunder, so that it is far more glorious here than on the plain. Hark!—someone at the door. Who is this that chooses a time of thunder for making calls ? And why don't he, man-fashion, use the knocker, instead of making that doleful undertaker's clatter with his fist against the hollow panel ? But let him in. Ah, here he comes. ' Good day, sir ' : an entire stranger. ' Pray be seated.' What is that strange-looking walking-stick he carries ? ' A fine thunderstorm, sir.'

' Fine ?—Awful ! '

' You are wet. Stand here on the hearth before the fire.'

' Not for worlds ! '

The stranger still stood in the exact middle of the cottage, where he had first planted himself. His singularity impelled a closer scrutiny. A lean, gloomy figure. Hair dark and lank, mattedly streaked over his brow. His sunken pitfalls of eyes were ringed by indigo halos, and played with an innocuous sort of lightning : the gleam without the bolt. The whole man was dripping.

171

He stood in a puddle on the bare oak floor : his strange
walking-stick vertically resting at his side.

It was a polished copper rod, four feet long, lengthwise attached to a neat wooden staff by insertion into
two balls of greenish glass, ringed with copper bands.
The metal rod terminated at the top tripodwise, in three
keen tines, brightly gilt. He held the thing by the
wooden part alone.

'Sir,' said I, bowing politely, 'have I the honour of
a visit from that illustrious god, Jupiter Tonans ? So
stood he in the Greek statue of old, grasping the lightning-
bolt. If you be he, or his viceroy, I have to thank
you for this noble storm you have brewed among our
mountains. Listen : That was a glorious peal. Ah,
to a lover of the majestic, it is a good thing to have the
Thunderer himself in one's cottage. The thunder grows
finer for that. But pray be seated. This old rush-
bottomed arm-chair, I grant, is a poor substitute for
your evergreen throne on Olympus ; but, condescend
to be seated.'

While I thus pleasantly spoke, the stranger eyed me,
half in wonder, and half in a strange sort of horror ;
but did not move a foot.

'Do, sir, be seated ; you need to be dried ere going
forth again.'

I planted the chair invitingly on the broad hearth,
where a little fire had been kindled that afternoon to
dissipate the dampness, not the cold ; for it was early
in the month of September.

But without heeding my solicitation, and still standing
in the middle of the floor, the stranger gazed at me
portentously and spoke.

'Sir,' said he, ' excuse me ; but instead of my accepting
your invitation to be seated on the hearth there, I
solemnly warn *you*, that you had best accept *mine*,

and stand with me in the middle of the room. Good
heavens ! ' he cried, starting—' there is another of those
awful crashes. I warn you, sir, quit the hearth.'

' Mr. Jupiter Tonans,' said I, quietly rolling my body
on the stone, ' I stand very well here.'

' Are you so horridly ignorant, then,' he cried, ' as
not to know, that by far the most dangerous part of a
house, during such a terrific tempest as this, is the fire-
place ? '

' Nay, I did not know that,' involuntarily stepping
upon the first board next to the stone.

The stranger now assumed such an unpleasant air of
successful admonition, that—quite involuntarily again—
I stepped back upon the hearth, and threw myself into
the erectest, proudest posture I could command. But
I said nothing.

' For heaven's sake,' he cried, with a strange mixture
of alarm and intimidation—' for heaven's sake, get off
the hearth ! Know you not, that the heated air and
soot are conductors ;—to say nothing of those immense
iron fire-dogs ? Quit the spot—I conjure—I command
you.'

' Mr. Jupiter Tonans, I am not accustomed to be
commanded in my own house.'

' Call me not by that pagan name. You are profane
in this time of terror.'

' Sir, will you be so good as to tell me your business ?
If you seek shelter from the storm, you are welcome,
so long as you be civil ; but if you come on business,
open it forthwith. Who are you ? '

' I am a dealer in lightning-rods,' said the stranger,
softening his tone ; ' my special business is—— Merciful
heaven ! what a crash !—Have you ever been struck—
your premises, I mean ? No ? It 's best to be provided ' ;—significantly rattling his metallic staff on the

floor ;—' by nature, there are no castles in thunder-
storms ; yet, say but the word, and of this cottage I
can make a Gibraltar by a few waves of this wand.
Hark, what Himalayas of concussions ! '

' You interrupted yourself ; your special business you
were about to speak of.'

' My special business is to travel the country for
orders for lightning - rods. This is my specimen
rod,' tapping his staff ; ' I have the best of references '—fumbling in his pockets. ' In Criggan last
month, I put up three-and-twenty rods on only five
buildings.'

' Let me see. Was it not at Criggan last week, about
midnight on Saturday, that the steeple, the big elm,
and the assembly-room cupola were struck ? Any of
your rods there ? '

' Not on the tree and cupola, but the steeple.'

' Of what use is your rod, then ? '

' Of life-and-death use. But my workman was heedless. In fitting the rod at top to the steeple, he allowed
a part of the metal to graze the tin sheeting. Hence
the accident. Not my fault, but his. Hark ! '

' Never mind. That clap burst quite loud enough
to be heard without finger-pointing. Did you hear of
the event at Montreal last year ? A servant girl struck
at her bedside with a rosary in her hand ; the beads
being metal. Does your beat extend into the Canadas ? '

' No. And I hear that there, iron rods only are in
use. They should have *mine*, which are copper. Iron
is easily fused. Then they draw out the rod so slender,
that it has not body enough to conduct the full electric
current. The metal melts ; the building is destroyed.
My copper rods never act so. Those Canadians are
fools. Some of them knob the rod at the top, which
risks a deadly explosion, instead of imperceptibly carry-

ing down the current into the earth, as this sort of rod does. *Mine* is the only true rod. Look at it. Only one dollar a foot.'

'This abuse of your own calling in another might make one distrustful with respect to yourself.'

'Hark! The thunder becomes less muttering. It is nearing us, and nearing the earth, too. Hark! One crammed crash! All the vibrations made one by nearness. Another flash. Hold!'

'What do you?' I said, seeing him now, instantaneously relinquishing his staff, lean intently forward toward the window, with his right fore and middle fingers on his left wrist.

But ere the words had well escaped me, another exclamation escaped him.

'Crash! only three pulses—less than a third of a mile off—yonder, somewhere in that wood. I passed three stricken oaks there, ripped out new and glittering. The oak draws lightning more than other timber, having iron in solution in its sap. Your floor here seems oak.'

'Heart-of-oak. From the peculiar time of your call upon me, I suppose you purposely select stormy weather for your journeys. When the thunder is roaring, you deem it an hour peculiarly favourable for producing impressions favourable to your trade.'

'Hark!—Awful!'

'For one who would arm others with fearlessness, you seem unbeseemingly timorous yourself. Common men choose fair weather for their travels; you choose thunder-storms; and yet——'

'That I travel in thunder-storms, I grant; but not without particular precautions, such as only a lightning-rod man may know. Hark! Quick—look at my specimen rod. Only one dollar a foot.'

'A very fine rod, I dare say. But what are these
particular precautions of yours ? Yet first let me close
yonder shutters ; the slanting rain is beating through
the sash. I will bar up.'

'Are you mad ? Know you not that yon iron bar
is a swift conductor ? Desist.'

'I will simply close the shutters, then, and call my
boy to bring me a wooden bar. Pray, touch the bell-
pull there.'

'Are you frantic ? That bell-wire might blast you.
Never touch bell-wire in a thunder-storm, nor ring a
bell of any sort.'

'Nor those in belfries ? Pray, will you tell me where
and how one may be safe in a time like this ? Is there
any part of my house I may touch with hopes of my
life ? '

'There is ; but not where you now stand. Come
away from the wall. The current will sometimes run
down a wall, and—a man being a better conductor than
a wall—it would leave the wall and run into him. Swoop !
That must have fallen very nigh. That must have been
globular lightning.'

'Very probably. Tell me at once, which is, in your
opinion, the safest part of this house ? '

'This room, and this one spot in it where I stand.
Come hither.'

'The reasons first.'

'Hark !—after the flash the gust—the sashes shiver—
the house, the house !—Come hither to me ! '

'The reasons, if you please.'

'Come hither to me ! '

'Thank you again, I think I will try my old stand—
the hearth. And now, Mr. Lightning-rod man, in the
pauses of the thunder, be so good as to tell me your
reasons for esteeming this one room of the house the

safest, and your own one standpoint there the safest
spot in it.'

There was now a little cessation of the storm for a
while. The Lightning-rod man seemed relieved, and
replied :

' Your house is a one-storied house, with an attic and
a cellar ; this room is between. Hence its comparative
safety. Because lightning sometimes passes from the
clouds to the earth, and sometimes from the earth
to the clouds. Do you comprehend ?—and I choose
the middle of the room, because, if the lightning should strike the house at all, it would come
down the chimney or walls ; so, obviously, the
further you are from them, the better. Come hither
to me, now.'

' Presently. Something you just said, instead of
alarming me, has strangely inspired confidence.'

' What have I said ? '

' You said that sometimes lightning flashes from the
earth to the clouds.'

' Ay, the returning-stroke, as it is called ; when the
earth, being overcharged with the fluid, flashes its surplus
upward.'

' The returning-stroke ; that is, from earth to sky.
Better and better. But come here on the hearth and
dry yourself.'

' I am better here, and better wet.'

' How ? '

' It is the safest thing you can do—Hark, again !—to
get yourself thoroughly drenched in a thunder-storm.
Wet clothes are better conductors than the body ; and
so, if the lightning strike, it might pass down the wet
clothes without touching the body. The storm deepens
again. Have you a rug in the house ? Rugs are non-
conductors. Get one, that I may stand on it here, and

M

you, too.　The skies blacken—it is dusk at noon.　Hark !
—the rug, the rug ! '

I gave him one ; while the hooded mountains seemed
closing and tumbling into the cottage.

' And now, since our being dumb will not help us,'
said I, resuming my place, ' let me hear your precautions
in travelling during thunder-storms.'

' Wait till this one is past.'

' Nay, proceed with the precautions.　You stand in
the safest possible place according to your own account.
Go on.'

' Briefly, then.　I avoid pine-trees, high houses, lonely
barns, upland pastures, running water, flocks of cattle
and sheep, a crowd of men.　If I travel on foot—as
to-day—I do not walk fast ; if in my buggy, I touch
not its back or sides ; if on horseback, I dismount and
lead the horse.　But of all things, I avoid tall men.'

' Do I dream ?　Man avoid man ?　and in danger-
time, too.'

' Tall men in a thunder-storm I avoid.　Are you so
grossly ignorant as not to know, that the height of a
six-footer is sufficient to discharge an electric cloud
upon him ?　Are not lonely Kentuckians, ploughing, smit
in the unfinished furrow ?　Nay, if the six-footer stand
by running water, the cloud will sometimes *select* him
as its conductor to that running water.　Hark !　Sure,
yon black pinnacle is split.　Yes, a man is a good
conductor.　The lightning goes through and through a
man, but only peels a tree.　But, sir, you have kept
me so long answering your questions that I have not
yet come to business.　Will you order one of my rods ?
Look at this specimen one.　See : it is of the best of
copper.　Copper 's the best conductor.　Your house is
low ; but being upon the mountains, that lowness does
not one whit depress it.　You mountaineers are most

exposed. In mountainous countries the lightning-rod
man should have most business. Look at the specimen,
sir. One rod will answer for a house so small as this.
Look over these recommendations. Only one rod, sir ;
cost, only twenty dollars. Hark ! There go all the
granite Taconics and Hoosics dashed together like
pebbles. By the sound, that must have struck something. An elevation of five feet above the house will
protect twenty feet radius all about the rod. Only
twenty dollars, sir—a dollar a foot. Hark !—Dreadful !—
Will you order ? Will you buy ? Shall I put down your
name ? Think of being a heap of charred offal, like a
haltered horse burnt in his stall ; and all in one
flash ! '

'You pretended envoy extraordinary and minister
plenipotentiary to and from Jupiter Tonans,' laughed I ;
' you mere man who come here to put you and your
pipe-stem between clay and sky, do you think that
because you can strike a bit of green light from the
Leyden jar, that you can thoroughly avert the supernal
bolt ? Your rod rusts, or breaks, and where are you ?
Who has empowered you, you Tetzel, to peddle round
your indulgences from divine ordinations ? The hairs
of our heads are numbered, and the days of our lives.
In thunder as in sunshine, I stand at ease in the hands
of my God. False negotiator, away ! See, the scroll
of the storm is rolled back ; the house is unharmed ;
and in the blue heavens I read in the rainbow, that
the Deity will not, of purpose, make war on man's
earth.'

'Impious wretch ! ' foamed the stranger, blackening
in the face as the rainbow beamed, ' I will publish your
infidel notions.'

The scowl grew blacker on his face ; the indigo
circles enlarged round his eyes as the storm-rings round

the midnight moon. He sprang upon me ; his tri-
forked thing at my heart.

I seized it ; I snapped it ; I dashed it ; I trod it ; and
dragging the dark lightning-king out of my door, flung
his elbowed, copper sceptre after him.

But spite of my treatment, and spite of my dissuasive
talk of him to my neighbours, the Lightning-rod man
still dwells in the land ; still travels in storm-time, and
drives a brave trade with the fears of man.

THE ENCANTADAS;

OR,

ENCHANTED ISLES

SKETCH FIRST

THE ISLES AT LARGE

' —That may not be, said then the ferryman,
Least we unweeting hap to be fordonne ;
For those same islands seeming now and than,
Are not firme land, nor any certein wonne,
But stragling plots which to and fro do ronne
In the wide waters ; therefore are they hight
The Wandering Islands ; therefore do them shonne ;
For they have oft drawne many a wandring wight
Into most deadly daunger and distressed plight ;
For whosoever once hath fastened
His foot thereon may never it secure
But wandreth evermore uncertein and unsure.'

    *   *   *   *   *

' Darke, dolefull, dreary, like a greedy grave,
That still for carrion carcasses doth crave ;
On top whereof ay dwelt the ghastly owl,
Shrieking his balefull note, which ever drave
Far from that haunt all other cheerful fowl,
And all about it wandring ghosts did wayle and howl.'

TAKE five-and-twenty heaps of cinders dumped here and
there in an outside city lot ; imagine some of them
magnified into mountains, and the vacant lot the sea ;
and you will have a fit idea of the general aspect of the
Encantadas, or Enchanted Isles. A group rather of
extinct volcanoes than of isles ; looking much as the
world at large might, after a penal conflagration.

It is to be doubted whether any spot of earth can, in desolateness, furnish a parallel to this group. Abandoned cemeteries of long ago, old cities by piecemeal tumbling to their ruin, these are melancholy enough; but, like all else which has but once been associated with humanity, they still awaken in us some thoughts of sympathy, however sad. Hence, even the Dead Sea, along with whatever other emotions it may at times inspire, does not fail to touch in the pilgrim some of his less unpleasurable feelings.

And as for solitariness; the great forests of the north, the expanses of unnavigated waters, the Greenland ice-fields, are the profoundest of solitudes to a human observer; still the magic of their changeable tides and seasons mitigates their terror; because, though unvisited by men, those forests are visited by the May; the remotest seas reflect familiar stars even as Lake Erie does; and in the clear air of a fine Polar day, the irradiated, azure ice shows beautifully as malachite.

But the special curse, as one may call it, of the Encantadas, that which exalts them in desolation above Idumea and the Pole, is, that to them change never comes; neither the change of seasons nor of sorrows. Cut by the Equator, they know not autumn, and they know not spring; while already reduced to the lees of fire, ruin itself can work little more upon them. The showers refresh the deserts; but in these isles rain never falls. Like split Syrian gourds left withering in the sun, they are cracked by an everlasting drought beneath a torrid sky. 'Have mercy upon me,' the wailing spirit of the Encantadas seems to cry, 'and send Lazarus that he may dip the tip of his finger in water and cool my tongue, for I am tormented in this flame.'

Another feature in these isles is their emphatic uninhabitableness. It is deemed a fit type of all-forsaken overthrow, that the jackal should den in the wastes of weedy Babylon ; but the Encantadas refuse to harbour even the outcasts of the beasts. Man and wolf alike disown them. Little but reptile life is here found : tortoises, lizards, immense spiders, snakes, and that strangest anomaly of outlandish nature, the *aguano*. No voice, no low, no howl is heard ; the chief sound of life here is a hiss.

On most of the isles where vegetation is found at all, it is more ungrateful than the blankness of Aracama. Tangled thickets of wiry bushes, without fruit and without a name, springing up among deep fissures of calcined rock, and treacherously masking them ; or a parched growth of distorted cactus trees.

In many places the coast is rock-bound, or, more properly, clinker-bound ; tumbled masses of blackish or greenish stuff like the dross of an iron-furnace, forming dark clefts and caves here and there, into which a ceaseless sea pours a fury of foam ; overhanging them with a swirl of gray, haggard mist, amidst which sail screaming flights of unearthly birds heightening the dismal din. However calm the sea without, there is no rest for those swells and those rocks ; they lash and are lashed, even when the outer ocean is most at peace with itself. On the oppressive, clouded days, such as are peculiar to this part of the watery Equator, the dark, vitrified masses, many of which raise themselves among white whirlpools and breakers in detached and perilous places off the shore, present a most Plutonian sight. In no world but a fallen one could such lands exist.

Those parts of the strand free from the marks of fire stretch away in wide level beaches of multitudinous dead shells, with here and there decayed bits of sugar-cane, bamboos, and cocoa-nuts, washed upon this other and darker world from the charming palm isles to the westward and southward ; all the way from Paradise to Tartarus ; while mixed with the relics of distant beauty you will sometimes see fragments of charred wood and mouldering ribs of wrecks. Neither will any-one be surprised at meeting these last, after observing the conflicting currents which eddy throughout nearly all the wide channels of the entire group. The capriciousness of the tides of air sympathises with those of the sea. Nowhere is the wind so light, baffling, and every way unreliable, and so given to perplexing calms, as at the Encantadas. Nigh a month has been spent by a ship going from one isle to another, though but ninety miles between ; for owing to the force of the current, the boats employed to tow barely suffice to keep the craft from sweeping upon the cliffs, but do nothing toward accelerating her voyage. Sometimes it is impossible for a vessel from afar to fetch up with the group itself, unless large allowances for prospective lee-way have been made ere its coming in sight. And yet, at other times, there is a mysterious indraft, which irresistibly draws a passing vessel among the isles, though not bound to them.

True, at one period, as to some extent at the present day, large fleets of whalemen cruised for spermaceti upon what some seamen call the Enchanted Ground. But this, as in due place will be described, was off the great outer isle of Albemarle, away from the intricacies of the smaller isles, where there is plenty of sea-room ; and hence, to that vicinity, the above remarks do not altogether apply ; though even there the current runs at times with singular force, shifting, too, with as singular a caprice.

Indeed, there are seasons when currents quite un-accountable prevail for a great distance round about the total group, and are so strong and irregular as to change a vessel's course against the helm, though sailing at the rate of four or five miles the hour. The difference in the reckonings of navigators, produced by these causes, along with the light and variable winds, long nourished a persuasion, that there existed two distinct clusters of isles in the parallel of the Encantadas, about a hundred leagues apart. Such was the idea of their earlier visitors, the Bucaniers ; and as late as 1750, the charts of that part of the Pacific accorded with the strange delusion. And this apparent fleetingness and unreality of the locality of the isles was most probably one reason for the Spaniards calling them the Encantada, or Enchanted Group.

But not uninfluenced by their character, as they now confessedly exist, the modern voyager will be inclined to fancy that the bestowal of this name might have in part originated in that air of spell-bound desertness which so significantly invests the isles. Nothing can better suggest the aspect of once living things malignly crumbled from ruddiness into ashes. Apples of Sodom, after touching, seem these isles.

However wavering their place may seem by reason of the currents, they themselves, at least to one upon the shore, appear invariably the same ; fixed, cast, glued into the very body of cadaverous death.

Nor would the appellation, enchanted, seem misapplied in still another sense. For concerning the peculiar reptile inhabitant of these wilds—whose presence gives the group its second Spanish name, Gallipagos—concerning the tortoises found here, most mariners have long cherished a superstition, not more frightful than grotesque. They earnestly believe that all wicked sea-officers, more especially commodores and captains, are at death (and, in some cases, before death) transformed

into tortoises ; thenceforth dwelling upon these hot
aridities, sole solitary lords of Asphaltum.

Doubtless, so quaintly dolorous a thought was originally inspired by the woebegone landscape itself ; but
more particularly, perhaps, by the tortoises. For, apart
from their strictly physical features, there is something
strangely self-condemned in the appearance of these
creatures. Lasting sorrow and penal hopelessness are
in no animal form so suppliantly expressed as in theirs ;
while the thought of their wonderful longevity does not
fail to enhance the impression.

Nor even at the risk of meriting the charge of absurdly
believing in enchantments, can I restrain the admission
that sometimes, even now, when leaving the crowded
city to wander out July and August among the Adiron-
dack Mountains, far from the influences of towns and
proportionally nigh to the mysterious ones of nature ;
when at such times I sit me down in the mossy head of
some deep-wooded gorge, surrounded by prostrate trunks
of blasted pines, and recall, as in a dream, my other and
far-distant rovings in the baked heart of the charmed
isles ; and remember the sudden glimpses of dusky
shells, and long languid necks protruded from the leafless
thickets ; and again have beheld the vitreous inland
rocks worn down and grooved into deep ruts by ages
and ages of the slow draggings of tortoises in quest of
pools of scanty water ; I can hardly resist the feeling
that in my time I have indeed slept upon evilly enchanted
ground.

Nay, such is the vividness of my memory, or the
magic of my fancy, that I know not whether I am not
the occasional victim of optical delusion concerning
the Gallipagos. For, often in scenes of social merriment, and especially at revels held by candle-light in
old-fashioned mansions, so that shadows are thrown into

the further recesses of an angular and spacious room, making them put on a look of haunted undergrowth of lonely woods, I have drawn the attention of my comrades by my fixed gaze and sudden change of air, as I have seemed to see, slowly emerging from those imagined solitudes, and heavily crawling along the floor, the ghost of a gigantic tortoise, with ' Memento * * * * * ' burning in live letters upon his back.

SKETCH SECOND

TWO SIDES TO A TORTOISE

' Most ugly shapes and horrible aspects,
Such as Dame Nature selfe mote feare to see,
Or shame, that ever should so fowle defects
From her most cunning hand escaped bee ;
All dreadfull pourtraicts of deformitee.
Ne wonder if these do a man appall ;
For all that here at home we dreadfull hold
Be but as bugs to fearen babes withall
Compared to the creatures in these isles' entrall.
  *   *   *   *
Fear naught, then said the palmer, well avized,
For these same monsters are not there indeed,
But are into these fearful shapes disguized.
  *   *   *   *   *
And lifting up his vertuous staffe on high,
Then all that dreadful armie fast gan flye
Into great Zethy's bosom, where they hidden lye.'

In view of the description given, may one be gay upon the Encantadas ? Yes : that is, find one the gaiety, and he will be gay. And, indeed, sackcloth and ashes as they are, the isles are not perhaps unmitigated gloom. For while no spectator can deny their claims to a most solemn and superstitious consideration, no more than my firmest resolutions can decline to behold the spectre-tortoise when emerging from its shadowy recess ; yet even the tortoise, dark and melancholy as it is upon the back, still possesses a bright side ; its calipee or breast-plate being sometimes of a faint yellowish or golden tinge. Moreover, everyone knows that tortoises as well as turtle are of such a make, that if you but put them on their backs you thereby expose their bright sides without the possibility of their recovering themselves, and turning into view the other. But after you have done this, and because you have done this, you should not swear that the tortoise has no dark side. Enjoy the bright, keep it turned up perpetually if you can, but be honest, and don't deny the black. Neither should he, who cannot turn the tortoise from its natural position so as to hide the darker and expose its livelier aspect, like a great October pumpkin in the sun, for that cause declare the creature to be one total inky blot. The tortoise is both black and bright. But let us to particulars.

Some months before my first stepping ashore upon the group, my ship was cruising in its close vicinity. One noon we found ourselves off the South Head of Albemarle, and not very far from the land. Partly by way of freak, and partly by way of spying out so strange a country, a boat's crew was sent ashore, with orders to see all they could, and besides, bring back whatever tortoises they could conveniently transport.

It was after sunset when the adventurers returned. I looked down over the ship's high side as if looking down over the curb of a well, and dimly saw the damp boat deep in the sea with some unwonted weight. Ropes were dropped over, and presently three huge antediluvian-looking tortoises, after much straining, were landed on deck. They seemed hardly of the seed of earth. We had been broad upon the waters for five long months, a period amply sufficient to make all things of the land wear a fabulous hue to the dreamy mind. Had three Spanish custom-house officers boarded us then, it is not unlikely that I should have curiously stared at them, felt of them, and stroked them much as savages serve civilised guests. But instead of three custom-house officers, behold these really wondrous tortoises—none of your schoolboy mud-turtles—but black as widower's weeds, heavy as chests of plate, with vast shells medallioned and orbed like shields, and dented and blistered like shields that have breasted a battle, shaggy, too, here and there, with dark green moss, and slimy with the spray of the sea. These mystic creatures, suddenly translated by night from unutterable solitudes to our peopled deck, affected me in a manner not easy to unfold. They seemed newly crawled forth from beneath the foundations of the world. Yea, they seemed the identical tortoises whereon the Hindu plants this total sphere. With a lantern I inspected them more closely. Such worshipful venerableness of aspect! Such furry greenness mantling the rude peelings and healing the fissures of their shattered shells. I no more saw three tortoises. They expanded — became transfigured. I seemed to see three Roman Coliseums in magnificent decay.

Ye oldest inhabitants of this, or any other isle, said I, pray, give me the freedom of your three-walled towns.

The great feeling inspired by these creatures was that of age :—dateless, indefinite endurance. And, in fact, that any other creature can live and breathe as long as the tortoise of the Encantadas, I will not readily believe. Not to hint of their known capacity of sustaining life, while going without food for an entire year, consider that impregnable armour of their living mail. What other bodily being possesses such a citadel wherein to resist the assaults of Time ?

As, lantern in hand, I scraped among the moss and beheld the ancient scars of bruises received in many a sullen fall among the marly mountains of the isle— scars strangely widened, swollen, half obliterate, and yet distorted like those sometimes found in the bark of very hoary trees, I seemed an antiquary of a geologist, studying the bird-tracks and ciphers upon the exhumed slates trod by incredible creatures whose very ghosts are now defunct.

As I lay in my hammock that night, overhead I heard the slow weary draggings of the three ponderous strangers along the encumbered deck. Their stupidity or their resolution was so great, that they never went aside for any impediment. One ceased his movements altogether just before the mid-watch. At sunrise I found him butted like a battering-ram against the immovable foot of the foremast, and still striving, tooth and nail, to force the impossible passage. That these tortoises are the victims of a penal, or malignant, or perhaps a downright diabolical enchanter, seems in nothing more likely than in that strange infatuation of hopeless toil which so often possesses them. I have known them in their journeyings ram themselves heroically against rocks, and long abide there, nudging, wriggling, wedging, in order to displace them, and so hold on their inflexible path. Their crowning curse is their drudging impulse to straightforwardness in a belittered world.

Meeting with no such hindrance as their companion did, the other tortoises merely fell foul of small stumbling-blocks—buckets, blocks, and coils of rigging—and at times in the act of crawling over them would slip with an astounding rattle to the deck. Listening to these draggings and concussions, I thought me of the haunt from which they came ; an isle full of metallic ravines and gulches, sunk bottomlessly into the hearts of splintered mountains, and covered for many miles with inextricable thickets. I then pictured these three straightforward monsters, century after century, writhing through the shades, grim as blacksmiths ; crawling so slowly and ponderously, that not only did toad-stools and all fungus things grow beneath their feet, but a sooty moss sprouted upon their backs. With them I lost myself in volcanic mazes ; brushed away endless boughs of rotting thickets ; till finally in a dream I found myself sitting cross-legged upon the foremost, a Brahmin similarly mounted upon either side, forming a tripod of foreheads which upheld the universal cope.

Such was the wild nightmare begot by my first impression of the Encantadas tortoise. But next evening, strange to say, I sat down with my shipmates, and made a merry repast from tortoise steaks and tortoise stews ; and supper over, out knife, and helped convert the three mighty concave shells into three fanciful souptureens, and polished the three flat yellowish calipees into three gorgeous salvers.

SKETCH THIRD

ROCK RODONDO

' For they this hight the Rock of vile Reproach,
A dangerous and dreadful place,
To which nor fish nor fowl did once approach,
But yelling meaws with sea-gulls hoars and bace
And cormoyrants with birds of ravenous race,
Which still sit waiting on that dreadful clift.'
* * * * *
' With that the rolling sea resounding soft
In his big base them fitly answered,
And on the Rock, the waves breaking aloft,
A solemn meane unto them measured.'
* * * * *
' Then he the boteman bad row easily,
And let him heare some part of that rare melody.'
* * * * *
' Suddeinly an innumerable flight
Of harmefull fowles about them fluttering cride,
And with their wicked wings them oft did smight
And sore annoyed, groping in that griesly night.'
* * * * *
' Even all the nation of unfortunate
And fatal birds about them flocked were.'

To go up into a high stone tower is not only a very fine thing in itself, but the very best mode of gaining a comprehensive view of the region round about. It is all the better if this tower stand solitary and alone, like that mysterious Newport one, or else be sole survivor of some perished castle.

Now, with reference to the Enchanted Isles, we are fortunately supplied with just such a noble point of observation in a remarkable rock, from its peculiar figure called of old by the Spaniards, Rock Rodondo, or Round Rock. Some two hundred and fifty feet high,

N

rising straight from the sea ten miles from land, with the whole mountainous group to the south and east, Rock Rodondo occupies, on a large scale, very much the position which the famous Campanile or detached Bell Tower of St. Mark does with respect to the tangled group of hoary edifices around it.

Ere ascending, however, to gaze abroad upon the Encantadas, this sea-tower itself claims attention. It is visible at the distance of thirty miles ; and, fully participating in that enchantment which pervades the group, when first seen afar invariably is mistaken for a sail. Four leagues away, of a golden, hazy noon, it seems some Spanish admiral's ship, stacked up with glittering canvas. Sail ho ! Sail ho ! Sail ho ! from all three masts. But coming nigh, the enchanted frigate is transformed apace into a craggy keep.

My first visit to the spot was made in the gray of the morning. With a view of fishing, we had lowered three boats, and pulling some two miles from our vessel, found ourselves just before dawn of day close under the moon-shadow of Rodondo. Its aspect was heightened, and yet softened, by the strange double twilight of the hour. The great full moon burned in the low west like a half-spent beacon, casting a soft mellow tinge upon the sea like that cast by a waning fire of embers upon a midnight hearth ; while along the entire east the invisible sun sent pallid intimations of his coming. The wind was light ; the waves languid ; the stars twinkled with a faint effulgence ; all nature seemed supine with the long night watch, and half-suspended in jaded expectation of the sun. This was the critical hour to catch Rodondo in his perfect mood. The twilight was just enough to reveal every striking point, without tearing away the dim investiture of wonder.

From a broken stair-like base, washed, as the steps

of a water-palace, by the waves, the tower rose in entablatures of strata to a shaven summit. These uniform layers, which compose the mass, form its most peculiar feature. For at their lines of junction they project flatly into encircling shelves, from top to bottom, rising one above another in graduated series. And as the eaves of any old barn or abbey are alive with swallows, so were all these rocky ledges with unnumbered seafowl. Eaves upon eaves, and nests upon nests. Here and there were long bird-lime streaks of a ghostly white staining the tower from sea to air, readily accounting for its sail-like look afar. All would have been bewitchingly quiescent, were it not for the demoniac din created by the birds. Not only were the eaves rustling with them, but they flew densely overhead, spreading themselves into a winged and continually shifting canopy. The tower is the resort of aquatic birds for hundreds of leagues around. To the north, to the east, to the west, stretches nothing but eternal ocean ; so that the man-of-war hawk coming from the coast of North America, Polynesia, or Peru, makes his first land at Rodondo. And yet though Rodondo be terra-firma, no land-bird ever lighted on it. Fancy a red-robin or a canary there ! What a falling into the hands of the Philistines, when the poor warbler should be surrounded by such locust-flights of strong bandit birds, with long bills cruel as daggers.

I know not where one can better study the natural history of strange sea-fowl than at Rodondo. It is the aviary of ocean. Birds light here which never touched mast or tree ; hermit-birds, which ever fly alone ; cloud-birds, familiar with unpierced zones of air.

Let us first glance low down to the lowermost shelf of all, which is the widest, too, and but a little space from high-water mark. What outlandish beings are these ? Erect as men, but hardly as symmetrical, they stand all round the rock like sculptured caryatides, supporting the next range of eaves above. Their bodies are grotesquely misshapen ; their bills short ; their feet seemingly legless ; while the members at their sides are neither fin, wing, nor arm. And truly neither fish, flesh, nor fowl is the penguin ; as an edible, pertaining neither to Carnival nor Lent ; without exception the most ambiguous and least lovely creature yet discovered by man. Though dabbling in all three elements, and indeed possessing some rudimental claims to all, the penguin is at home in none. On land it stumps ; afloat it sculls ; in the air it flops. As if ashamed of her failure, nature keeps this ungainly child hidden away at the ends of the earth, in the Straits of Magellan, and on the abased sea-story of Rodondo.

But look, what are yon woebegone regiments drawn up on the next shelf above ? what rank and file of large strange fowl ? what sea Friars of Orders Gray ? Pelicans. Their elongated bills, and heavy leathern pouches suspended thereto, give them the most lugubrious expression. A pensive race, they stand for hours together without motion. Their dull, ashy plumage imparts an aspect as if they had been powdered over with cinders. A penitential bird, indeed, fitly haunting the shores of the clinkered Encantadas, whereon tormented Job himself might have well sat down and scraped himself with potsherds.

Higher up now we mark the gony, or gray albatross, anomalously so called, an unsightly unpoetic bird, unlike its storied kinsman, which is the snow-white ghost of the haunted Capes of Hope and Horn.

As we still ascend from shelf to shelf, we find the tenants of the tower serially disposed in order of their magnitude :—gannets, black and speckled haglets, jays,

sea-hens, sperm-whale-birds, gulls of all varieties :—
thrones, princedoms, powers, dominating one above
another in senatorial array ; while, sprinkled over all,
like an ever-repeated fly in a great piece of broidery,
the stormy petrel or Mother Carey's chicken sounds his
continual challenge and alarm. That this mysterious
humming-bird of ocean—which, had it but brilliancy of
hue, might, from its evanescent liveliness, be almost
called its butterfly, yet whose chirrup under the stern
is ominous to mariners as to the peasant the death-tick
sounding from behind the chimney jamb—should have
its special haunt at the Encantadas, contributes, in the
seaman's mind, not a little to their dreary spell.

As day advances the dissonant din augments. With
ear-splitting cries the wild birds celebrate their matins.
Each moment, flights push from the tower, and join
the aerial choir hovering overhead, while their places
below are supplied by darting myriads. But down
through all this discord of commotion, I hear clear,
silver, bugle-like notes unbrokenly falling, like oblique
lines of swift-slanting rain in a cascading shower. I
gaze far up, and behold a snow-white angelic thing, with
one long, lance-like feather thrust out behind. It is the
bright, inspiriting chanticleer of ocean, the beauteous
bird, from its bestirring whistle of musical invocation,
fitly styled the ' Boatswain's Mate.'

The winged, life-clouding Rodondo had its full counter-
part in the finny hosts which peopled the waters at
its base. Below the water-line, the rock seemed one
honeycomb of grottoes, affording labyrinthine lurking-
places for swarms of fairy-fish. All were strange ; many
exceedingly beautiful ; and would have well graced the
costliest glass globes in which gold-fish are kept for a
show. Nothing was more striking than the complete
novelty of many individuals of this multitude. Here

hues were seen as yet unpainted, and figures which are unengraved.

To show the multitude, avidity, and nameless fearlessness and tameness of these fish, let me say, that often, marking through clear spaces of water—temporarily made so by the concentric dartings of the fish above the surface—certain larger and less unwary wights, which swam slow and deep ; our anglers would cautiously essay to drop their lines down to these last. But in vain ; there was no passing the uppermost zone. No sooner did the hook touch the sea, than a hundred infatuates contended for the honour of capture. Poor fish of Rodondo ! in your victimised confidence, you are of the number of those who inconsiderately trust, while they do not understand, human nature.

But the dawn is now fairly day. Band after band, the sea-fowl sail away to forage the deep for their food. The tower is left solitary, save the fish-caves at its base. Its bird-lime gleams in the golden rays like the whitewash of a tall lighthouse, or the lofty sails of a cruiser. This moment, doubtless, while we know it to be a dead desert rock, other voyagers are taking oaths it is a glad populous ship.

But ropes now, and let us ascend. Yet soft, this is not so easy.

SKETCH FOURTH

A PISGAH VIEW FROM THE ROCK

' —That done, he leads him to the highest mount,
From whence far off he unto him did show : '—

If you seek to ascend Rock Rodondo, take the following prescription. Go three voyages round the world
as a main-royal man of the tallest frigate that floats ;
then serve a year or two apprenticeship to the guides
who conduct strangers up the Peak of Teneriffe ; and
as many more respectively to a rope-dancer, an Indian
juggler, and a chamois. This done, come and be re-
warded by the view from our tower. How we got there,
we alone know. If we sought to tell others, what the
wiser were they ? Suffice it, that here at the summit
you and I stand. Does any balloonist, does the out-
looking man in the moon, take a broader view of space ?
Much thus, one fancies, looks the universe from Milton's
celestial battlements. A boundless watery Kentucky.
Here Daniel Boone would have dwelt content.

Never heed for the present yonder Burnt District of
the Enchanted Isles. Look edgeways, as it were, past
them, to the south. You see nothing ; but permit me
to point out the direction, if not the place, of certain
interesting objects in the vast sea, which, kissing this
tower's base, we behold unscrolling itself toward the
Antarctic Pole.

We stand now ten miles from the Equator. Yonder,
to the east, some six hundred miles, lies the continent ;
this Rock being just about on the parallel of Quito.

Observe another thing here. We are at one of three
uninhabited clusters, which, at pretty nearly uniform

distances from the main, sentinel, at long intervals from
each other, the entire coast of South America. In a
peculiar manner, also, they terminate the South American
character of country. Of the unnumbered Polynesian
chains to the westward, not one partakes of the qualities
of the Encantadas or Gallipagos, the isles of St. Felix
and St. Ambrose, the isles Juan Fernandez and Massafuero. Of the first, it needs not here to speak. The
second lie a little above the Southern Tropic; lofty,
inhospitable, and uninhabitable rocks, one of which,
presenting two round hummocks connected by a low
reef, exactly resembles a huge double-headed shot.
The last lie in the latitude of 33°; high, wild, and
cloven. Juan Fernandez is sufficiently famous without further description. Massafuero is a Spanish name,
expressive of the fact that the isle so called lies *more
without*, that is, further off the main than its neighbour
Juan. This isle Massafuero has a very imposing aspect
at a distance of eight or ten miles. Approached in one
direction, in cloudy weather, its great overhanging height
and rugged contour, and more especially a peculiar slope
of its broad summits, give it much the air of a vast iceberg
drifting in tremendous poise. Its sides are split with
dark cavernous recesses, as an old cathedral with its
gloomy lateral chapels. Drawing nigh one of these
gorges from sea, after a long voyage, and beholding some
tatterdemalion outlaw, staff in hand, descending its
steep rocks toward you, conveys a very queer emotion
to a lover of the picturesque.

On fishing parties from ships, at various times, I have
chanced to visit each of these groups. The impression
they give to the stranger pulling close up in his boat
under their grim cliffs is, that surely he must be their
first discoverer, such, for the most part, is the unim-
paired . . . silence and solitude. And here, by the

way, the mode in which these isles were really first lighted upon by Europeans is not unworthy of mention, especially as what is about to be said likewise applies to the original discovery of our Encantadas.

Prior to the year 1563, the voyages made by Spanish ships from Peru to Chili were full of difficulty. Along this coast, the winds from the south most generally prevail ; and it had been an invariable custom to keep close in with the land, from a superstitious conceit on the part of the Spaniards, that were they to lose sight of it, the eternal Trade wind would waft them into unending waters, from whence would be no return. Here, involved among tortuous capes and headlands, shoals and reefs, beating, too, against a continual head wind, often light, and sometimes for days and weeks sunk into utter calm, the provincial vessels, in many cases, suffered the extremest hardships, in passages, which at the present day seem to have been incredibly protracted. There is on record in some collections of nautical disasters, an account of one of these ships, which, starting on a voyage whose duration was esti- mated at ten days, spent four months at sea, and indeed never again entered harbour, for in the end she was cast away. Singular to tell, this craft never encountered a gale, but was the vexed sport of malicious calms and currents. Thrice, out of provisions, she put back to an intermediate port, and started afresh, but only yet again to return. Frequent fogs enveloped her ; so that no observation could be had of her place, and once, when all hands were joyously anticipating sight of their destination, lo ! the vapours lifted and disclosed the mountains from which they had taken their first de- parture. In the like deceptive vapours she at last struck upon a reef, whence ensued a long series of calamities too sad to detail.

It was the famous pilot, Juan Fernandez, immortalised
by the island named after him, who put an end to these
coasting tribulations, by boldly venturing the experiment—as Da Gama did before him with respect to
Europe—of standing broad out from land.   Here he found
the winds favourable for getting to the south, and by
running westward till beyond the influences of the
Trades, he regained the coast without difficulty ; making
the passage which, though in a high degree circuitous,
proved far more expeditious than the nominally direct
one.   Now it was upon these new tracks, and about the
year 1670, or thereabouts, that the Enchanted Isles,
and the rest of the sentinel groups, as they may be
called, were discovered.   Though I know of no account
as to whether any of them were found inhabited or no,
it may be reasonably concluded that they had been
immemorial solitudes.   But let us return to Rodondo.

South-west from our tower lies all Polynesia, hundreds
of leagues away ; but straight west, on the precise
line of his parallel, no land rises till your keel is breached
upon the Kingsmills, a nice little sail of, say, 5000 miles.

Having thus by such distant references—with Rodondo
the only possible ones—settled our relative place on the
sea, let us consider objects not quite so remote.   Behold
the grim and charred Enchanted Isles.   This nearest
crater-shaped headland is part of Albemarle, the largest
of the group, being some sixty miles or more long, and
fifteen broad.   Did you ever lay eye on the real genuine
Equator ?   Have you ever, in the largest sense, toed
the Line ?   Well, that identical crater-shaped headland
there, all yellow lava, is cut by the Equator exactly as
a knife cuts straight through the centre of a pumpkin
pie.   If you could only see so far, just to one side of
that same headland, across yon low dikey ground, you
would catch sight of the isle of Narborough, the loftiest

land of the cluster ; no soil whatever ; one seamed
clinker from top to bottom ; abounding in black caves
like smithies ; its metallic shore ringing under foot
like plates of iron ; its central volcanoes standing grouped
like a gigantic chimney-stack.

Narborough and Albemarle are neighbours after a
quite curious fashion. A familiar diagram will illustrate
this strange neighbourhood :—

ⴹ

Cut a channel at the above letter joint, and the
middle transverse limb is Narborough, and all the rest
is Albemarle. Volcanic Narborough lies in the black
jaws of Albemarle like a wolf's red tongue in his open
mouth.

If now you desire the population of Albemarle, I will
give you, in round numbers, the statistics, according
to the most reliable estimates made upon the spot :—

Men	none
Ant-eaters	unknown
Man-haters	unknown
Lizards	500,000
Snakes	500,000
Spiders	10,000,000
Salamanders	unknown
Devils	unknown
Making a clean total of . . .	11,000,000

exclusive of an incomputable host of fiends, ant-eaters,
man-haters, and salamanders.

Albemarle opens his mouth toward the setting sun.
His distended jaws form a great bay, which Narborough,
his tongue, divides into halves, one whereof is called
Weather Bay, the other Lee Bay ; while the volcanic

promontories, terminating his coasts, are styled South
Head and North Head. I note this, because these bays
are famous in the annals of the Sperm Whale Fishery.
The whales come here at certain seasons to calve. When
ships first cruised hereabouts, I am told, they used to
blockade the entrance of Lee Bay, when their boats
going round by Weather Bay, passed through Narborough
channel, and so had the leviathans very neatly in
a pen.

The day after we took fish at the base of this Round
Tower, we had a fine wind, and shooting round the north
headland, suddenly descried a fleet of full thirty sail,
all beating to windward like a squadron in line. A
brave sight as ever man saw. A most harmonious
concord of rushing keels. Their thirty kelsons hummed
like thirty harp-strings, and looked as straight whilst
they left their parallel traces on the sea. But there
proved too many hunters for the game. The fleet
broke up, and went their separate ways out of sight,
leaving my own ship and two trim gentlemen of London.
These last, finding no luck either, likewise vanished ;
and Lee Bay, with all its appurtenances, and without a
rival, devolved to us.

The way of cruising here is this. You keep hovering
about the entrance of the bay, in one beat and out the
next. But at times—not always, as in other parts of
the group—a race-horse of a current sweeps right across
its mouth. So, with all sails set, you carefully ply your
tacks. How often, standing at the foremast-head at
sunrise, with our patient prow pointed in between these
isles, did I gaze upon that land, not of cakes, but of
clinkers, not of streams of sparkling water, but arrested
torrents of tormented lava.

As the ship runs in from the open sea, Narborough
presents its side in one dark craggy mass, soaring up

some five or six thousand feet, at which point it hoods itself in heavy clouds, whose lowest level fold is as clearly defined against the rocks as the snow-line against the Andes. There is dire mischief going on in that upper dark. There toil the demons of fire, who, at intervals, irradiate the nights with a strange spectral illumination for miles and miles around, but unaccompanied by any further demonstration ; or else, suddenly announce themselves by terrific concussions, and the full drama of a volcanic eruption. The blacker that cloud by day, the more may you look for light by night. Often whale-men have found themselves cruising nigh that burning mountain when all aglow with a ballroom blaze. Or, rather, glass-works, you may call this same vitreous isle of Narborough, with its tall chimney-stacks.

Where we still stand, here on Rodondo, we cannot see all the other isles, but it is a good place from which to point out where they lie. Yonder, though, to the E.N.E., I mark a distant dusky ridge. It is Abington Isle, one of the most northerly of the group ; so solitary, remote, and blank, it looks like No-Man's Land seen off our northern shore. I doubt whether two human beings ever touched upon that spot. So far as yon Abington Isle is concerned, Adam and his billions of posterity remain uncreated.

Ranging south of Abington, and quite out of sight behind the long spine of Albemarle, lies James's Isle, so called by the early bucaniers after the luckless Stuart, Duke of York. Observe here, by the way, that, excepting the isles particularised in comparatively recent times, and which mostly received the names of famous admirals, the Encantadas were first christened by the Spaniards ; but these Spanish names were generally effaced on English charts by the subsequent christenings of the bucaniers, who, in the middle of

the seventeenth century, called them after English noble-
men and kings. Of these loyal freebooters and the
things which associate their name with the Encantadas,
we shall hear anon. Nay, for one little item, immediately; for between James's Isle and Albemarle lies a
fantastic islet, strangely known as ' Cowley's Enchanted
Isle.' But, as all the group is deemed enchanted, the
reason must be given for the spell within a spell involved
by this particular designation. The name was bestowed
by that excellent bucanier himself, on his first visit
here. Speaking in his published voyages of this spot,
he says—' My fancy led me to call it Cowley's Enchanted
Isle, for, we having had a sight of it upon several points
of the compass, it appeared always in so many different
forms; sometimes like a ruined fortification; upon
another point like a great city,' etc. No wonder, though,
that among the Encantadas all sorts of ocular decep-
tions and mirages should be met.

That Cowley linked his name with this self-trans-
forming and bemocking isle, suggests the possibility that
it conveyed to him some meditative image of himself.
At least, as is not impossible, if he were any relative of
the mildly thoughtful and self-upbraiding poet Cowley,
who lived about his time, the conceit might seem un-
warranted; for that sort of thing evinced in the naming
of this isle runs in the blood, and may be seen in pirates
as in poets.

Still south of James's Isle lie Jervis Isle, Duncan
Isle, Crossman's Isle, Brattle Isle, Wood's Isle, Chatham
Isle, and various lesser isles, for the most part an archi-
pelago of aridities, without inhabitant, history, or hope
of either in all time to come. But not far from these
are rather notable isles—Barrington, Charles's, Norfolk,
and Hood's. Succeeding chapters will reveal some
ground for their notability.

SKETCH FIFTH

THE FRIGATE, AND SHIP FLYAWAY

‘ Looking far forth into the ocean wide,
A goodly ship with banners bravely dight,
And flag in her top-gallant I espide,
Through the main sea making her merry flight.’

Ere quitting Rodondo, it must not be omitted that
here, in 1813, the U.S. frigate *Essex*, Captain David
Porter, came near leaving her bones. Lying becalmed
one morning with a strong current setting her rapidly
toward the rock, a strange sail was descried, which—not
out of keeping with alleged enchantments of the neighbourhood—seemed to be staggering under a violent
wind, while the frigate lay lifeless as if spellbound. But
a light air springing up, all sail was made by the frigate
in chase of the enemy, as supposed—he being deemed
an English whale-ship—but the rapidity of the current
was so great, that soon all sight was lost of him ; and,
at meridian, the *Essex*, spite of her drags, was driven so
close under the foam-lashed cliffs of Rodondo that, for
a time, all hands gave her up. A smart breeze, however,
at last helped her off, though the escape was so critical
as to seem almost miraculous.

Thus saved from destruction herself, she now made
use of that salvation to destroy the other vessel, if
possible. Renewing the chase in the direction in which
the stranger had disappeared, sight was caught of him
the following morning. Upon being descried he hoisted
American colours and stood away from the *Essex*. A
calm ensued ; when, still confident that the stranger
was an Englishman, Porter dispatched a cutter, not to
board the enemy, but drive back his boats engaged in

towing him. The cutter succeeded. Cutters were subsequently sent to capture him ; the stranger now showing English colours in place of American. But, when the frigate's boats were within a short distance of their hoped-for prize, another sudden breeze sprang up ; the stranger, under all sail, bore off to the westward, and, ere night, was hull down ahead of the *Essex*, which, all this time, lay perfectly becalmed.

This enigmatic craft—American in the morning, and English in the evening—her sails full of wind in a calm—was never again beheld. An enchanted ship no doubt. So, at least, the sailors swore.

This cruise of the *Essex* in the Pacific during the war of 1812 is, perhaps, the strangest and most stirring to be found in the history of the American navy. She captured the furthest wandering vessels ; visited the remotest seas and isles ; long hovered in the charmed vicinity of the enchanted group ; and, finally, valiantly gave up the ghost fighting two English frigates in the harbour of Valparaiso. Mention is made of her here for the same reason that the bucaniers will likewise receive record ; because, like them, by long cruising among the isles, tortoise-hunting upon their shores, and generally exploring them ; for these and other reasons, the *Essex* is peculiarly associated with the Encantadas.

Here be it said that you have but three eye-witness authorities worth mentioning touching the Enchanted Isles :—Cowley, the bucanier (1684) ; Colnet, the whaling-ground explorer (1798) ; Porter, the post-captain (1813). Other than these you have but barren, bootless allusions from some few passing voyagers or compilers.

SKETCH SIXTH

BARRINGTON ISLE AND THE BUCANIERS

' Let us all servile base subjection scorn,
And as we be sons of the earth so wide,
Let us our father's heritage divide,
And challenge to ourselves our portions dew
Of all the patrimony, which a few
Now hold on hugger-mugger in their hand.'

* * * * *

' Lords of the world, and so will wander free,
Whereso us listeth, uncontroll'd of any.'

* * * * *

' How bravely now we live, how jocund, how near the first
inheritance, without fear, how free from little troubles ! '

Near two centuries ago Barrington Isle was the resort
of that famous wing of the West Indian bucaniers,
which, upon their repulse from the Cuban waters, crossing
the Isthmus of Darien, ravaged the Pacific side of the
Spanish colonies, and, with the regularity and timing
of a modern mail, waylaid the royal treasure-ships
plying between Manilla and Acapulco. After the toils
of piratic war, here they came to say their prayers,
enjoy their free-and-easies, count their crackers from
the cask, their doubloons from the keg, and measure
their silks of Asia with long Toledos for their yard-
sticks.

As a secure retreat, an undiscoverable hiding-place,
no spot in those days could have been better fitted.
In the centre of a vast and silent sea, but very little
traversed—surrounded by islands, whose inhospitable
aspect might well drive away the chance navigator—
and yet within a few days' sail of the opulent countries
which they made their prey—the unmolested bucaniers

o

found here that tranquillity which they fiercely denied to every civilised harbour in that part of the world. Here, after stress of weather, or a temporary drubbing at the hands of their vindictive foes, or in swift flight with golden booty, those old marauders came, and lay snugly out of all harm's reach. But not only was the place a harbour of safety, and a bower of ease, but for utility in other things it was most admirable.

Barrington Isle is, in many respects, singularly adapted to careening, refitting, refreshing, and other seamen's purposes. Not only has it good water, and good anchorage, well sheltered from all winds by the high land of Albemarle, but it is the least unproductive isle of the group. Tortoises good for food, trees good for fuel, and long grass good for bedding, abound here, and there are pretty natural walks, and several landscapes to be seen. Indeed, though in its locality belonging to the Enchanted Group, Barrington Isle is so unlike most of its neighbours, that it would hardly seem of kin to them.

' I once landed on its western side,' says a sentimental voyager long ago, ' where it faces the black buttress of Albemarle. I walked beneath groves of trees—not very lofty, and not palm-trees, or orange-trees, or peach-trees, to be sure—but, for all that, after long seafaring, very beautiful to walk under, even though they supplied no fruit. And here, in calm spaces at the heads of glades, and on the shaded tops of slopes commanding the most quiet scenery—what do you think I saw ? Seats which might have served Brahmins and presidents of peace societies. Fine old ruins of what had once been symmetric lounges of stone and turf, they bore every mark both of artificialness and age, and were, undoubtedly, made by the bucaniers. One had been a long sofa, with back and arms, just such a sofa as the poet Gray might have loved to throw himself upon, his Crebillon in hand.

'Though they sometimes tarried here for months at a time, and used the spot for a storing-place for spare spars, sails, and casks ; yet it is highly improbable that the bucaniers ever erected dwelling-houses upon the isle. They never were here except their ships remained, and they would most likely have slept on board. I mention this, because I cannot avoid the thought, that it is hard to impute the construction of these romantic seats to any other motive than one of pure peaceful-ness and kindly fellowship with nature. That the bucaniers perpetrated the greatest outrages is very true—that some of them were mere cut-throats is not to be denied ; but we know that here and there among their host was a Dampier, a Wafer, and a Cowley, and likewise other men, whose worst reproach was their desperate fortunes—whom persecution, or adversity, or secret and unavengeable wrongs, had driven from Christian society to seek the melancholy solitude or the guilty adventures of the sea. At any rate, long as those ruins of seats on Barrington remain, the most singular monuments are furnished to the fact, that all of the bucaniers were not unmitigated monsters.

'But during my ramble on the isle I was not long in discovering other tokens, of things quite in accord-ance with those wild traits, popularly, and no doubt truly enough, imputed to the freebooters at large. Had I picked up old sails and rusty hoops I would only have thought of the ship's carpenter and cooper. But I found old cutlasses and daggers reduced to mere threads of rust, which, doubtless, had stuck between Spanish ribs ere now. These were signs of the murderer and robber ; the reveller likewise had left his trace. Mixed with shells, fragments of broken jars were lying here and there, high up upon the beach. They were precisely like the jars now used upon the Spanish coast for the wine and Pisco spirits of that country.

' With a rusty dagger-fragment in one hand, and a bit of a wine-jar in another, I sat me down on the ruinous green sofa I have spoken of, and bethought me long and deeply of these same bucaniers. Could it be possible, that they robbed and murdered one day, revelled the next, and rested themselves by turning meditative philosophers, rural poets, and seat-builders on the third ? Not very improbable, after all. For consider the vacillations of a man. Still, strange as it may seem, I must also abide by the more charitable thought ; namely, that among these adventurers were some gentlemanly, companionable souls, capable of genuine tranquillity and virtue.'

SKETCH SEVENTH

CHARLES'S ISLE AND THE DOG-KING

' —So with outragious cry,
A thousand villeins round about him swarmed
Out of the rocks and caves adjoining nye ;
Vile caitive wretches, ragged, rude, deformed ;
All threatning death, all in straunge manner armed ;
Some with unweldy clubs, some with long speares,
Some rusty knives, some staves in fier warmd.'
  * * * * *
' We will not be of any occupation,
Let such vile vassals, born to base vocation,
Drudge in the world, and for their living droyle,
Which have no wit to live withouten toyle.'

South-west of Barrington lies Charles's Isle. And hereby hangs a history which I gathered long ago from a shipmate learned in all the lore of outlandish life.

During the successful revolt of the Spanish provinces from Old Spain, there fought on behalf of Peru a certain Creole adventurer from Cuba, who, by his bravery and good fortune, at length advanced himself to high rank in the patriot army. The war being ended, Peru found itself like many valorous gentlemen, free and independent enough, but with few shot in the locker. In other words, Peru had not wherewithal to pay off its troops. But the Creole—I forget his name—volunteered to take his pay in lands. So they told him he might have his pick of the Enchanted Isles, which were then, as they still remain, the nominal appanage of Peru. The soldier straightway embarks thither, explores the group, returns to Callao, and says he will take a deed of Charles's Isle. Moreover, this deed must stipulate that thenceforth Charles's Isle is not only the sole property of the Creole, but is forever free of Peru, even as Peru of Spain. To be short, this adventurer procures himself to be made in effect Supreme Lord of the Island, one of the princes of the powers of the earth.[1]

He now sends forth a proclamation inviting subjects to his as yet unpopulated kingdom. Some eighty souls, men and women, respond ; and being provided by their leader with necessaries, and tools of various sorts, together with a few cattle and goats, take ship for the promised land ; the last arrival on board, prior to sailing, being the Creole himself, accompanied, strange to say, by a disciplined cavalry company of large grim dogs. These, it was observed on the passage, refusing to consort with the emigrants, remained aristocratically grouped around their master on the elevated quarter-deck, casting disdainful glances forward upon the inferior rabble there ; much as, from the ramparts, the soldiers of a garrison, thrown into a conquered town, eye the inglorious citizen-mob over which they are set to watch.

Now Charles's Isle not only resembles Barrington Isle in being much more inhabitable than other parts of the group, but it is double the size of Barrington, say forty or fifty miles in circuit.

Safely debarked at last, the company, under direction of their lord and patron, forthwith proceed to build their capital city. They make considerable advance in the way of walls of clinkers, and lava floors, nicely sanded with cinders. On the least barren hills they pasture their cattle, while the goats, adventurers by

---

[1] The American Spaniards have long been in the habit of making presents of islands to deserving individuals. The pilot Juan Fernandez procured a deed of the isle named after him, and for some years resided there before Selkirk came. It is supposed, however, that he eventually contracted the blues upon his princely property, for after a time he returned to the main, and, as report goes, became a very garrulous barber in the city of Lima.

nature, explore the far inland solitudes for a scanty livelihood of lofty herbage. Meantime, abundance of fish and tortoises supply their other wants.

The disorders incident to settling all primitive regions, in the present case were heightened by the peculiarly untoward character of many of the pilgrims. His Majesty was forced at last to proclaim martial law, and actually hunted and shot with his own hand several of his rebellious subjects, who, with most questionable intentions, had clandestinely encamped in the interior, whence they stole by night, to prowl barefooted on tiptoe round the precincts of the lava-palace. It is to be remarked, however, that prior to such stern proceedings, the more reliable men had been judiciously picked out for an infantry bodyguard, subordinate to the cavalry bodyguard of dogs. But the state of politics in this unhappy nation may be somewhat imagined, from the circumstance that all who were not of the bodyguard were downright plotters and malignant traitors. At length the death-penalty was tacitly abolished, owing to the timely thought, that were strict sportsman's justice to be dispensed among such subjects, ere long the Nimrod King would have little or no remaining game to shoot. The human part of the lifeguard was now disbanded, and set to work cultivating the soil and raising potatoes ; the regular army now solely consisting of the dog-regiment. These, as I have heard, were of a singularly ferocious character, though by severe training rendered docile to their master. Armed to the teeth, the Creole now goes in state, surrounded by his canine janizaries, whose terrific bayings prove quite as serviceable as bayonets in keeping down the surgings of revolt.

But the census of the isle, sadly lessened by the dispensation of justice, and not materially recruited by matrimony, began to fill his mind with sad mistrust. Some way the population must be increased. Now, from its possessing a little water, and its comparative pleasantness of aspect, Charles's Isle at this period was occasionally visited by foreign whalers. These His Majesty had always levied upon for port charges, thereby contributing to his revenue. But now he had additional designs. By insidious arts he, from time to time, cajoles certain sailors to desert their ships, and enlist beneath his banner. Soon as missed, their captains crave permission to go and hunt them up. Whereupon His Majesty first hides them very carefully away, and then freely permits the search. In consequence, the delinquents are never found, and the ships retire without them.

Thus, by a two-edged policy of this crafty monarch, foreign nations were crippled in the number of their subjects, and his own were greatly multiplied. He particularly petted these renegado strangers. But alas for the deep-laid schemes of ambitious princes, and alas for the vanity of glory. As the foreign-born Pretorians, unwisely introduced into the Roman state, and still more unwisely made favourites of the emperors, at last insulted and overturned the throne, even so these lawless mariners, with all the rest of the bodyguard and all the populace, broke out into a terrible mutiny, and defied their master. He marched against them with all his dogs. A deadly battle ensued upon the beach. It raged for three hours, the dogs fighting with determined valour, and the sailors reckless of everything but victory. Three men and thirteen dogs were left dead upon the field, many on both sides were wounded, and the king was forced to fly with the remainder of his canine regiment. The enemy pursued, stoning the dogs with their master into the wilderness of the interior.

Discontinuing the pursuit, the victors returned to the
village on the shore, stove the spirit casks, and proclaimed a Republic. The dead men were interred with
the honours of war, and the dead dogs ignominiously
thrown into the sea. At last, forced by stress of suffering, the fugitive Creole came down from the hills and
offered to treat for peace. But the rebels refused it
on any other terms than his unconditional banishment.
Accordingly, the next ship that arrived carried away
the ex-king to Peru.

The history of the king of Charles's Island furnishes
another illustration of the difficulty of colonising barren
islands with unprincipled pilgrims.

Doubtless for a long time the exiled monarch, pen-
sively ruralising in Peru, which afforded him a safe
asylum in his calamity, watched every arrival from the
Encantadas, to hear news of the failure of the Republic,
the consequent penitence of the rebels, and his own recall
to royalty. Doubtless he deemed the Republic but a
miserable experiment which would soon explode. But
no, the insurgents had confederated themselves into a
democracy neither Grecian, Roman, nor American.
Nay, it was no democracy at all, but a permanent *Rioto-
cracy*, which gloried in having no law but lawlessness.
Great inducements being offered to deserters, their ranks
were swelled by accessions of scamps from every ship
which touched their shores. Charles's Island was proclaimed the asylum of the oppressed of all navies. Each
runaway tar was hailed as a martyr in the cause of
freedom, and became immediately installed a ragged
citizen of this universal nation. In vain the captains
of absconding seamen strove to regain them. Their
new compatriots were ready to give any number of
ornamental eyes in their behalf. They had few cannon,
but their fists were not to be trifled with. So at last

it came to pass that no vessels acquainted with the
character of that country durst touch there, however
sorely in want of refreshment. It became Anathema—
a sea Alsatia—the unassailed lurking-place of all sorts
of desperadoes, who in the name of liberty did just
what they pleased. They continually fluctuated in
their numbers. Sailors, deserting ships at other islands,
or in boats at sea anywhere in that vicinity, steered for
Charles's Isle, as to their sure home of refuge ; while,
sated with the life of the isle, numbers from time to
time crossed the water to the neighbouring ones, and
there presenting themselves to strange captains as ship-
wrecked seamen, often succeeded in getting on board
vessels bound to the Spanish coast, and having a compassionate purse made up for them on landing there.

One warm night during my first visit to the group,
our ship was floating along in languid stillness, when
someone on the forecastle shouted, 'Light ho!' We
looked and saw a beacon burning on some obscure land
off the beam. Our third mate was not intimate with
this part of the world. Going to the captain he said,
'Sir, shall I put off in a boat ? These must be ship-
wrecked men.'

The captain laughed rather grimly, as, shaking his
fist toward the beacon, he rapped out an oath, and
said, 'No, no, you precious rascals, you don't juggle
one of my boats ashore this blessed night. You do
well, you thieves—you do benevolently to hoist a light
yonder as on a dangerous shoal. It tempts no wise
man to pull off and see what's the matter, but bids
him steer small and keep off shore—that is Charles's
Island ; brace up, Mr. Mate, and keep the light astern.'

SKETCH EIGHTH

NORFOLK ISLE AND THE CHOLA WIDOW

' At last they in an island did espy
A seemly woman sitting by the shore,
That with great sorrow and sad agony
Seemed some great misfortune to deplore,
And loud to them for succor called evermore.'

' Black his eye as the midnight sky,
White his neck as the driven snow,
Red his cheek as the morning light ;—
Cold he lies in the ground below.
    My love is dead,
    Gone to his death-bed, ys
All under the cactus tree.'

' Each lonely scene shall thee restore,
For thee the tear be duly shed ;
Belov'd till life can charm no more,
And mourned till Pity's self be dead.'

Far to the north-east of Charles's Isle, sequestered from the rest, lies Norfolk Isle ; and, however insignificant to most voyagers, to me, through sympathy, that lone island has become a spot made sacred by the strangest trials of humanity.

It was my first visit to the Encantadas. Two days had been spent ashore in hunting tortoises. There was not time to capture many ; so on the third afternoon we loosed our sails. We were just in the act of getting under way, the uprooted anchor yet suspended and invisibly swaying beneath the wave, as the good ship gradually turned her heel to leave the isle behind, when the seaman who heaved with me at the windlass paused suddenly, and directed my attention to something moving on the land, not along the beach, but somewhat back, fluttering from a height.

In view of the sequel of this little story, be it here narrated how it came to pass, that an object which partly from its being so small was quite lost to every other man on board, still caught the eye of my hand-spike companion. The rest of the crew, myself included, merely stood up to our spikes in heaving, whereas, unwontedly exhilarated, at every turn of the ponderous windlass, my belted comrade leaped atop of it, with might and main giving a downward, thewey, perpendicular heave, his raised eye bent in cheery animation upon the slowly receding shore. Being high lifted above all others was the reason he perceived the object, otherwise unperceivable; and this elevation of his eye was owing to the elevation of his spirits; and this again— for truth must out—to a dram of Peruvian Pisco, in guerdon for some kindness done, secretly administered to him that morning by our mulatto steward. Now, certainly, Pisco does a deal of mischief in the world; yet seeing that, in the present case, it was the means, though indirect, of rescuing a human being from the most dreadful fate, must we not also needs admit that sometimes Pisco does a deal of good?

Glancing across the water in the direction pointed out, I saw some white thing hanging from an inland rock, perhaps half a mile from the sea.

'It is a bird; a white-winged bird; perhaps a—no; it is—it is a handkerchief!'

'Ay, a handkerchief!' echoed my comrade, and with a louder shout apprised the captain.

Quickly now—like the running out and training of a great gun—the long cabin spy-glass was thrust through the mizen-rigging from the high platform of the poop; whereupon a human figure was plainly seen upon the inland rock, eagerly waving toward us what seemed to be the handkerchief.

Our captain was a prompt, good fellow. Dropping the glass, he lustily ran forward, ordering the anchor to be dropped again ; hands to stand by a boat, and lower away.

In a half-hour's time the swift boat returned. It went with six and came with seven ; and the seventh was a woman.

It is not artistic heartlessness, but I wish I could but draw in crayons ; for this woman was a most touching sight ; and crayons, tracing softly melancholy lines, would best depict the mournful image of the dark-damasked Chola widow.

Her story was soon told, and though given in her own strange language was as quickly understood ; for our captain, from long trading on the Chilian coast, was well versed in the Spanish. A Cholo, or half-breed Indian woman of Payta in Peru, three years gone by, with her young new-wedded husband Felipe, of pure Castilian blood, and her one only Indian brother, Truxill, Hunilla had taken passage on the main in a French whaler, commanded by a joyous man ; which vessel, bound to the cruising-grounds beyond the Enchanted Isles, proposed passing close by their vicinity. The object of the little party was to procure tortoise oil, a fluid which for its great purity and delicacy is held in high estimation wherever known ; and it is well known all along this part of the Pacific coast. With a chest of clothes, tools, cooking utensils, a rude apparatus for trying out the oil, some casks of biscuit, and other things, not omitting two favourite dogs, of which faithful animal all the Cholos are very fond, Hunilla and her companions were safely landed at their chosen place ; the Frenchman, according to the contract made ere sailing, engaged to take them off upon returning from a four months' cruise in the westward seas ; which

interval the three adventurers deemed quite sufficient
for their purposes.

On the isle's lone beach they paid him in silver for
their passage out, the stranger having declined to carry
them at all except upon that condition ; though willing
to take every means to ensure the due fulfilment of his
promise.   Felipe had striven hard to have this payment
put off to the period of the ship's return.   But in vain.
Still they thought they had, in another way, ample
pledge of the good faith of the Frenchman.   It was
arranged that the expenses of the passage home should
not be payable in silver, but in tortoises ;   one hundred
tortoises ready captured to the returning captain's hand.
These the Cholos meant to secure after their own work
was done, against the probable time of the Frenchman's coming back ;   and no doubt in prospect already
felt, that in those hundred tortoises—now somewhere
ranging the isle's interior—they possessed one hundred
hostages.   Enough : the vessel sailed ;   the gazing three
on shore answered the loud glee of the singing crew ;
and ere evening, the French craft was hull down in the
distant sea, its masts three faintest lines which quickly
faded from Hunilla's eye.

The stranger had given a blithesome promise, and
anchored it with oaths ;   but oaths and anchors equally
will drag ;   naught else abides on fickle earth but unkept
promises of joy.   Contrary winds from out unstable
skies, or contrary moods of his more varying mind, or
shipwreck and sudden death in solitary waves ;   whatever
was the cause, the blithe stranger never was seen again.

Yet, however dire a calamity was here in store, misgivings of it ere due time never disturbed the Cholos'
busy mind, now all intent upon the toilsome matter
which had brought them hither.   Nay, by swift doom
coming like a thief at night, ere seven weeks went by,

two of the little party were removed from all anxieties of land or sea. No more they sought to gaze with feverish fear, or still more feverish hope, beyond the present's horizon line ; but into the furthest future their own silent spirits sailed. By persevering labour beneath that burning sun, Felipe and Truxill had brought down to their hut many scores of tortoises, and tried out the oil, when, elated with their good success, and to reward themselves for such hard work, they, too hastily, made a catamaran, or Indian raft, much used on the Spanish main, and merrily started on a fishing trip, just without a long reef with many jagged gaps, running parallel with the shore, about half a mile from it. By some bad tide or hap, or natural negligence of joyfulness (for though they could not be heard, yet by their gestures they seemed singing at the time) forced in deep water against that iron bar, the ill-made catamaran was overset, and came all to pieces ; when dashed by broad-chested swells between their broken logs and the sharp teeth of the reef, both adventurers perished before Hunilla's eyes.

Before Hunilla's eyes they sank. The real woe of this event passed before her sight as some sham tragedy on the stage. She was seated on a rude bower among the withered thickets, crowning a lofty cliff, a little back from the beach. The thickets were so disposed, that in looking upon the sea at large she peered out from among the branches as from the lattice of a high balcony. But upon the day we speak of here, the better to watch the adventure of those two hearts she loved, Hunilla had withdrawn the branches to one side, and held them so. They formed an oval frame, through which the bluely boundless sea rolled like a painted one. And there, the invisible painter painted to her view the wave-tossed and disjointed raft, its once level logs slantingly upheaved, as raking masts, and the four struggling arms undistinguishable among them; and then all subsided into smooth-flowing creamy waters, slowly drifting the splintered wreck; while first and last, no sound of any sort was heard. Death in a silent picture; a dream of the eye; such vanishing shapes as the mirage shows.

So instant was the scene, so trance-like its mild pictorial effect, so distant from her blasted bower and her common sense of things, that Hunilla gazed and gazed, nor raised a finger or a wail. But as good to sit thus dumb, in stupor staring on that dumb show, for all that otherwise might be done. With half a mile of sea between, how could her two enchanted arms aid those four fated ones? The distance long, the time one sand. After the lightning is beheld, what fool shall stay the thunder-bolt? Felipe's body was washed ashore, but Truxill's never came; only his gay, braided hat of golden straw—that same sunflower thing he waved to her, pushing from the strand—and now, to the last gallant, it still saluted her. But Felipe's body floated to the marge, with one arm encirclingly outstretched. Lock-jawed in grim death, the lover-husband softly clasped his bride, true to her even in death's dream. Ah, heaven, when man thus keeps his faith, wilt thou be faithless who created the faithful one? But they cannot break faith who never plighted it.

It needs not to be said what nameless misery now wrapped the lonely widow. In telling her own story she passed this almost entirely over, simply recounting the event. Construe the comment of her features as you might, from her mere words little would you have weened that Hunilla was herself the heroine of her tale. But not thus did she defraud us of our tears. All hearts bled that grief could be so brave.

She but showed us her soul's lid, and the strange
ciphers thereon engraved; all within, with pride's
timidity, was withheld. Yet was there one exception.
Holding out her small olive hand before our captain,
she said in mild and slowest Spanish, 'Señor, I buried
him'; then paused, struggled as against the writhed
coilings of a snake, and cringing suddenly, leaped up,
repeating in impassioned pain, 'I buried him, my life,
my soul!'

Doubtless, it was by half-unconscious, automatic
motions of her hands, that this heavy-hearted one
performed the final office for Felipe, and planted a rude
cross of withered sticks—no green ones might be had—
at the head of that lonely grave, where rested now in
lasting uncomplaint and quiet haven he whom un-
tranquil seas had overthrown.

But some dull sense of another body that should be
interred, of another cross that should hallow another
grave—unmade as yet—some dull anxiety and pain
touching her undiscovered brother, now haunted the
oppressed Hunilla. Her hands fresh from the burial
earth, she slowly went back to the beach, with unshaped
purposes wandering there, her spell-bound eye bent upon
the incessant waves. But they bore nothing to her but
a dirge, which maddened her to think that murderers
should mourn. As time went by, and these things
came less dreamingly to her mind, the strong persuasions
of her Romish faith, which sets peculiar store by conse-
crated urns, prompted her to resume in waking earnest
that pious search which had but been begun as in
somnambulism. Day after day, week after week, she
trod the cindery beach, till at length a double motive
edged every eager glance. With equal longing she now
looked for the living and the dead; the brother and
the captain; alike vanished, never to return. Little

P

accurate note of time had Hunilla taken under such
emotions as were hers, and little, outside herself, served
for calendar or dial. As to poor Crusoe in the self-same
sea, no saint's bell pealed forth the lapse of week or
month ; each day went by unchallenged ; no chanticleer
announced those sultry dawns, no lowing herds those
poisonous nights. All wonted and steadily recurring
sounds, human, or humanised by sweet fellowship with
man, but one stirred that torrid trance—the cry of
dogs ; save which naught but the rolling sea invaded
it, an all-pervading monotone ; and to the widow that
was the least loved voice she could have heard.

No wonder, that as her thoughts now wandered to the
unreturning ship, and were beaten back again, the hope
against hope so struggled in her soul, that at length
she desperately said, ' Not yet, not yet ; my foolish
heart runs on too fast.' So she forced patience for
some further weeks. But to those whom earth's sure
indraft draws, patience or impatience is still the same.

Hunilla now sought to settle precisely in her mind,
to an hour, how long it was since the ship had sailed ;
and then, with the same precision, how long a space
remained to pass. But this proved impossible. What
present day or month it was she could not say. Time
was her labyrinth, in which Hunilla was entirely
lost.

And now follows——

Against my own purposes a pause descends upon me
here. One knows not whether nature doth not impose
some secrecy upon him who has been privy to certain
things. At least, it is to be doubted whether it be good
to blazon such. If some books are deemed most baneful
and their sale forbid, how, then, with deadlier facts, not
dreams of doting men ? Those whom books will hurt
will not be proof against events. Events, not books,

should be forbid. But in all things man sows upon the wind, which bloweth just there whither it listeth ; for ill or good, man cannot know. Often ill comes from the good, as good from ill.

When Hunilla——

Dire sight it is to see some silken beast long dally with a golden lizard ere she devour. More terrible, to see how feline Fate will sometimes dally with a human soul, and by a nameless magic make it repulse a sane despair with a hope which is but mad. Unwittingly I imp this cat-like thing, sporting with the heart of him who reads ; for if he feel not he reads in vain.

—' The ship sails this day, to-day,' at last said Hunilla to herself ; ' this gives me certain time to stand on ; without certainty I go mad. In loose ignorance I have hoped and hoped ; now in firm knowledge I will but wait. Now I live and no longer perish in bewilderings. Holy Virgin, aid me ! Thou wilt waft back the ship. Oh, past length of weary weeks—all to be dragged over—to buy the certainty of to-day, I freely give ye, though I tear ye from me ! '

As mariners, tossed in tempest on some desolate ledge, patch them a boat out of the remnants of their vessel's wreck, and launch it in the self-same waves, see here Hunilla, this lone ship-wrecked soul, out of treachery invoking trust. Humanity, thou strong thing, I worship thee, not in the laurelled victor, but in this vanquished one.

Truly Hunilla leaned upon a reed, a real one ; no metaphor ; a real Eastern reed. A piece of hollow cane, drifted from unknown isles, and found upon the beach, its once jagged ends rubbed smoothly even as by sandpaper ; its golden glazing gone. Long ground between the sea and land, upper and nether stone, the unvarnished substance was filed bare, and wore another polish now, one with itself, the polish of its agony. Circular lines at intervals cut all round this surface, divided it into six panels of unequal length. In the first were scored the days, each tenth one marked by a longer and deeper notch ; the second was scored for the number of sea-fowl eggs for sustenance, picked out from the rocky nests ; the third, how many fish had been caught from the shore ; the fourth, how many small tortoises found inland ; the fifth, how many days of sun ; the sixth, of clouds ; which last, of the two, was the greater one. Long night of busy numbering, misery's mathematics, to weary her too-wakeful soul to sleep ; yet sleep for that was none.

The panel of the days was deeply worn—the long tenth notches half effaced, as alphabets of the blind. Ten thousand times the longing widow had traced her finger over the bamboo—dull flute, which played on, gave no sound—as if counting birds flown by in air would hasten tortoises creeping through the woods.

After the one hundred and eightieth day no further mark was seen ; that last one was the faintest, as the first the deepest.

'There were more days,' said our captain ; 'many, many more ; why did you not go on and notch them, too, Hunilla ? '

' Señor, ask me not.'

' And meantime, did no other vessel pass the isle ? '

' Nay, señor ;—but——'

' You do not speak ; but *what*, Hunilla ? '

' Ask me not, señor.'

' You saw ships pass, far away ; you waved to them ; they passed on ;—was that it, Hunilla ? '

' Señor, be it as you say.'

Braced against her woe, Hunilla would not, durst not

trust the weakness of her tongue. Then when our captain asked whether any whale-boats had——

But no, I will not file this thing complete for scoffing souls to quote, and call it firm proof upon their side. The half shall here remain untold. Those two unnamed events which befell Hunilla on this isle, let them abide between her and her God. In nature, as in law, it may be libellous to speak some truths.

Still, how it was that, although our vessel had lain three days anchored nigh the isle, its one human tenant should not have discovered us till just upon the point of sailing, never to revisit so lone and far a spot, this needs explaining ere the sequel come.

The place where the French captain had landed the little party was on the further and opposite end of the isle. There, too, it was that they had afterward built their hut. Nor did the widow in her solitude desert the spot where her loved ones had dwelt with her, and where the dearest of the twain now slept his last long sleep, and all her plaints awaked him not, and he of husbands the most faithful during life.

Now, high broken land rises between the opposite extremities of the isle. A ship anchored at one side is invisible from the other. Neither is the isle so small, but a considerable company might wander for days through the wilderness of one side, and never be seen, or their halloos heard, by any stranger holding aloof on the other. Hence Hunilla, who naturally associated the possible coming of ships with her own part of the isle, might to the end have remained quite ignorant of the presence of our vessel, were it not for a mysterious presentiment, borne to her, so our mariners averred, by this isle's enchanted air. Nor did the widow's answer undo the thought.

'How did you come to cross the isle this morning, then, Hunilla ? ' said our captain.

'Señor, something came flitting by me. It touched my cheek, my heart, señor.'

'What do you say, Hunilla ? '

'I have said, señor, something came through the air.'

It was a narrow chance. For when in crossing the isle Hunilla gained the high land in the centre, she must then for the first have perceived our masts, and also marked that their sails were being loosed, perhaps even heard the echoing chorus of the windlass song. The strange ship was about to sail, and she behind. With all haste she now descends the height on the hither side, but soon loses sight of the ship among the sunken jungles at the mountain's base. She struggles on through the withered branches, which seek at every step to bar her path, till she comes to the isolated rock, still some way from the water. This she climbs, to re-assure herself. The ship is still in plainest sight. But now, worn out with over-tension, Hunilla all but faints ; she fears to step down from her giddy perch ; she is fain to pause, there where she is, and as a last resort catches the turban from her head, unfurls and waves it over the jungles toward us.

During the telling of her story the mariners formed a voiceless circle round Hunilla and the captain ; and when at length the word was given to man the fastest boat, and pull round to the isle's thither side, to bring away Hunilla's chest and the tortoise-oil, such alacrity of both cheery and sad obedience seldom before was seen. Little ado was made. Already the anchor had been recommitted to the bottom, and the ship swung calmly to it.

But Hunilla insisted upon accompanying the boat

as indispensable pilot to her hidden hut. So being refreshed with the best the steward could supply, she started with us. Nor did ever any wife of the most famous admiral, in her husband's barge, receive more silent reverence of respect than poor Hunilla from this boat's crew.

Rounding many a vitreous cape and bluff, in two hours' time we shot inside the fatal reef ; wound into a secret cove, looked up along a green many-gabled lava wall, and saw the island's solitary dwelling.

It hung upon an impending cliff, sheltered on two sides by tangled thickets, and half screened from view in front by juttings of the rude stairway, which climbed the precipice from the sea. Built of canes, it was thatched with long, mildewed grass. It seemed an abandoned hay-rick, whose haymakers were now no more. The roof inclined but one way ; the eaves coming to within two feet of the ground. And here was a simple apparatus to collect the dews, or rather doubly distilled and finest winnowed rains, which, in mercy or in mockery, the night-skies sometimes drop upon these blighted Encantadas. All along beneath the eaves, a spotted sheet, quite weather-stained, was spread, pinned to short, upright stakes, set in the shallow sand. A small clinker, thrown into the cloth, weighed its middle down, thereby straining all moisture into a calabash placed below. This vessel supplied each drop of water ever drunk upon the isle by the Cholos. Hunilla told us the calabash would sometimes, but not often, be half filled overnight. It held six quarts, perhaps. ' But,' said she, ' we were used to thirst. At sandy Payta, where I live, no shower from heaven ever fell ; all the water there is brought on mules from the inland vales.'

Tied among the thickets were some twenty moaning tortoises, supplying Hunilla's lonely larder ; while hundreds of vast tableted black bucklers, like displaced, shattered tombstones of dark slate, were also scattered round. These were the skeleton backs of those great tortoises from which Felipe and Truxill had made their precious oil. Several large calabashes and two goodly kegs were filled with it. In a pot near by were the caked crusts of a quantity which had been permitted to evaporate. 'They meant to have strained it off next day,' said Hunilla, as she turned aside.

I forgot to mention the most singular sight of all, though the first that greeted us after landing.

Some ten small, soft-haired, ringleted dogs, of a beautiful breed, peculiar to Peru, set up a concert of glad welcomings when we gained the beach, which was responded to by Hunilla. Some of these dogs had, since her widowhood, been born upon the isle, the progeny of the two brought from Payta. Owing to the jagged steeps and pitfalls, tortuous thickets, sunken clefts, and perilous intricacies of all sorts in the interior, Hunilla, admonished by the loss of one favourite among them, never allowed these delicate creatures to follow her in her occasional birds'-nests climbs and other wanderings; so that, through long habituation, they offered not to follow, when that morning she crossed the land, and her own soul was then too full of other things to heed their lingering behind. Yet, all along she had so clung to them, that, besides what moisture they lapped up at early daybreak from the small scoop-holes among the adjacent rocks, she had shared the dew of her calabash among them; never laying by any considerable store against those prolonged and utter droughts which, in some disastrous seasons, warp these isles.

Having pointed out, at our desire, what few things she would like transported to the ship—her chest, the

oil, not omitting the live tortoises which she intended
for a grateful present to our captain—we immediately
set to work, carrying them to the boat down the long,
sloping stair of deeply shadowed rock. While my
comrades were thus employed, I looked and Hunilla had
disappeared.

It was not curiosity alone, but, it seems to me, something different mingled with it, which prompted me to
drop my tortoise, and once more gaze slowly around.
I remembered the husband buried by Hunilla's hands.
A narrow pathway led into a dense part of the thickets.
Following it through many mazes, I came out upon a
small, round, open space, deeply chambered there.

The mound rose in the middle ; a bare heap of finest
sand, like that unverdured heap found at the bottom
of an hour-glass run out. At its head stood the cross
of withered sticks ; the dry, peeled bark still fraying
from it ; its transverse limb tied up with rope, and
forlornly adroop in the silent air.

Hunilla was partly prostrate upon the grave ; her
dark head bowed, and lost in her long, loosened Indian
hair ; her hands extended to the cross-foot, with a little
brass crucifix clasped between ; a crucifix worn feature-
less, like an ancient graven knocker long plied in vain.
She did not see me, and I made no noise, but slid aside,
and left the spot.

A few moments ere all was ready for our going, she
reappeared among us. I looked into her eyes, but
saw no tear. There was something which seemed
strangely haughty in her air, and yet it was the air of
woe. A Spanish and an Indian grief, which would not
visibly lament. Pride's height in vain abased to proneness on the rack ; nature's pride subduing nature's
torture.

Like pages the small and silken dogs surrounded her,

as she slowly descended toward the beach. She caught the two most eager creatures in her arms :—' Mia Teeta ! Mia Tomoteeta ! ' and fondling them, inquired how many could we take on board.

The mate commanded the boat's crew ; not a hard-hearted man, but his way of life had been such that in most things, even in the smallest, simple utility was his leading motive.

' We cannot take them all, Hunilla ; our supplies are short ; the winds are unreliable ; we may be a good many days going to Tombez. So take those you have, Hunilla ; but no more.'

She was in the boat ; the oarsmen, too, were seated ; all save one, who stood ready to push off and then spring himself. With the sagacity of their race, the dogs now seemed aware that they were in the very instant of being deserted upon a barren strand. The gunwales of the boat were high ; its prow—presented inland—was lifted ; so owing to the water, which they seemed instinctively to shun, the dogs could not well leap into the little craft. But their busy paws hard scraped the prow, as it had been some farmer's door shutting them out from shelter in a winter storm. A clamorous agony of alarm. They did not howl, or whine ; they all but spoke.

' Push off ! Give way ! ' cried the mate. The boat gave one heavy drag and lurch, and next moment shot swiftly from the beach, turned on her heel, and sped. The dogs ran howling along the water's marge ; now pausing to gaze at the flying boat, then motioning as if to leap in chase, but mysteriously withheld themselves ; and again ran howling along the beach. Had they been human beings, hardly would they have more vividly inspired the sense of desolation. The oars were plied as confederate feathers of two wings. No one spoke.

I looked back upon the beach, and then upon Hunilla, but her face was set in a stern dusky calm. The dogs crouching in her lap vainly licked her rigid hands. She never looked behind her; but sat motionless, till we turned a promontory of the coast and lost all sights and sounds astern. She seemed as one who, having experienced the sharpest of mortal pangs, was henceforth content to have all lesser heartstrings riven, one by one. To Hunilla, pain seemed so necessary, that pain in other beings, though by love and sympathy made her own, was unrepiningly to be borne. A heart of yearning in a frame of steel. A heart of earthly yearning, frozen by the frost which falleth from the sky.

The sequel is soon told. After a long passage, vexed by calms and baffling winds, we made the little port of Tombez in Peru, there to recruit the ship. Payta was not very distant. Our captain sold the tortoise oil to a Tombez merchant; and adding to the silver a contribution from all hands, gave it to our silent passenger, who knew not what the mariners had done.

The last seen of lone Hunilla she was passing into Payta town, riding upon a small gray ass; and before her on the ass's shoulders, she eyed the jointed workings of the beast's armorial cross.

SKETCH NINTH

HOOD'S ISLE AND THE HERMIT OBERLUS

'That darkesome glen they enter, where they find
That cursed man low sitting on the ground,
Musing full sadly in his sullein mind;
His griesly lockes long grouen and unbound,
Disordered hong about his shoulders round,
And hid his face, through which his hollow eyne
Lookt deadly dull, and stared as astound;
His raw-bone cheekes, through penurie and pine,
Were shronke into the jawes, as he did never dine
His garments nought but many ragged clouts,
With thornes together pind and patched reads,
The which his naked sides he wrapt abouts.'

South-east of Crossman's Isle lies Hood's Isle, or McCain's Beclouded Isle; and upon its south side is a vitreous cove with a wide strand of dark pounded black lava, called Black Beach, or Oberlus's Landing. It might fitly have been styled Charon's.

It received its name from a wild white creature who spent many years here; in the person of a European bringing into this savage region qualities more diabolical than are to be found among any of the surrounding cannibals.

About half a century ago, Oberlus deserted at the above-named island, then, as now, a solitude. He built himself a den of lava and clinkers, about a mile from the Landing, subsequently called after him, in a vale, or expanded gulch, containing here and there among the rocks about two acres of soil capable of rude cultivation; the only place on the isle not too blasted for that purpose. Here he succeeded in raising a sort of degenerate potatoes and pumpkins, which from time to time he exchanged with needy whalemen passing, for spirits or dollars.

His appearance, from all accounts, was that of the victim of some malignant sorceress ; he seemed to have drunk of Circe's cup ; beastlike ; rags insufficient to hide his nakedness ; his befreckled skin blistered by continual exposure to the sun ; nose flat ; countenance contorted, heavy, earthy ; hair and beard unshorn, profuse, and of fiery red. He struck strangers much as if he were a volcanic creature thrown up by the same convulsion which exploded into sight the isle. All be-patched and coiled asleep in his lonely lava den among the mountains, he looked, they say, as a heaped drift of withered leaves, torn from autumn trees, and so left in some hidden nook by the whirling halt for an instant of a fierce night-wind, which then ruthlessly sweeps on, somewhere else to repeat the capricious act. It is also reported to have been the strangest sight, this same Oberlus, of a sultry, cloudy morning, hidden under his shocking old black tarpaulin hat, hoeing potatoes among the lava. So warped and crooked was his strange nature, that the very handle of his hoe seemed gradually to have shrunk and twisted in his grasp, being a wretched bent stick, elbowed more like a savage's war-sickle than a civilised hoe-handle. It was his mysterious custom upon a first encounter with a stranger ever to present his back ; possibly, because that was his better side, since it revealed the least. If the encounter chanced in his garden, as it sometimes did—the new-landed strangers going from the seaside straight through the gorge, to hunt up the queer greengrocer reported doing business here—Oberlus for a time hoed on, unmindful of all greeting, jovial or bland ; as the curious stranger would turn to face him, the recluse, hoe in hand, as diligently would avert himself ; bowed over, and sullenly revolving round his murphy hill. Thus far for hoeing. When planting, his whole aspect and all his gestures were so malevolently and uselessly sinister and secret, that he seemed rather in act of dropping poison into wells than potatoes into soil. But among his lesser and more harmless marvels was an idea he ever had, that his visitors came equally as well led by longings to behold the mighty hermit Oberlus in his royal state of solitude, as simply to obtain potatoes, or find whatever company might be upon a barren isle. It seems incredible that such a being should possess such vanity; a misanthrope be conceited; but he really had his notion; and upon the strength of it, often gave himself amusing airs to captains. But after all, this is somewhat of a piece with the well-known eccentricity of some convicts, proud of that very hatefulness which makes them notorious. At other times, another unaccountable whim would seize him, and he would long dodge advancing strangers round the clinkered corners of his hut; sometimes like a stealthy bear, he would slink through the withered thickets up the mountains, and refuse to see the human face.

Except his occasional visitors from the sea, for a long period, the only companions of Oberlus were the crawling tortoises; and he seemed more than degraded to their level, having no desires for a time beyond theirs, unless it were for the stupor brought on by drunkenness. But sufficiently debased as he appeared, there yet lurked in him, only awaiting occasion for discovery, a still further proneness. Indeed, the sole superiority of Oberlus over the tortoises was his possession of a larger capacity of degradation; and along with that, something like an intelligent will to it. Moreover, what is about to be revealed, perhaps will show, that selfish ambition, or the love of rule for its own sake, far from being the peculiar infirmity of noble minds, is shared by beings which have no mind at all. No creatures are so selfishly tyrannical as some brutes ; as anyone who has observed the tenants of the pasture must occasionally have observed.

'This island's mine by Sycorax my mother,' said Oberlus to himself, glaring round upon his haggard solitude. By some means, barter or theft—for in those days ships at intervals still kept touching at his Landing—he obtained an old musket, with a few charges of powder and ball. Possessed of arms, he was stimulated to enterprise, as a tiger that first feels the coming of its claws. The long habit of sole dominion over every object round him, his almost unbroken solitude, his never encountering humanity except on terms of misanthropic independence, or mercantile craftiness, and even such encounters being comparatively but rare ; all this must have gradually nourished in him a vast idea of his own importance, together with a pure animal sort of scorn for all the rest of the universe.

The unfortunate Creole, who enjoyed his brief term of royalty at Charles's Isle, was perhaps in some degree influenced by not unworthy motives ; such as prompt other adventurous spirits to lead colonists into distant regions and assume political pre-eminence over them. His summary execution of many of his Peruvians is quite pardonable, considering the desperate characters he had to deal with ; while his offering canine battle to the banded rebels seems under the circumstances altogether just. But for this King Oberlus and what shortly follows, no shade of palliation can be given. He acted out of mere delight in tyranny and cruelty, by virtue of a quality in him inherited from Sycorax his mother. Armed now with that shocking blunderbuss, strong in the thought of being master of that horrid isle, he panted for a chance to prove his potency upon the first specimen of humanity which should fall unbefriended into his hands.

Nor was he long without it. One day he spied a boat upon the beach, with one man, a negro, standing by it. Some distance off was a ship, and Oberlus immediately knew how matters stood. The vessel had put in for wood, and the boat's crew had gone into the thickets for it. From a convenient spot he kept watch of the boat, till presently a straggling company appeared loaded with billets. Throwing these on the beach, they again went into the thickets, while the negro proceeded to load the boat.

Oberlus now makes all haste and accosts the negro, who, aghast at seeing any living being inhabiting such a solitude, and especially so horrific a one, immediately falls into a panic, not at all lessened by the ursine suavity of Oberlus, who begs the favour of assisting him in his labours. The negro stands with several billets on his shoulder, in act of shouldering others ; and Oberlus, with a short cord concealed in his bosom, kindly proceeds to lift those other billets to their place. In so doing, he persists in keeping behind the negro, who, rightly suspicious of this, in vain dodges about to gain the front of Oberlus ; but Oberlus dodges also ; till at last, weary of this bootless attempt at treachery, or fearful of being surprised by the remainder of the party, Oberlus runs off a little space to a bush, and fetching his blunderbuss, savagely commands the negro to desist work and follow him. He refuses. Whereupon, presenting his piece, Oberlus snaps at him. Luckily the blunderbuss misses fire ; but by this time, frightened out of his wits, the negro, upon a second intrepid summons, drops his billets, surrenders at discretion, and follows on. By a narrow defile familiar to him, Oberlus speedily removes out of sight of the water.

On their way up the mountains, he exultingly informs
the negro, that henceforth he is to work for him, and be
his slave, and that his treatment would entirely depend
on his future conduct. But Oberlus, deceived by the
first impulsive cowardice of the black, in an evil moment
slackens his vigilance. Passing through a narrow way,
and perceiving his leader quite off his guard, the negro,
a powerful fellow, suddenly grasps him in his arms,
throws him down, wrests his musketoon from him, ties
his hands with the monster's own cord, shoulders him,
and returns with him down to the boat. When the rest
of the party arrive, Oberlus is carried on board the ship.
This proved an Englishman, and a smuggler; a sort of
craft not apt to be over-charitable. Oberlus is severely
whipped, then handcuffed, taken ashore, and compelled
to make known his habitation and produce his property.
His potatoes, pumpkins, and tortoises, with a pile of
dollars he had hoarded from his mercantile operations,
were secured on the spot. But while the too vindictive
smugglers were busy destroying his hut and garden,
Oberlus makes his escape into the mountains, and conceals himself there in impenetrable recesses, only known
to himself, till the ship sails, when he ventures back,
and by means of an old file which he sticks into a tree,
contrives to free himself from his handcuffs.

Brooding among the ruins of his hut, and the desolate
clinkers and extinct volcanoes of this outcast isle, the
insulted misanthrope now meditates a signal revenge
upon humanity, but conceals his purposes. Vessels still
touch the Landing at times; and by and by Oberlus is
enabled to supply them with some vegetables.

Warned by his former failure in kidnapping strangers,
he now pursues a quite different plan. When seamen
come ashore, he makes up to them like a free-and-easy
comrade, invites them to his hut, and with whatever

Q

affability his red-haired grimness may assume, entreats
them to drink his liquor and be merry. But his guests
need little pressing ; and so, soon as rendered insensible,
are tied hand and foot, and pitched among the clinkers,
are there concealed till the ship departs, when, finding
themselves entirely dependent upon Oberlus, alarmed
at his changed demeanour, his savage threats, and
above all, that shocking blunderbuss, they willingly
enlist under him, becoming his humble slaves, and
Oberlus the most incredible of tyrants. So much so,
that two or three perish beneath his initiating process.
He sets the remainder—four of them—to breaking the
caked soil ; transporting upon their backs loads of
loamy earth, scooped up in moist clefts among the mountains ; keeps them on the roughest fare ; presents his
piece at the slightest hint of insurrection ; and in all
respects converts them into reptiles at his feet—plebeian
garter-snakes to this Lord Anaconda.

At last, Oberlus contrives to stock his arsenal with
four rusty cutlasses, and an added supply of powder
and ball intended for his blunderbuss. Remitting in
good part the labour of his slaves, he now approves
himself a man, or rather devil, of great abilities in the
way of cajoling or coercing others into acquiescence
with his own ulterior designs, however at first abhorrent
to them. But indeed, prepared for almost any eventual
evil by their previous lawless life, as a sort of ranging
Cow-Boys of the sea, which had dissolved within them
the whole moral man, so that they were ready to con-
crete in the first offered mould of baseness now ; rotted
down from manhood by their hopeless misery on the
isle ; wonted to cringe in all things to their lord, himself the worst of slaves ; these wretches were now
become wholly corrupted to his hands. He used them
as creatures of an inferior race ; in short, he gaffles his

four animals, and makes murderers of them ; out of cowards fitly manufacturing bravos.

Now, sword or dagger, human arms are but artificial claws and fangs, tied on like false spurs to the fighting cock. So, we repeat, Oberlus, czar of the isle, gaffles his four subjects ; that is, with intent of glory, puts four rusty cutlasses into their hands. Like any other autocrat, he had a noble army now.

It might be thought a servile war would hereupon ensue. Arms in the hands of trodden slaves ? how indiscreet of Emperor Oberlus ! Nay, they had but cutlasses—sad old scythes enough—he a blunderbuss, which by its blind scatterings of all sorts of boulders, clinkers, and other scoria would annihilate all four mutineers, like four pigeons at one shot. Besides, at first he did not sleep in his accustomed hut ; every lurid sunset, for a time, he might have been seen wending his way among the riven mountains, there to secrete himself till dawn in some sulphurous pitfall, undiscoverable to his gang ; but finding this at last too troublesome, he now each evening tied his slaves hand and foot, hid the cutlasses, and thrusting them into his barracks, shut to the door, and lying down before it, beneath a rude shed lately added, slept out the night, blunderbuss in hand.

It is supposed that not content with daily parading over a cindery solitude at the head of his fine army, Oberlus now meditated the most active mischief ; his probable object being to surprise some passing ship touching at his dominions, massacre the crew, and run away with her to parts unknown. While these plans were simmering in his head, two ships touch in company at the isle, on the opposite side to his ; when his designs undergo a sudden change.

The ships are in want of vegetables, which Oberlus

promises in great abundance, provided they send their boats round to his landing, so that the crews may bring the vegetables from his garden ; informing the two captains, at the same time, that his rascals—slaves and soldiers—had become so abominably lazy and good-for-nothing of late, that he could not make them work by ordinary inducements, and did not have the heart to be severe with them.

The arrangement was agreed to, and the boats were sent and hauled upon the beach. The crews went to the lava hut ; but to their surprise nobody was there. After waiting till their patience was exhausted, they returned to the shore, when lo, some stranger—not the Good Samaritan either—seems to have very recently passed that way. Three of the boats were broken in a thousand pieces, and the fourth was missing. By hard toil over the mountains and through the clinkers, some of the strangers succeeded in returning to that side of the isle where the ships lay, when fresh boats are sent to the relief of the rest of the hapless party.

However amazed at the treachery of Oberlus, the two captains, afraid of new and still more mysterious atrocities—and indeed, half imputing such strange events to the enchantments associated with these isles—perceive no security but in instant flight ; leaving Oberlus and his army in quiet possession of the stolen boat.

On the eve of sailing they put a letter in a keg, giving the Pacific Ocean intelligence of the affair, and moored the keg in the bay. Some time subsequent, the keg was opened by another captain chancing to anchor there, but not until after he had dispatched a boat round to Oberlus's Landing. As may be readily surmised, he felt no little inquietude till the boat's return ; when another letter was handed him, giving Oberlus's version of the affair. This precious document had been found pinned half-mildewed to the clinker wall of the sulphurous and deserted hut. It ran as follows : showing that Oberlus was at least an accomplished writer, and no mere boor ; and what is more, was capable of the most trustful eloquence.

' SIR,—I am the most unfortunate ill-treated gentleman that lives. I am a patriot, exiled from my country by the cruel hand of tyranny.

' Banished to these Enchanted Isles, I have again and again besought captains of ships to sell me a boat, but always have been refused, though I offered the handsomest prices in Mexican dollars. At length an opportunity presented of possessing myself of one, and I did not let it slip.

' I have been long endeavouring, by hard labour and much solitary suffering, to accumulate something to make myself comfortable in a virtuous though unhappy old age ; but at various times have been robbed and beaten by men professing to be Christians.

' To-day I sail from the Enchanted group in the good boat *Charity* bound to the Feejee Isles.
'FATHERLESS OBERLUS.

' *P.S.*—Behind the clinkers, nigh the oven, you will find the old fowl. Do not kill it ; be patient ; I leave it setting ; if it shall have any chicks, I hereby bequeath them to you, whoever you may be. But don't count your chicks before they are hatched.'

The fowl proved a starveling rooster, reduced to a sitting posture by sheer debility.

Oberlus declares that he was bound to the Feejee Isles ; but this was only to throw pursuers on a false scent. For, after a long time, he arrived, alone in his open boat, at Guayaquil. As his miscreants were never again beheld on Hood's Isle, it is supposed, either that they perished for want of water on the passage to Guayaquil, or, what is quite as probable, were thrown overboard by Oberlus, when he found the water growing scarce.

From Guayaquil Oberlus proceeded to Payta; and there, with that nameless witchery peculiar to some of the ugliest animals, wound himself into the affections of a tawny damsel; prevailing upon her to accompany him back to his Enchanted Isle; which doubtless he painted as a Paradise of flowers, not a Tartarus of clinkers.

But unfortunately for the colonisation of Hood's Isle with a choice variety of animated nature, the extra-ordinary and devilish aspect of Oberlus made him to be regarded in Payta as a highly suspicious character. So that being found concealed one night, with matches in his pocket, under the hull of a small vessel just ready to be launched, he was seized and thrown into jail.

The jails in most South American towns are generally of the least wholesome sort. Built of huge cakes of sun-burnt brick, and containing but one room, without windows or yard, and but one door heavily grated with wooden bars, they present both within and without the grimmest aspect. As public edifices they con-spicuously stand upon the hot and dusty Plaza, offering to view, through the gratings, their villainous and hope-less inmates, burrowing in all sorts of tragic squalor. And here, for a long time, Oberlus was seen; the central figure of a mongrel and assassin band; a creature whom it is religion to detest, since it is philanthropy to hate a misanthrope.

Note.—They who may be disposed to question the possibility of the character above depicted, are referred to the second volume of Porter's *Voyage into the Pacific*, where they will recognise many sentences, for expedition's sake derived verbatim from thence, and incorporated here; the main difference—save a few passing reflections—between the two accounts being, that the present writer has added to Porter's facts accessory ones picked up in the Pacific from reliable sources; and where facts conflict, has naturally preferred his own authorities to Porter's. As, for instance, *his* authorities place Oberlus on Hood's Isle: Porter's, on Charles's Isle. The letter found in the hut is also somewhat different; for while at the Encantadas he was informed that, not only did it evince a certain clerkliness, but was full of the strangest satiric effontery which does not adequately appear in Porter's version. I accordingly altered it to suit the general character of its author.

SKETCH TENTH

RUNAWAYS, CASTAWAYS, SOLITARIES, GRAVE-STONES, ETC.

' And all about old stocks and stubs of trees,
  Whereon nor fruit nor leaf was ever seen,
  Did hang upon ragged knotty knees,
  On which had many wretches hanged been.'

Some relics of the hut of Oberlus partially remain to
this day at the head of the clinkered valley.   Nor does
the stranger, wandering among other of the Enchanted
Isles, fail to stumble upon still other solitary abodes
long abandoned to the tortoise and the lizard.   Probably
few parts of earth have, in modern times, sheltered so
many solitaries.   The reason is, that these isles are
situated in a distant sea, and the vessels which occasionally visit them are mostly all whalers, or ships bound
on dreary and protracted voyages, exempting them in
a good degree from both the oversight and the memory
of human law.   Such is the character of some commanders
and some seamen, that under these untoward circumstances, it is quite impossible but that scenes of un-
pleasantness and discord should occur between them.
A sullen hatred of the tyrannic ship will seize the sailor,
and he gladly exchanges it for isles, which, though
blighted as by a continual sirocco and burning breeze,
still offer him, in their labyrinthine interior, a retreat
beyond the possibility of capture.   To flee the ship in
any Peruvian or Chilian port, even the smallest and
most rustical, is not unattended with great risk of
apprehension, not to speak of jaguars.   A reward of
five pesos sends fifty dastardly Spaniards into the woods,
who, with long knives, scour them day and night in
eager hopes of securing their prey.   Neither is it, in

general, much easier to escape pursuit at the isles of Polynesia. Those of them which have felt a civilising influence present the same difficulty to the runaway with the Peruvian ports, the advanced natives being quite as mercenary and keen of knife and scent as the retrograde Spaniards; while, owing to the bad odour in which all Europeans lie, in the minds of aboriginal savages who have chanced to hear aught of them, to desert the ship among primitive Polynesians, is, in most cases, a hope not unforlorn. Hence the Enchanted Isles become the voluntary tarrying places of all sorts of refugees; some of whom too sadly experience the fact, that flight from tyranny does not of itself ensure a safe asylum, far less a happy home.

Moreover, it has not seldom happened that hermits have been made upon the isles by the accidents incident to tortoise-hunting. The interior of most of them is tangled and difficult of passage beyond description; the air is sultry and stifling; an intolerable thirst is provoked, for which no running stream offers its kind relief. In a few hours, under an equatorial sun, reduced by these causes to entire exhaustion, woe betide the straggler at the Enchanted Isles! Their extent is such as to forbid an adequate search, unless weeks are devoted to it. The impatient ship waits a day or two; when, the missing man remaining undiscovered, up goes a stake on the beach, with a letter of regret, and a keg of crackers and another of water tied to it, and away sails the craft.

Nor have there been wanting instances where the inhumanity of some captains has led them to wreak a secure revenge upon seamen who have given their caprice or pride some singular offence. Thrust ashore upon the scorching marl, such mariners are abandoned to perish outright, unless by solitary labours they succeed in discovering some precious dribblets of moisture oozing from a rock or stagnant in a mountain pool.

I was well acquainted with a man, who, lost upon the Isle of Narborough, was brought to such extremes by thirst, that at last he only saved his life by taking that of another being. A large hair-seal came upon the beach. He rushed upon it, stabbed it in the neck, and then throwing himself upon the panting body quaffed at the living wound ; the palpitations of the creature's dying heart injected life into the drinker.

Another seaman, thrust ashore in a boat upon an isle at which no ship ever touched, owing to its peculiar sterility and the shoals about it, and from which all other parts of the group were hidden—this man, feeling that it was sure death to remain there, and that nothing worse than death menaced him in quitting it, killed two seals, and inflating their skins, made a float, upon which he transported himself to Charles's Island, and joined the republic there.

But men, not endowed with courage equal to such desperate attempts, find their only resource in forthwith seeking some watering-place, however precarious or scanty ; building a hut ; catching tortoises and birds ; and in all respects preparing for a hermit life, till tide or time, or a passing ship arrives to float them off.

At the foot of precipices on many of the isles, small rude basins in the rocks are found, partly filled with rotted rubbish or vegetable decay, or overgrown with thickets, and sometimes a little moist ; which upon examination, reveal plain tokens of artificial instruments employed in hollowing them out, by some poor castaway or still more miserable runaway. These basins are made in places where it was supposed some scanty drops of dew might exude into them from the upper crevices.

The relics of hermitages and stone basins are not the only signs of vanishing humanity to be found upon the isles. And, curious to say, that spot which of all others in settled communities is most animated, at the Enchanted Isles presents the most dreary of aspects. And though it may seem very strange to talk of post-offices in this barren region, yet post-offices are occasionally to be found there. They consist of a stake and a bottle, the letters being not only sealed but corked. They are generally deposited by captains of Nantucketers for the benefit of passing fishermen, and contain statements as to what luck they had in whaling or tortoise-hunting. Frequently, however, long months and months, whole years glide by and no applicant appears. The stake rots and falls, presenting no very exhilarating object.

If now it be added that grave-stones, or rather grave-boards, are also discovered upon some of the isles, the picture will be complete.

Upon the beach of James's Isle, for many years, was to be seen a rude finger-post, pointing inland. And, perhaps, taking it for some signal of possible hospitality in this otherwise desolate spot—some good hermit living there with his maple dish—the stranger would follow on in the path thus indicated, till at last he would come out in a noiseless nook, and find his only welcome, a dead man—his sole greeting the inscription over a grave. Here, in 1813, fell, in a daybreak duel, a lieutenant of the U.S. frigate *Essex*, aged twenty-one: attaining his majority in death.

It is but fit that, like those old monastic institutions of Europe, whose inmates go not out of their own walls to be inurned, but are entombed there where they die, the Encantadas, too, should bury their own dead, even as the great general monastery of earth does hers.

It is known that burial in the ocean is a pure necessity of seafaring life, and that it is only done when land is far astern, and not clearly visible from the bow. Hence, to vessels cruising in the vicinity of the Enchanted Isles, they afford a convenient Potter's Field. The interment over, some good-natured forecastle poet and artist seizes his paint-brush, and inscribes a doggerel epitaph. When, after a long lapse of time, other good-natured seamen chance to come upon the spot, they usually make a table of the mound, and quaff a friendly can to the poor soul's repose.

As a specimen of these epitaphs, take the following, found in a bleak gorge of Chatham Isle :—

> ' Oh, Brother Jack, as you pass by,
> As you are now, so once was I.
> Just so game, and just so gay,
> But now, alack, they 've stopped my pay.
> No more I peep out of my blinkers,
> Here I be—tucked in with clinkers ! '

THE BELL-TOWER

In the south of Europe, nigh a once frescoed capital, now with dank mould cankering its bloom, central in a plain, stands what, at distance, seems the black mossed stump of some immeasurable pine, fallen in forgotten days, with Anak and the Titan.

As all along where the pine-tree falls, its dissolution leaves a mossy mound—last-flung shadow of the perished trunk ; never lengthening, never lessening ; unsubject to the fleet falsities of the sun ; shade immutable, and true gauge which cometh by prostration—so westward from what seems the stump, one steadfast spear of lichened ruin veins the plain.

From that tree-top, what birded chimes of silver throats had rung. A stone pine ; a metallic aviary in its crown : the Bell-Tower, built by the great mechanician, the unblest foundling, Bannadonna.

Like Babel's, its base was laid in a high hour of renovated earth, following the second deluge, when the waters of the Dark Ages had dried up, and once more the green appeared. No wonder that, after so long and deep submersion, the jubilant expectation of the race should, as with Noah's sons, soar into Shinar aspiration.

In firm resolve, no man in Europe at that period went beyond Bannadonna. Enriched through commerce with the Levant, the state in which he lived voted to have the noblest Bell-Tower in Italy. His repute assigned him to be architect.

Stone by stone, month by month, the tower rose.

Higher, higher ; snail-like in pace, but torch or rocket in its pride.

After the masons would depart, the builder, standing alone upon its ever-ascending summit, at close of every day, saw that he overtopped still higher walls and trees. He would tarry till a late hour there, wrapped in schemes of other and still loftier piles. Those who of saints' days thronged the spot—hanging to the rude poles of scaffolding, like sailors on yards, or bees on boughs, unmindful of lime and dust, and falling chips of stone— their homage not the less inspirited him to self-esteem.

At length the holiday of the Tower came. To the sound of viols, the climax-stone slowly rose in air, and, amid the firing of ordnance, was laid by Bannadonna's hands upon the final course. Then mounting it, he stood erect, alone, with folded arms, gazing upon the white summits of blue inland Alps, and whiter crests of bluer Alps off-shore—sights invisible from the plain. Invisible, too, from thence was that eye he turned below, when, like the cannon booms, came up to him the people's combustions of applause.

That which stirred them so was, seeing with what serenity the builder stood three hundred feet in air, upon an unrailed perch. This none but he durst do. But his periodic standing upon the pile, in each stage of its growth—such discipline had its last result.

Little remained now but the bells. These, in all respects, must correspond with their receptacle.

The minor ones were prosperously cast. A highly enriched one followed, of a singular make, intended for suspension in a manner before unknown. The purpose of this bell, its rotary motion, and connection with the clock-work, also executed at the time, will, in the sequel, receive mention.

In the one erection, bell-tower and clock-tower were

united, though, before that period, such structures had commonly been built distinct ; as the Campanile and Torre del 'Orologio of St. Mark to this day attest.

But it was upon the great state-bell that the founder lavished his more daring skill. In vain did some of the less elated magistrates here caution him ; saying that though truly the tower was Titanic, yet limit should be set to the dependent weight of its swaying masses. But undeterred, he prepared his mammoth mould, dented with mythological devices ; kindled his fires of balsamic firs ; melted his tin and copper, and, throwing in much plate, contributed by the public spirit of the nobles, let loose the tide.

The unleashed metals bayed like hounds. The workmen shrunk. Through their fright, fatal harm to the bell was dreaded. Fearless as Shadrach, Bannadonna, rushing through the glow, smote the chief culprit with his ponderous ladle. From the smitten part, a splinter was dashed into the seething mass, and at once was melted in.

Next day a portion of the work was heedfully uncovered. All seemed right. Upon the third morning, with equal satisfaction, it was bared still lower. At length, like some old Theban king, the whole cooled casting was disinterred. All was fair except in one strange spot. But as he suffered no one to attend him in these inspections, he concealed the blemish by some preparation which none knew better to devise.

The casting of such a mass was deemed no small triumph for the caster ; one, too, in which the state might not scorn to share. The homicide was overlooked. By the charitable that deed was but imputed to sudden transports of aesthetic passion, not to any flagitious quality. A kick from an Arabian charger ; not sign of vice, but blood.

His felony remitted by the judge, absolution given

him by the priest, what more could even a sickly conscience have desired.

Honouring the tower and its builder with another holiday, the republic witnessed the hoisting of the bells and clock-work amid shows and pomps superior to the former.

Some months of more than usual solitude on Bannadonna's part ensued. It was not unknown that he was engaged upon something for the belfry, intended to complete it, and surpass all that had gone before. Most people imagined that the design would involve a casting like the bells. But those who thought they had some further insight, would shake their heads, with hints, that not for nothing did the mechanician keep so secret. Meantime, his seclusion failed not to invest his work with more or less of that sort of mystery pertaining to the forbidden.

Ere long he had a heavy object hoisted to the belfry, wrapped in a dark sack or cloak—a procedure sometimes had in the case of an elaborate piece of sculpture, or statue, which, being intended to grace the front of a new edifice, the architect does not desire exposed to critical eyes, till set up, finished, in its appointed place. Such was the impression now. But, as the object rose, a statuary present observed, or thought he did, that it was not entirely rigid, but was, in a manner, pliant. At last, when the hidden thing had attained its final height, and, obscurely seen from below, seemed almost of itself to step into the belfry, as if with little assistance from the crane, a shrewd old blacksmith present ventured the suspicion that it was but a living man. This surmise was thought a foolish one, while the general interest failed not to augment.

Not without demur from Bannadonna, the chief magistrate of the town, with an associate—both elderly men—followed what seemed the image up the tower. But, arrived at the belfry, they had little recompense. Plausibly entrenching himself behind the conceded mysteries of his art, the mechanician withheld present explanation. The magistrates glanced toward the cloaked object, which, to their surprise, seemed now to have changed its attitude, or else had before been more perplexingly concealed by the violent muffling action of the wind without. It seemed now seated upon some sort of frame, or chair, contained within the domino. They observed that nigh the top, in a sort of square, the web of the cloth, either from accident or design, had its warp partly withdrawn, and the cross threads plucked out here and there, so as to form a sort of woven grating. Whether it were the low wind or no, stealing through the stone lattice-work, or only their own perturbed imaginations, is uncertain, but they thought they discerned a slight sort of fitful, spring-like motion, in the domino. Nothing, however incidental or insignificant, escaped their uneasy eyes. Among other things, they pried out, in a corner, an earthen cup, partly corroded and partly encrusted, and one whispered to the other, that this cup was just such a one as might, in mockery, be offered to the lips of some brazen statue, or, perhaps, still worse.

But, being questioned, the mechanician said, that the cup was simply used in his founder's business, and described the purpose; in short, a cup to test the condition of metals in fusion. He added, that it had got into the belfry by the merest chance.

Again, and again, they gazed at the domino, as at some suspicious incognito at a Venetian mask. All sorts of vague apprehensions stirred them. They even dreaded lest, when they should descend, the mechanician, though without a flesh and blood companion, for all that, would not be left alone.

R

Affecting some merriment at their disquietude, he begged to relieve them, by extending a coarse sheet of workman's canvas between them and the object.

Meantime he sought to interest them in his other work ; nor, now that the domino was out of sight, did they long remain insensible to the artistic wonders lying round them ; wonders hitherto beheld but in their unfinished state ; because, since hoisting the bells, none but the caster had entered within the belfry. It was one trait of his, that, even in details, he would not let another do what he could, without too great loss of time, accomplish for himself. So, for several preceding weeks, whatever hours were unemployed in his secret design, had been devoted to elaborating the figures on the bells.

The clock-bell, in particular, now drew attention. Under a patient chisel, the latent beauty of its enrichments, before obscured by the cloudings incident to casting, that beauty in its shyest grace, was now revealed. Round and round the bell, twelve figures of gay girls, garlanded, hand-in-hand, danced in a choral ring—the embodied hours.

' Bannadonna,' said the chief, ' this bell excels all else. No added touch could here improve. Hark ! ' hearing a sound, ' was that the wind ? '

' The wind, Excellenza,' was the light response. ' But the figures, they are not yet without their faults. They need some touches yet. When those are given, and the—block yonder,' pointing toward the canvas screen, ' when Haman there, as I merrily call him,—him ? *it*, I mean—when Haman is fixed on this, his lofty tree, then, gentlemen, will I be most happy to receive you here again.'

The equivocal reference to the object caused some return of restlessness. However, on their part, the visitors forbore further allusion to it, unwilling, perhaps, to let the foundling see how easily it lay within his plebeian art to stir the placid dignity of nobles.

' Well, Bannadonna,' said the chief, ' how long ere you are ready to set the clock going, so that the hour shall be sounded ? Our interest in you, not less than in the work itself, makes us anxious to be assured of your success. The people, too,—why, they are shouting now. Say the exact hour when you will be ready.'

' To-morrow, Excellenza, if you listen for it,—or should you not, all the same—strange music will be heard. The stroke of one shall be the first from yonder bell,' pointing to the bell adorned with girls and gar-lands, ' that stroke shall fall there, where the hand of Una clasps Dua's. The stroke of one shall sever that loved clasp. To-morrow, then, at one o'clock, as struck here, precisely here,' advancing and placing his finger upon the clasp, ' the poor mechanic will be most happy once more to give you liege audience, in this his littered shop. Farewell till then, illustrious magnificoes, and hark ye for your vassal's stroke.'

His still, Vulcanic face hiding its burning brightness like a forge, he moved with ostentatious deference toward the scuttle, as if so far to escort their exit. But the junior magistrate, a kind-hearted man, troubled at what seemed to him a certain sardonical disdain, lurking beneath the foundling's humble mien, and in Christian sympathy more distressed at it on his account than on his own, dimly surmising what might be the final fate of such a cynic solitaire, nor perhaps uninfluenced by the general strangeness of surrounding things, this good magistrate had glanced sadly, sideways from the speaker, and thereupon his foreboding eye had started at the expression of the unchanging face of the hour Una.

' How is this, Bannadonna ? ' he lowly asked, ' Una looks unlike her sisters.'

'In Christ's name, Bannadonna,' impulsively broke in the chief, his attention, for the first attracted to the figure, by his associate's remark, 'Una's face looks just like that of Deborah, the prophetess, as painted by the Florentine, Del Fonca.'

'Surely, Bannadonna,' lowly resumed the milder magistrate, 'you meant the twelve should wear the same jocundly abandoned air. But see, the smile of Una seems but a fatal one. 'Tis different.'

While his mild associate was speaking, the chief glanced, inquiringly, from him to the caster, as if anxious to mark how the discrepancy would be accounted for. As the chief stood, his advanced foot was on the scuttle's curb.

Bannadonna spoke.

'Excellenza, now that, following your keener eye, I glance upon the face of Una, I do indeed perceive some little variance. But look all round the bell, and you will find no two faces entirely correspond. Because there is a law in art—but the cold wind is rising more ; these lattices are but a poor defence. Suffer me, magnificoes, to conduct you, at least, partly on your way. Those in whose well-being there is a public stake, should be heedfully attended.'

'Touching the look of Una, you were saying, Bannadonna, that there was a certain law in art,' observed the chief, as the three now descended the stone shaft, 'pray, tell me, then——'

'Pardon ; another time, Excellenza ;—the tower is damp.'

'Nay, I must rest, and hear it now. Here,—here is a wide landing, and through this leeward slit, no wind, but ample light. Tell us of your law ; and at large.'

'Since, Excellenza, you insist, know that there is a law in art, which bars the possibility of duplicates. Some

years ago, you may remember, I graved a small seal
for your republic, bearing, for its chief device, the head
of your own ancestor, its illustrious founder. It becoming necessary, for the customs' use, to have innumerable impressions for bales and boxes, I graved an entire
plate, containing one hundred of the seals. Now, though,
indeed, my object was to have those hundred heads
identical, and though, I dare say, people think them so,
yet, upon closely scanning an uncut impression from
the plate, no two of those five-score faces, side by side,
will be found alike. Gravity is the air of all; but,
diversified in all. In some, benevolent; in some,
ambiguous; in two or three, to a close scrutiny, all but
incipiently malign, the variation of less than a hair's-
breadth in the linear shadings round the mouth sufficing
to all this. Now, Excellenza, transmute that general
gravity into joyousness, and subject it to twelve of
those variations I have described, and tell me, will you
not have my hours here, and Una one of them? But
I like——'

'Hark! is that—a footfall above?'

'Mortar, Excellenza; sometimes it drops to the
belfry floor from the arch where the stonework was left
undressed. I must have it seen to. As I was about to
say: for one, I like this law forbidding duplicates. It
evokes fine personalities. Yes, Excellenza, that strange,
and—to you—uncertain smile, and those fore-looking
eyes of Una, suit Bannadonna very well.'

'Hark!—sure we left no soul above?'

'No soul, Excellenza; rest assured, no *soul*.—Again
the mortar.'

'It fell not while we were there.'

'Ah, in your presence, it better knew its place,
Excellenza,' blandly bowed Bannadonna.

'But, Una,' said the milder magistrate, 'she seemed

intently gazing on you ; one would have almost sworn
that she picked you out from among us three.'

' If she did, possibly, it might have been her finer
apprehension, Excellenza.'

' How, Bannadonna ?   I do not understand you.'

' No consequence, no consequence, Excellenza—but
the shifted wind is blowing through the slit.   Suffer me
to escort you on ; and then, pardon, but the toiler must
to his tools.'

' It may be foolish, signor,' said the milder magistrate, as, from the third landing, the two now went
down unescorted, ' but, somehow, our great mechanician
moves me strangely.   Why, just now, when he so super-
ciliously replied, his walk seemed Sisera's, God's vain
foe, in Del Fonca's painting.   And that young, sculptured
Deborah, too.   Ay, and that——'

' Tush, tush, signor ! ' returned the chief.   ' A passing
whim.   Deborah ?—Where's Jael, pray ? '

' Ah,' said the other, as they now stepped upon the
sod, ' Ah, signor, I see you leave your fears behind you
with the chill and gloom ; but mine, even in this sunny
air, remain.   Hark ! '

It was a sound from just within the tower door,
whence they had emerged.   Turning, they saw it
closed.

He has slipped down and barred us out,' smiled the
chief ; ' but it is his custom.'

Proclamation was now made, that the next day, at
one hour after meridian, the clock would strike, and—
thanks to the mechanician's powerful art—with unusual
accompaniments.   But what those should be, none as
yet could say.   The announcement was received with
cheers.

By the looser sort, who encamped about the tower
all night, lights were seen gleaming through the topmost

blind-work, only disappearing with the morning sun. Strange sounds, too, were heard, or were thought to be, by those whom anxious watching might not have left mentally undisturbed—sounds, not only of some ringing implement, but also—so they said—half-suppressed screams and plainings, such as might have issued from some ghostly engine, overplied.

Slowly the day drew on ; part of the concourse chasing the weary time with songs and games, till, at last, the great blurred sun rolled, like a football, against the plain.

At noon, the nobility and principal citizens came from the town in cavalcade, a guard of soldiers, also, with music, the more to honour the occasion.

Only one hour more. Impatience grew. Watches were held in hands of feverish men, who stood, now scrutinising their small dial-plates, and then, with neck thrown back, gazing toward the belfry, as if the eye might foretell that which could only be made sensible to the ear ; for, as yet, there was no dial to the tower-clock.

The hour hands of a thousand watches now verged within a hair's-breadth of the figure 1. A silence, as of the expectation of some Shiloh, pervaded the swarming plain. Suddenly a dull, mangled sound—naught ringing in it ; scarcely audible, indeed, to the outer circles of the people—that dull sound dropped heavily from the belfry. At the same moment, each man stared at his neighbour blankly. All watches were upheld. All hour hands were at—had passed—the figure 1. No bell-stroke from the tower. The multitude became tumultuous.

Waiting a few moments, the chief magistrate, commanding silence, hailed the belfry, to know what thing unforeseen had happened there.

No response.

He hailed again and yet again.

All continued hushed.

By his order, the soldiers burst in the tower door ; when, stationing guards to defend it from the now surging mob, the chief, accompanied by his former associate, climbed the winding stairs. Half-way up, they stopped to listen. No sound. Mounting faster, they reached the belfry ; but, at the threshold, started at the spectacle disclosed. A spaniel, which, unbeknown to them, had followed them thus far, stood shivering as before some unknown monster in a brake : or, rather, as if it snuffed footsteps leading to some other world.

Bannadonna lay, prostrate and bleeding, at the base of the bell which was adorned with girls and garlands. He lay at the feet of the hour Una ; his head coinciding, in a vertical line, with her left hand, clasped by the hour Dua. With downcast face impending over him, like Jael over nailed Sisera in the tent, was the domino ; now no more becloaked.

It had limbs, and seemed clad in a scaly mail, lustrous as a dragon-beetle's. It was manacled, and its clubbed arms were uplifted, as if, with its manacles, once more to smite its already smitten victim. One advanced foot of it was inserted beneath the dead body, as if in the act of spurning it.

Uncertainty falls on what now followed.

It were but natural to suppose that the magistrates would, at first, shrink from immediate personal contact with what they saw. At the least, for a time, they would stand in involuntary doubt ; it may be, in more or less of horrified alarm. Certain it is, that an arquebus was called for from below. And some add, that its report, followed by a fierce whiz, as of the sudden snapping of a mainspring, with a steely din, as if a stack of sword-blades should be dashed upon a pavement, these blended sounds came ringing to the plain, attracting every eye far upward to the belfry, whence, through the lattice-work, thin wreaths of smoke were curling.

Some averred that it was the spaniel, gone mad by fear, which was shot. This, others denied. True it was, the spaniel never more was seen ; and, probably, for some unknown reason, it shared the burial now to be related of the domino. For, whatever the preceding circumstances may have been, the first instinctive panic over, or else all ground of reasonable fear removed, the two magistrates, by themselves, quickly rehooded the figure in the dropped cloak wherein it had been hoisted. The same night, it was secretly lowered to the ground, smuggled to the beach, pulled far out to sea, and sunk. Nor to any after urgency, even in free convivial hours, would the twain ever disclose the full secrets of the belfry.

From the mystery unavoidably investing it, the popular solution of the foundling's fate involved more or less of supernatural agency. But some few less unscientific minds pretended to find little difficulty in otherwise accounting for it. In the chain of circumstantial inferences drawn, there may, or may not, have been some absent or defective links. But, as the explanation in question is the only one which tradition has explicitly preserved, in dearth of better, it will here be given. But, in the first place, it is requisite to present the supposition entertained as to the entire motive and mode, with their origin, of the secret design of Bannadonna ; the minds above-mentioned assuming to penetrate as well into his soul as into the event. The disclosure will indirectly involve reference to peculiar matters, none of the clearest, beyond the immediate subject.

At that period, no large bell was made to sound otherwise than as at present, by agitation of a tongue within, by means of ropes, or percussion from without, either from cumbrous machinery, or stalwart watchmen, armed with heavy hammers, stationed in the belfry, or in sentry-boxes on the open roof, according as the bell was sheltered or exposed.

It was from observing these exposed bells, with their watchmen, that the foundling, as was opined, derived the first suggestion of his scheme. Perched on a great mast or spire, the human figure, viewed from below, undergoes such a reduction in its apparent size, as to obliterate its intelligent features. It evinces no personality. Instead of bespeaking volition, its gestures rather resemble the automatic ones of the arms of a telegraph.

Musing, therefore, upon the purely Punchinello aspect of the human figure thus beheld, it had indirectly occurred to Bannadonna to devise some metallic agent, which should strike the hour with its mechanic hand, with even greater precision than the vital one. And, moreover, as the vital watchman on the roof, sallying from his retreat at the given periods, walked to the bell with uplifted mace, to smite it, Bannadonna had resolved that his invention should likewise possess the power of locomotion, and, along with that, the appearance, at least, of intelligence and will.

If the conjectures of those who claimed acquaintance with the intent of Bannadonna be thus far correct, no unenterprising spirit could have been his. But they stopped not here ; intimating that though, indeed, his design had, in the first place, been prompted by the sight of the watchman, and confined to the devising of a subtle substitute for him : yet, as is not seldom the case with projectors, by insensible gradations, pro-

ceeding from comparatively pigmy aims to Titanic ones,
the original scheme had, in its anticipated eventualities,
at last, attained to an unheard-of degree of daring.
He still bent his efforts upon the locomotive figure for
the belfry, but only as a partial type of an ulterior
creature, a sort of elephantine Helot, adapted to further,
in a degree scarcely to be imagined, the universal con-
veniences and glories of humanity ; supplying nothing
less than a supplement to the Six Days' Work ; stocking
the earth with a new serf, more useful than the ox,
swifter than the dolphin, stronger than the lion, more
cunning than the ape, for industry an ant, more fiery
than serpents, and yet, in patience, another ass. All
excellences of all God-made creatures, which served
man, were here to receive advancement, and then to be
combined in one. Talus was to have been the all-
accomplished Helot's name. Talus, iron slave to Bannadonna, and, through him, to man.

Here, it might well be thought that, were these last
conjectures as to the foundling's secrets not erroneous,
then must he have been hopelessly infected with the
craziest chimeras of his age ; far outgoing Albert Magus
and Cornelius Agrippa. But the contrary was averred.
However marvellous his design, however apparently
transcending not alone the bounds of human invention,
but those of divine creation, yet the proposed means to
be employed were alleged to have been confined within
the sober forms of sober reason. It was affirmed that,
to a degree of more than sceptic scorn, Bannadonna had
been without sympathy for any of the vain-glorious
irrationalities of his time. For example, he had not
concluded, with the visionaries among the metaphysicians,
that between the finer mechanic forces and the ruder
animal vitality some germ of correspondence might
prove discoverable. As little did his scheme partake

of the enthusiasm of some natural philosophers, who hoped, by physiological and chemical inductions, to arrive at a knowledge of the source of life, and so qualify themselves to manufacture and improve upon it. Much less had he aught in common with the tribe of alchemists, who sought, by a species of incantations, to evoke some surprising vitality from the laboratory. Neither had he imagined, with certain sanguine theosophists, that, by faithful adoration of the Highest, unheard-of powers would be vouchsafed to man. A practical materialist, what Bannadonna had aimed at was to have been reached, not by logic, not by crucible, not by conjuration, not by altars ; but by plain vice-bench and hammer. In short, to solve nature, to steal into her, to intrigue beyond her, to procure someone else to bind her to his hand ;—these, one and all, had not been his objects ; but, asking no favours from any element or any being, of himself, to rival her, outstrip her, and rule her. He stooped to conquer. With him, common-sense was theurgy ;   machinery, miracle ; Prometheus, the heroic name for machinist ; man, the true God.

Nevertheless, in his initial step, so far as the experimental automaton for the belfry was concerned, he allowed fancy some little play ; or, perhaps, what seemed his fancifulness was but his utilitarian ambition collaterally extended. In figure, the creature for the belfry should not be likened after the human pattern, nor any animal one, nor after the ideals, however wild, of ancient fable, but equally in aspect as in organism be an original production ; the more terrible to behold, the better.

Such, then, were the suppositions as to the present scheme, and the reserved intent. How, at the very threshold, so unlooked for a catastrophe overturned all,

or rather, what was the conjecture here, is now to be
set forth.

It was thought that on the day preceding the fatality,
his visitors having left him, Bannadonna had unpacked
the belfry image, adjusted it, and placed it in the retreat
provided—a sort of sentry-box in one corner of the
belfry ; in short, throughout the night, and for some
part of the ensuing morning, he had been engaged in
arranging everything connected with the domino ; the
issuing from the sentry-box each sixty minutes ; sliding
along a grooved way, like a railway ; advancing to the
clock-bell, with uplifted manacles ; striking it at one
of the twelve junctions of the four-and-twenty hands ;
then wheeling, circling the bell, and retiring to its post,
there to bide for another sixty minutes, when the same
process was to be repeated ; the bell, by a cunning
mechanism, meantime turning on its vertical axis, so as
to present, to the descending mace, the clasped hands
of the next two figures, when it would strike two, three,
and so on, to the end.   The musical metal in this time-
bell being so managed in the fusion, by some art, perishing
with its originator, that each of the clasps of the four-
and-twenty hands should give forth its own peculiar
resonance when parted.

But on the magic metal, the magic and metallic
stranger never struck but that one stroke, drove but
that one nail, served but that one clasp, by which
Bannadonna clung to his ambitious life.   For, after
winding up the creature in the sentry-box, so that, for
the present, skipping the intervening hours, it should
not emerge till the hour of one, but should then infallibly
emerge, and, after deftly oiling the grooves whereon it
was to slide, it was surmised that the mechanician must
then have hurried to the bell, to give his final touches to
its sculpture.   True artist, he here became absorbed ;

and absorption still further intensified, it may be, by
his striving to abate that strange look of Una ; which,
though, before others, he had treated with such un-
concern, might not, in secret, have been without its
thorn.

And so, for the interval, he was oblivious of his
creature ; which, not oblivious of him, and true to its
creation, and true to its heedful winding up, left its
post precisely at the given moment ; along its well-oiled
route, slid noiselessly toward its mark ; and, aiming at
the hand of Una, to ring one clangorous note, dully smote
the intervening brain of Bannadonna, turned backward to it ; the manacled arms then instantly upspring-
ing to their hovering poise. The falling body clogged
the thing's return ; so there it stood, still impending
over Bannadonna, as if whispering some post-mortem
terror. The chisel lay dropped from the hand, but
beside the hand ; the oil-flask spilled across the iron
track.

In his unhappy end, not unmindful of the rare genius
of the mechanician, the republic decreed him a stately
funeral. It was resolved that the great bell—the one
whose casting had been jeopardised through the timidity
of the ill-starred workman—should be rung upon the
entrance of the bier into the cathedral. The most
robust man of the country round was assigned the office
of bell-ringer.

But as the pall-bearers entered the cathedral porch,
naught but a broken and disastrous sound, like that
of some lone Alpine landslide, fell from the tower upon
their ears. And then, all was hushed.

Glancing backward, they saw the groined belfry
crashed sideways in. It afterward appeared that the
powerful peasant, who had the bell-rope in charge,
wishing to test at once the full glory of the bell, had

swayed down upon the rope with one concentrate jerk.
The mass of quaking metal, too ponderous for its frame,
and strangely feeble somewhere at its top, loosed from
its fastening, tore sideways down, and tumbling in one
sheer fall, three hundred feet to the soft sward below,
buried itself inverted and half out of sight.

Upon its disinterment, the main fracture was found
to have started from a small spot in the ear ; which,
being scraped, revealed a defect, deceptively minute,
in the casting ; which defect must subsequently have
been pasted over with some unknown compound.

The remolten metal soon reassumed its place in the
tower's repaired superstructure. For one year the
metallic choir of birds sang musically in its belfry-bough-
work of sculptured blinds and traceries. But on the
first anniversary of the tower's completion—at early
dawn, before the concourse had surrounded it—an earth-
quake came ; one loud crash was heard. The stone-
pine, with all its bower of songsters, lay overthrown
upon the plain.

So the blind slave obeyed its blinder lord ; but, in
obedience, slew him. So the creator was killed by the
creature. So the bell was too heavy for the tower.
So the bell's main weakness was where man's blood
had flawed it. And so pride went before the fall.

THE END